# Going to the Top

VIKING
75 years

# GOING
## *TO THE*
# TOP

*A Road Map for Success*

*from America's Leading*

*Women Executives*

**Carol Gallagher, Ph.D.**

WITH

**Susan K. Golant, M.A.**

*VIKING*

To contact the author with comments or to inquire about
speaking, seminars, or consulting, write to her at:

Carol_Gallagher@amsinc.com

VIKING
Published by the Penguin Group
Penguin Putnam Inc., 375 Hudson Street,
New York, New York 10014, U.S.A.
Penguin Books Ltd, 27 Wrights Lane, London W8 5TZ, England
Penguin Books Australia Ltd, Ringwood, Victoria, Australia
Penguin Books Canada Ltd, 10 Alcorn Avenue,
Toronto, Ontario, Canada M4V 3B2
Penguin Books (N.Z.) Ltd, 182–190 Wairau Road,
Auckland 10, New Zealand

Penguin Books Ltd, Registered Offices:
Harmondsworth, Middlesex, England

First published in 2000 by Viking Penguin,
a member of Penguin Putnam Inc.

1 2 3 4 5 6 7 8 9 10

"Your Career Road Map" on pages 294–295 by Janet Schatzman.

LIBRARY OF CONGRESS CATALOGING IN PUBLICATION DATA
Gallagher, Carol, date.
Going to the top : a road map for success from America's
leading women executives / Carol Gallagher with Susan K. Golant.
p.   cm.
ISBN 0-670-89151-7
1. Women executives—United States.
2. Success in business—United States.   I. Golant, Susan K.   II. Title.
HD6054.3 .G35      2000
658.4'09'0820973—dc21         99-054183

This book is printed on acid-free paper. ∞

Printed in the United States of America
Set in Adobe Garamond  •  Designed by Francesca Belanger

To my parents, Don and Jerry Gallagher,
who have taught me to see the possibilities in life

# Acknowledgments

As I began to put my acknowledgments down on paper, I realized how many people contributed to this book in one way or another. I truly appreciate all of the encouragement, time, and help each person provided.

I am enormously thankful for Susan Golant, without whom this book would never have become a reality. I have enjoyed working with such a brilliant writer and compassionate human being. I am delighted that our working relationship has blossomed into a lovely friendship with both Susan and Mitch, her husband.

I want to express my deepest gratitude to all of the senior executive women and CEOs I interviewed for this book. Their vulnerability, openness, and passion provided the catalyst and content for this book. I am constantly inspired by their generosity.

I want to thank American Management Systems, specifically Donna Morea, Fred Forman, Fred Nader, Frank Nicolai, Paul Brands, Sandy Devine, Joy Moody, and Lavonna Green, for providing me with the encouragement and support to pursue my dream while contributing to AMS.

I am grateful for our literary agent and my new friend, Bob Tabian. Through Bob's keen sense of intuition, guidance, and strong relationships, he helped us develop a proposal that was of interest to many publishers. I am very grateful, however, that it was of utmost interest to Viking Penguin. I have thoroughly enjoyed working with Janet Goldstein, our executive editor, who believed in my ideas and advocated for them. I also want to thank the executives and staff at Viking Penguin for making this process a pleasurable experience.

Thanks go to Jo Sanzgiri, Julie Indvik, Sharon Gadberry, Ginny Corsi, Cynthia Scott, Susan Wels, RHR International, and the staff and professors of The California School of Professional Psychology for helping me to spark and kindle the flame for this research and book.

I am so blessed by my biological and extended family: Don, Jerry, Charlette, Tom, Randy, and Patti Gallagher, John Allred, David Waters, Sherry Long, and Sue Goddard. They have truly been the wind beneath my wings. Through their steadfast love and dedication, they have helped my life and work unfold.

I also want to thank a special group of friends who provided constant emotional support and encouragement during my research and doctoral studies: Dr. Charles Mullen, Rev. Faye Orton Matthews, Fran Baskin, Corinne Petrich, Susan Slone, Brigit Garabedian, Mari Cyphers, and Kerry Silverstone. They also granted me the alone time I needed to complete this undertaking.

Most important, I want to thank my God for giving me courage and wisdom. I know that I have been guided in this process to fulfill a much bigger vision than my own. I pray that this book will touch other people's lives as much as the process of writing it has influenced mine.

—Carol Gallagher, Ph.D.

What a wonderful experience this has been, from start to finish! I have only the deepest respect for my partner, Carol Gallagher. Her insight, sense of humor, quick mind, and sincere commitment to women's advancement have made the creation of this book a joy. I am also most grateful to Janet Goldstein, our editor at Viking Penguin, who immediately grasped what we were all about and has steadfastly championed the project from its inception. Her incisive comments helped us to bring the best out of the great wealth of material that Carol had amassed. And, as always, I'm deeply indebted to our agent, Bob Tabian, without whose enthusiastic support none of this would have been possible.

My husband, Dr. Mitch Golant, and my family always play a vital role, as their constant love and support provide the wellsprings from which I draw strength.

Finally, Elizabeth Mehren, staff writer for the *Los Angeles Times,* deserves a special mention since she was instrumental in this collaboration. After a chance meeting a year or two earlier, she had the foresight to recommend me to Carol as a writing partner. How could I have known then that an hour spent idly chatting with her would lead to this wonderful opportunity? Hers was a gift for which I will be forever grateful.

—Susan K. Golant, M.A.

# Contents

# PART I

# WINDOWS IN THE GLASS CEILING

# 1 ‖ Women Who Ride the T-Rex

**M**uch has been written about the high numbers of women—some 30 percent—who drop out of the corporate game, selecting themselves out of the management track and choosing part-time or entrepreneurial work. This book is for the other 70 percent of women managers who want to win, who love the power and complexity of big business, and who dream about finding and climbing through the windows in the glass ceiling. It is also for the millions of women who want to make the next strategic move in their career or who simply want to know what it takes to make it to the highest corporate levels—so they can evaluate whether they have the desire and the personal and professional skills to make it.

No book could present the ideal formula, the perfect combination of abilities, behaviors, and decisions that will guarantee your advancement to the top executive tier. Every individual, every company is different. What this book will do is point out the commonalities that 200 of America's highest-level executive women share and the advice they want to impart to those coming up behind them. You will be able to use their insights to plan your ideal career at whatever level is right for you.

## Who Are T-Rex Women?

The women in this book are courageous, adventurous, and strong. They are able to stay atop some of the most powerful corporations in the world. They are among the pioneers. They are part of the first significant wave of professional women to take their place in the executive suites of major corporations. With an average of twenty years' experience behind them, this small vanguard, now mainly in their mid-forties to mid-fifties, are in many cases the first and only women who have ever reached the senior levels of their corporations.

They are women like Carlene Ellis, a Vice President at Intel Corporation. In her early fifties, Carlene is decisive, direct, and candid. When I first met her, she was dressed casually in slacks and a tailored cotton blouse, her graying blond hair carefully coiffed, a navy blazer draped neatly over the back of her chair. Seated behind the desk in a minimalist ten-by-fifteen cubicle (all Intel employees, even executives, have cubicles), decorated only with a laptop and table and chair for visitors, she seemed bright, challenging—a forward thinker. At any given moment during our conversation, she was two thoughts ahead of me.

The c    ) win motivates Ellis every day. "I want to be the person making the decisions," she told me matter-of-factly, "and I love the challenge of meeting seemingly impossible goals. Running this organization," she added, "is not at all like riding a tiger. It's more like riding a T-Rex. You can't control it, but you try to stay on top of it and guide it in the right direction. The thrill for me is to try to keep the organization disciplined, creative, and ahead of the curve."

I like that analogy. Corporations, like the *Tyrannosaurus rex,* can be fierce, unpredictable, unwieldy, lumbering, archaic, commanding, and not easily understood. They are often difficult to get one's arms around—and it's a tough climb to the top. Like never before, some of the largest corporations are even faced with extinction—through acquisition, deregulation, or changing technological, economic, or consumer trends. Yet the women who have made it into the highest executive ranks seek out and relish the challenge. They even revel in it.

Liz Fetter, former senior executive at Pacific Telesis, SBC, and US West Communications, and now President and Chief Operating Officer of NorthPoint Communications, is such a woman. In her late thirties, Liz sat in a beautiful corner office, chicly dressed in a designer suit and scarf when I first met her, and she exuded femininity. But she was also direct, thoughtful, assertive. I could sense that she valued protocol and enjoyed the power and prestige of her position. Liz has been motivated by her desire to influence results on a large scale. "I love to lead," she declared, "and I love to win. I work like a dog. I am very clear about what I want to do, and I do what it takes to fulfill my ambitions. To make it, you really have to know yourself, the system, and the game you're playing."

Anne McNamara, General Counsel of American Airlines; Karen Elliott House, President of International for Dow Jones/Wall Street Journal; Linda Keene, Vice President of Market Development at American Express; Ellen Gordon, President of Tootsie Roll Industries; Terri Dial, President of Wells Fargo Bank—these are all women who have found a way to achieve the highest levels of success. Their successes have been celebrated and studied. They have been singled out as curiosities, and praised and criticized for storming the barricades of a man's world. And standing right behind them, emerging from their shadow, is the next generation: thousands, perhaps millions of women just like you who are crowding the mid-management ranks of corporations and thinking about their next move.

In the 1960s, fewer than 30 percent of college women believed that they would be working at age thirty. Perhaps this is partially attributable to the fact that women were denied access to the nation's most prestigious undergraduate programs—Harvard did not admit female students until 1963, Yale until 1969, and Columbia until 1983. (Although it's true that women's colleges developed many professional pioneers, their alumni networks were not as powerful as those emanating from the men's colleges because they had few graduates in the upper echelons of business.) But today, women earn more than 35 percent of MBAs and more than 42 percent of law degrees (that's up from 3.6 and 5.4 percent, respectively, in 1970), many from Ivy League institutions that were closed to them as recently as thirty or forty years ago. Their overwhelming numbers are dramatically changing the face of corporations. Women now make up 48.9 percent of all managerial and professional jobs—fully double the percentage they held two decades ago.

Common sense dictates that, in time, many women should make it to the top of the corporate pyramid—the prized corner offices of CEO, chairman, president, and other top executives. The plain fact is, however, that only a handful has leaped from mid-management to the highest corporate levels. In 1997, merely 3 percent of top executives in America's 500 largest companies were women.

Does this mean that there is still a glass ceiling? Many mid-level women believe that it exists because they feel they've hit it, and they're struggling to get through. However, most of the senior executive women with whom I've spoken don't believe there is a glass ceiling because they never encountered it! That's not to say that there weren't obstacles in their way or behaviors they had to learn. Although progress for women at the upper echelons of the corporate world is still slow, I too am beginning to see that today the glass ceiling is no longer the impenetrable barrier it once was—a barrier that had to be shattered by law or custom. In reality, it has a few windows through which an increasing number of female executives like Carlene Ellis and Liz Fetter are making their way to the top.

In this book you will learn about the common characteristics, behaviors, and experiences of these outstanding women. In their own words, they will tell you what helped them succeed and which pitfalls you would be wise to avoid. They will provide you with a composite role model and a road map for your own corporate climb.

The top executive women whom you will meet in these pages are all enthusiastic about sharing their insights and experiences. All of them know from personal experience how very difficult it is for women to make their way through the corporate labyrinth. Now they want to share their knowledge with those coming up behind them. Most agree with Gale Duff-Bloom, President of Company Communications and Corporate Image at J. C. Penney, who told me, "Women need courage and support to go for the top jobs. We need to help empower other corporate women—to influence their success and give them the confidence and tools it will take for them to be leaders."

## Questions and Confusions

In her mid-thirties, Sara Drozdowski is a fast-rising product manager for Fannie Mae in Washington, D.C. "I'm ambitious," Drozdowski insisted. "I want to keep moving up the corporate ladder. But I know that competence and intelligence by themselves won't get me there. I think that today things are easier for women in corporations than they were ten or fifteen years ago, but at the same time I believe that advancing to the next level is still harder for women than it is for men. What I need to know is, what are the unwritten rules? What are the qualities I need to cultivate to move up? How did other women do it?"

Like Drozdowski, you too may be hungry for knowledge that will help you evaluate your career choices and increase your odds of attaining the highest corporate levels. You too may benefit from other women's hindsight and experience as you reach crucial decision points in your career. You may be confused by questions such as:

- What does it take to reach the upper levels of my company? Do I measure up? Is this even something I want to do?

- Should I make a lateral move to broaden my base of experience—or take a prestigious or lucrative promotion that might not, in the long run, take me to the top levels?

- Should I make a risky career move, perhaps to a far-flung location, that would give me profit-and-loss experience—or go for a safer staff promotion at corporate headquarters?

- Where should I draw the line between my business and personal lives? Is it even possible to reach the upper tiers and have a personal life or family?

Until now there were few answers. Unfortunately, the lessons that the current wave of women executives have learned—and the passages through the windows in the glass ceiling they created—have not yet been passed along to the next generation. In truth, the women who have reached the corporate pinnacle are so few and often so burdened with obligations that they cannot effectively serve as coaches and mentors to the many women coming up behind them.

In this book, I will present the crucial guidance that potential executive women need to go to the top. Drawing on in-depth interviews that I conducted with 200 top executive women positioned within one or two steps of the CEOs at Fortune 1000 companies (with annual revenues over $800 million), I have created a road map for you, the aspiring executive on the rise. I will instruct you on how to recognize and pass through the gaps in the glass ceiling that others have identified before you.

This is a forward-looking book, one that focuses on what works rather than on the many impediments to advancement. And I have consciously written it that way. Consider this: In a high-performance driving school I recently attended, the instructor warned us that we tend to steer toward what we're looking at. For instance, if the car goes into a spin, and we focus on not hitting a tree, simply by looking at the tree we tend to point the car in that direction. The same principle can be applied to our careers. Indeed, I have often found that *we achieve what we focus on.* If we focus on obstacles, that may be exactly what we encounter!

Consequently, throughout this book I emphasize the ways that you *can* succeed rather than dwelling, like so many others do, on the reasons why you may not. That's not to say that the road to the top is smooth. There are barriers. However, if we concentrate too much on those barriers to advancement, we may become paralyzed and frustrated. Worse yet, we may head directly for the walls or ceiling rather than the openings.

> REMEMBER, WE ACHIEVE WHAT WE FOCUS ON: *Reframe your thoughts and reposition your energies toward identifying and creating pathways to the top, rather than focusing on obstacles.*

## How Did They Make It Through the Glass Ceiling?

The glass ceiling that my interviewees encountered on their way up was real, but clearly, it was *not* impenetrable. Those whom I have studied found a way through it. In the process, most didn't use confrontation or force to shatter barriers, wounding themselves or others as they rose to the top. Instead of trying to change their company, they thoroughly understood its rules and played by them. Rather than blaming themselves or their organizations when thwarted, these women pragmatically found routes around the hurdles blocking their advancement—paths that propelled them through openings in the glass ceiling.

And, perhaps most important, all of them used three vital strategies to get ahead:

**1. *They analyzed themselves and what they wanted.*** Liz Fetter said, "I am very clear about what I want to do, and I do what it takes to fulfill my ambitions. To make it, you really have to know yourself, the system, and the game you're playing." Liz was demonstrating this first characteristic. When you do a self-assessment, you ask, "Who am I? What do I value? What do I want to do with my life?" Maybe you don't even want to move into the senior ranks—that's good to know as you plan your career road map. But maybe you do, with gusto.

Indeed, virtually all of the executive women whom I interviewed understood themselves exceptionally well. They were realistic about their strengths and weaknesses. They were determined to "stay in the game," and they loved to win. They thrived on the complexity and competitiveness of big companies, on making a large-scale difference, and they were energized by the controlled chaos of running America's largest corporations.

Moreover, most of the executives I interviewed were not in it solely for the money. They wanted to effect a large-scale change, to impact global society. They loved their jobs and were passionate about what they did—they wanted to get up every morning because of it. With upswept honey-blond hair and a tanned, sunny face, Sue Swenson, President of Leap Wireless International and former CEO of Cellular One, exemplified this positive attitude. "My job is fun," she told me. "I mean, it is really fun. I like coming to work every day. I like the challenges. I like the way people approach problem-solving. I like to see how they all work together."

The corporate world is a much more enjoyable place to be when you truly know yourself, your capabilities, and why you are there. Throughout this book, you will have opportunities to assess your own strengths and weaknesses, and you will find particular help in Chapters 2, 3, and 13.

**2. *They learned about their companies, including its unwritten rules, and how to get to where they were trying to go.*** Knowing themselves, these women acknowledged, was only the first step.

They also needed to understand, intimately, the unwritten rules of their corporation. They could only glean that knowledge by seeking the guidance of others who had been around long enough to understand the game.

Learning about your company means asking your boss or a mentor, "What competencies do I need to master in order to move up? What outcomes should I produce? What relationships should I develop? And how can I do all this and stay sane?"

When Liz Fetter joined Pacific Telesis, prior to her positions at US West Communications and NorthPoint Communications, she took the advice of a manager who had been with the company a long time. He told her, "Be humble, learn, become a student of this business. You're smart, but you don't know everything." Fetter took his counsel to heart—and after two years, she was the only executive who had been hired from outside at her level who was still with the telecommunications firm. Even today, as President of NorthPoint Communications, she actively seeks the advice of those who know the organization, the ropes, and the players well. "There are a few people in this company," she noted, "who feel committed to helping me be successful. I can count on them to take me aside and tell me what's really going on." Chapter 13 will guide you toward understanding yourself vis-à-vis your company's unwritten rules.

**3. They emulated successful role models.** Most of the women in my study honed their skills and corporate style by carefully watching and emulating the behavior of top executives. They asked themselves, "How did those people make it?" "What makes them different?" They analyzed the behavior of people not only within their company, but also at other, similar companies.

However, they did not consider these individuals "mentors" in the usual sense. In fact, they largely avoided linking themselves too closely with a single powerful person. Instead, they emulated specifically chosen qualities of different people as they progressed in their careers. They called these individuals "advisers," "role models," and "influencers." Throughout this book, the voices of the many women whom I interviewed will coalesce into a composite role model for you to emulate in your quest for advancement.

## A Word About My Research

My interest in the human side of business began some years ago when, after having worked on Wall Street as a financial analyst for Goldman Sachs & Company, I was hired by IBM as a sales representative responsible for selling mainframe computer systems to strategic accounts.

After I had worked for IBM for about six months, the company acquired Rolm Telecommunications. Talk about a culture clash! All IBM employees were required to don suits and starched white shirts every day. The men wore their power ties, and the women sported those cute little rosettes at the collar. (Weren't those lovely!) But the telecommunications specialist on my team was from Rolm, and he often came to work dressed *in jeans and a casual shirt.* Right away I knew something was amiss. Our Rolm colleagues had company-sponsored beer busts on Fridays, while we weren't even allowed to *drink* at corporate parties. They got sabbaticals every few years—a concept that was quite foreign to an IBMer.

After working with my Rolm colleagues for a while, I became curious about the kinds of due diligence companies perform when considering a merger or acquisition. I approached several business-development people to better understand the rationale. When I looked at the checklists many of them followed, I immediately understood why one-third to one-half of all mergers fail. Of the hundred or so questions on the checklists, I found only one having to do with the compatibility of people and corporate cultures. Everything else was related to market, legal, and financial issues. In fact, as I might have predicted, IBM's merger with Rolm didn't work out either. They spun off the company a few years later.

But all of this set me to thinking about the psychology of business. So in 1993 I returned to school for a Ph.D. in Organizational Psychology. One of my areas of interest was leadership. I wanted to understand how business leaders attained their success and how they make decisions. This was sparked, in part, by my branch manager at IBM—Amal Johnson. There was something different about her that led me to believe that she was on the fast track to the top, which indeed she was. I wanted to understand what made Amal and other executive women so different—what made them tick! What could I learn from her and people like her that I might use to advance my own career? And did I have the stuff to make it too?

There had been a good deal of research on breaking the glass ceiling, but most of it focused on the obstacles to women's success rather than on helpful strategies. And even the few researchers and authors who did study success strategies typically looked at mid-level management women whose skills had not yet been proven for the executive level. It seemed to me that a more efficient approach would be to discover what actually worked for the few women who had found those windows through the glass ceiling. What did they deem useful? What could they recommend to other women who aspire to the executive suite?

And so I began conducting in-depth interviews with top executive women positioned within one or two steps of the CEOs at Fortune 1000 companies. I met with them in their offices. My original research involved seventy of these extremely high-level women, but I was so fascinated by their responses that I have continued this work, and to date have collected the stories and observed the behaviors and characteristics of more than 200 top-level executive women. In fact, I've spoken with many of their bosses—usually male CEOs—to gather additional insights.

## A Hunger for Connection

Surprisingly, some of the interviews lasted more than four or five hours. Why did they go on for so long? After all, these are very busy, highly responsible people. I believe the answer lies in the fact that many of the women I interviewed feel isolated. They are starved for someone to talk with who understands them as executives and as women, who can relate to what they face, who will maintain their privacy, and who is outside their companies. Because I met these criteria (I have received their permission to tell their stories in this book or have masked their identities by changing their names, industries, or other identifying characteristics, where necessary), they wanted to share their experiences and advice with me.

My interview allowed them to stop in the middle of their hectic day to touch a different part of themselves—an emotional and reflective part. They usually shut that off at work, where they know they must wear a veneer of firmness that conceals their vulnerabilities. I was able to speak their language. And, I admit, I also posed some pointed questions that unlocked their hearts.

People sometimes ask me, "Do you really feel these women were honest with you? Aren't they just telling you what you want to hear?" For some, perhaps, this was true; however, most were much too emotional for that. Indeed, several of my interviewees became tearful during our conversations. For the first time, someone else truly understood and was genuinely interested in what was going on inside them. Because many of their spouses were involved in different types of careers and didn't fully grasp the demands of their jobs, these women couldn't share all of themselves with their partners, even if the relationships were strong. And, as you'll see in Chapter 4, they also didn't feel they should completely confide in anyone at work.

So I became a sounding board for them. "Am I alone, or are there other women struggling with the same issues?" they wanted to know. They also wanted to talk to one another. Many of the interviewees felt the need to share their experiences with other senior executive women, but not with women in their own companies.

To address this need, I founded the Executive Women's Alliance™ in 1996. Its mission is, in part, to provide a forum for senior executive women to discuss key business and leadership strategies and personal issues.

Immediately after the first Executive Women's Alliance Conference in 1996, Gale Duff-Bloom, President of Company Communications and Corporate Image at J. C. Penney, confided in me that getting together with other senior executive women had changed her life. She no longer felt as isolated. She could see that others were dealing with similar issues, and that gave her the courage to stand up to her own convictions and to be more candid and forthright. There is an inherent strength in numbers.

Participation in the Executive Women's Alliance Conferences has also helped some of the women to legitimize their feeling that they belong in the positions they hold. Think of it this way: If you're the only woman on the men's basketball team, you soon feel that you don't belong there. Similarly, if you're the only women on the executive team, you may feel out of step as well. A great many of my interviewees didn't truly own their successes, but attributed their lofty status within their organizations to luck or to merely being in the right place at the right time. Seeing that other women had attained those same levels validated their position and gave them perspective. Maybe it wasn't a fluke or just good luck that they had made it. Maybe they were not an anomaly.

Another goal of the Executive Women's Alliance is to retain and advance talented women in leadership positions. To that end, I conduct Windows in the Glass Ceiling® seminars for mid-management women. During these workshops, the more-senior executive women talk candidly with high-potential female managers about their successes and, perhaps more important, their failures and how they bounced back. As a Senior Principal at American Management Systems (a billion-dollar international consulting firm specializing in business re-engineering, organization development, change management, and systems integration), I manage executive development programs that assist American Management Systems and other progressive companies in their promotion and retention of talented women.

As time goes on, I keep adding more and more data. All of the interviews, conferences, seminars, executive coaching, and consulting that I continue to provide help to keep my research current and evolving.

## Some Demographics

My interviews were as varied as the women with whom I spoke. The shortest, with Ellen Gordon, President of Tootsie Roll Industries, took about thirty minutes. Ellen was running late and needed to take a conference call from Hong Kong, which cut our time short. But after providing me with thirty minutes of solid content, she handed me a shopping bag into which she had tossed several pounds of Tootsie Rolls, Dots, Charm Blow Pops, and other assorted goodies. Like all of the executive women, Ellen had her own unique personality and identity. The longest interview was with Anne McNamara, the General Counsel at American Airlines; it lasted more than four hours.

Eighty-three percent of the women in my original study were Caucasian; 17 percent were women of color. This, of course, does not reflect the current situation in our society, since only 0.1 percent of all senior executive women are minorities. I feel fortunate in having had the opportunity to speak with so many executive women of color; you will find their insights and suggestions in Chapter 11. The average age of the women with whom I spoke was forty-four. The youngest was thirty-three, while the oldest was sixty-seven. Some of the women are still on their way up; some, perhaps, will be CEOs of Fortune 500 companies in the not-so-distant future. Others, particularly those in their late fifties and older, have likely reached the highest positions they will hold.

From the time they started their professional business careers to the point at which they crossed into the executive ranks, it took the women an average of eleven and a half years to make it into the executive level. (Many of them had already been executives for more than ten years when I spoke with them.) You might consider this to be a long time, or you might think it's short. Your perspective depends on your own personal experience and on the rate of advancement at your company. But I found it most interesting that the length of time it took for a woman to make it into the executive ranks did not depend on her age, education, marital status, number of children, or race. Rather, it had more to do with her understanding and adopting four critical success factors (I call them C.O.R.E. characteristics) early in her career. You will read about these factors in Chapter 3.

Eighty-one percent of the women I interviewed have earned graduate degrees, with 53 percent having a master's and 28 percent doctorate-level degrees (of the latter, 19 percent were attorneys). Seventeen percent had bachelor's degrees, and two executive women had only high school diplomas.

Ninety percent of the women I interviewed were or had been married, but many had either chosen not to have children or had limited the size of their families. Some 45 percent had no children, 44 percent had one or two, and only 11 percent had three or more. More than half the women were over thirty when they gave birth to their first child. These statistics dispel the belief that there is no

room for a full life at the top executive level. I'll explore these issues—and especially how the executives came to these choices and
manage their busy lives—in greater depth in Chapters 9 and 10.

As I researched their career advancement, I asked the women in
my study many questions, including the following:

- Why do you think you made it into the executive ranks and
  others didn't?

- What were the key decision points in your career?

- What have been your biggest failures? What did you learn
  from them? How did you bounce back?

- What would you do differently if you had the opportunity?

- What advice do you have for other women who aspire to the
  executive ranks?

And I was quite surprised by their responses. In fact, I discovered that many of the advancement-related convictions I had held
early in my career and had heard other women espouse simply did
not hold up. They were myths. I identified six common themes that
dispelled the beliefs most of us hold even today. These myths
include:

MYTH #1: The results speak for themselves.
MYTH #2: You have to network to get ahead.
MYTH #3: You have to be ruthless to succeed.
MYTH #4: If you keep your head down, you won't get shot.
MYTH #5: You need to "play the man's game" to get ahead.
MYTH #6: You need to find a mentor who will pave the way for
        your career.

I will be exploring these myths and the reality behind them
throughout Part II of this book. I will also let you in on the back-
stage—what male and female CEOs have observed about their up-
and-coming women employees. Because of the top-level contacts
I've developed through my research, I have unique access to these

corporate leaders and was able to conduct face-to-face interviews with twenty CEOs from large corporations. I asked them about the success factors needed to reach the higher-echelon corporate jobs, the mistakes they felt women made that could derail them in their quest for success, and the advice they would offer women to increase their chances of advancement.

The CEOs were impressive in their candor. They were observant of women and had put much thought into how to help their top female employees succeed. I will share with you their valuable insights throughout the pages of this book.

## How This Book Can Help You

Because self-knowledge is crucial to career success, you will have the opportunity to discover what you know about yourself and your path to success in Chapter 2, where you will focus on a short but penetrating self-assessment. And like many upwardly mobile female managers whom I have encountered in my seminars, perhaps you too will be surprised to see how far along the road you have already traveled.

In Part II, we will examine in depth the six myths and the realities associated with each myth. In Part III, we will take the view from the top, as successful executive women reflect candidly on the choices they have made, the demands and satisfactions of their work, their future goals, and the strategies they used to advance their careers. In Chapters 9 and 10, for instance, I pose the question, "Can you have it all and still have a full life?" The answer, it seems, is a resounding "Yes, but perhaps not all at once." How the executive women in my study made the choices they did and how they manage their busy lives can give you insight into making those tough decisions yourself. In Chapter 11, we will explore the unique roadblocks that women of color face in their career climbs. And in Chapter 12, I will summarize, by providing you with fifteen proven strategies for career success.

Finally, we will examine your personal steppingstones along your path to career success. I found it fascinating that a good many of the executive women whom I interviewed ascribed their success to "being in the right place at the right time." They seemed to chalk up their career advances to luck. In fact, the majority tended to not plan their careers. Only 27 percent of Caucasian women in my study had well-defined career goals. But today I firmly believe that if more women want to become executives, they must aggressively plan their futures. They need to envision where they want to go and assertively ask for what they want. In fact, I don't believe a laissez-faire career strategy will work for you if you're moving up in the twenty-first century.

In Chapter 13, the workbook section of this book, you will find interactive exercises to help you determine what you want for yourself, what your company requires, and also how far you have come. These activities will help you construct your own career road map. Their purpose is to help you concretely visualize what you have already achieved, and what still remains to be done. They will also help you identify your long-term and short-term goals and provide you with a list of what you need to focus on now and in the future. With this road map in mind, you can increase your chances of finding the windows in the glass ceiling that can lead you into the executive suite.

All in all, this book will:

- debunk six popular myths about what it takes to make it into the executive suite and set you on the right track;

- explain the four C.O.R.E. characteristics that you must have to reach the highest corporate levels;

- emphasize the many executive virtues that are necessary for success—such as responsibility, forthrightness, flexibility, curiosity, realism, and graciousness;

- explore the personal and career choices that executive women have made;

- discuss the specific barriers to career advancement that minority women face;

- provide you with a personalized career road map;

- include the candid reflections of top corporate women on the demands and satisfactions of their work, their future goals, the impact of their choices on their personal lives, and whether they would have made different decisions if they could do it all over.

## Why the Time Is Right for You

There was a time when the notion of a female CEO was totally foreign to most of us. Indeed, Carol Bartz, CEO of Autodesk, recently told me that she has what she calls "zoo status." When you see a rare and exotic animal in the zoo, you look and point. You think, "Boy, this animal is extremely unique!" You may like it, think it is weird-looking, or believe that it just doesn't belong there. Carol felt that perfectly described her situation as a female CEO when compared to her male peers.

But times are changing. With the advice the senior executive women proffer in these pages and the myths about female advancement that I will shatter in the next several chapters, more and more women will be moving, perhaps sooner than we think, into positions of corporate leadership. That, at least, is my fondest hope.

Besides, as I spoke with various CEOs from large corporations, they explained that one of the biggest challenges their companies will face during the next decade is the recruitment and retention of talented employees. There is an enormous demand for all kinds of people of both genders and all races, and companies don't currently have the talent in house (or in this country, for that matter!) to sustain themselves. For instance, in the state of California, of the three largest employers—the entertainment industry, technology (Silicon Valley and the like), and the penal system—two must go outside the United States to attract high-level, skilled people. The penal system is the only industry that can fully recruit from its own population.

Part of this has to do with demographics—the big dip in population after the baby boom. There are actually fewer people to train in the next generations. Jobs are not being filled because there simply aren't enough applicants. As a consequence, there is a great deal of competition among companies for talented workers. As one CEO in high tech told me, "We're fighting for the ability to retain high-quality resources today, and looking five to ten years out, that is the battleground worldwide. That's the number one, two, and three wars to fight in our industry. It's not technology, it's not chemistry, it's intellectual resources." That is, people.

When I asked if any specific skills were missing, the consensus among the CEOs was adeptness in management and leadership. For instance, Rick Belluzzo, Group Vice President at Microsoft and former CEO of Silicon Graphics (SGI), told me, "We need people with technical talent—and from a financial reward standpoint, high-tech engineering is probably the best career a young woman can contemplate—but we also need people to lead businesses. You can teach someone technical skills more easily than you can train someone to become a leader."

What does all of this mean to you as an aspiring businesswoman? If you have the leadership skills and the know-how, understand that companies are desperate to hire and promote you. The time is right for advancement.

But be deliberate and strategic about charting your course. The CEOs whom I interviewed suggested that women could do a better job at stepping back and taking an honest inventory of their careers. It's important to look at where you are and see how you can leverage your position in interesting ways. As women, we don't do a lot of that. In fact, men are more likely to construct a careful career plan: "In two years I want to be this, and in three years I want to be here." They're willing to either bulldoze their way through it or figure out how to reinvent themselves to get there—to take charge of their careers and set long-term goals.

---

THE TIME IS RIGHT FOR ADVANCEMENT: *If you have the leadership and know-how, understand that companies are desperate to hire and promote you.*

---

This may be due to the fact that we don't often ask for what we want. Or maybe we're so busy trying to manage everything else in our lives—the family, husband, and household—that we put ourselves and our career-planning goals last. Or perhaps it's a question of perfectionism. If we say we're going to do something, then we stick to it, no matter what. Men may be more flexible. They might treat their careers a bit like a pinball game. They go down one path, but if they hit a bumper they'll say, "Okay, let's try another way," and careen off in a new direction.

In this book, I will help you take ownership of your career. Today, a scant twenty years since the windows to the glass ceiling began creaking open to admit women, the possibilities seem limitless. So what are we waiting for? Let's get started!

# 2 | What You Know About Yourself and Your Company

Gloria Everett, Senior Vice President of Operations at Globalstar, emphatically told me, "I know if I like what I'm doing. And I'm not going to do what I don't like to do!" She is not alone in her strong sense of self-knowledge. Virtually all the top executive women whom I interviewed and have spoken with are quite introspective and understood themselves exceptionally well. And they have said that when it comes to moving ahead, self-assessment is Job Number One. As you plan your career advancement, you must ask yourself, "Who am I really? What am I capable of doing? What is it that I want to do?"

Such introspection requires a bit of creativity, and that involves allowing yourself the time and internal space to let your ideas flow at will. Your creativity evolves from the ability to play, but you can use it quite successfully in solving business problems, moving your career forward, and envisioning your next steps up the rungs of the corporate ladder.

## Know Thyself

Self-reflection is essential when it comes to evaluating where you want to go in your career. People derail or plateau when they don't understand themselves in terms of what they really want out of a career, what they want out of their job, or what they are capable of or willing to produce. When you're out of touch with what you need and who you are, you can easily fall into the Peter Principle trap (that is, being promoted beyond your level of expertise). Patricia

Martin, an astute mid-level manager who seems to be on the fast track at Clorox, told me about an officer at a company she once worked for who confessed that he wished he'd never become an officer. "He wanted to go back to being a director again because of the personal toll his new job took and the amount of stress he was dealing with," she explained.

The ongoing requirements of this man's job were more than he thought they would be and more than he had the personal capacity to handle. But there was no turning back. His only escape was to leave the company and work for someone else. You've got to know what a job is going to entail and whether you really want it before you get into it. And you also need to know what your capacities are.

> KNOW YOURSELF: *People derail or plateau when they don't understand themselves in terms of what they really want out of a career, what they want out of their job, or what they are capable of or willing to produce.*

## Self-Reflection to the Rescue

Knowing yourself can also save you from a difficult situation. One senior executive woman shared an enlightening story about how her knowledge of her own strengths, weaknesses, and motivations helped her salvage her career after a disastrous failure.

When Jennifer had first marketed herself to the finance department of a large petroleum company in the mid-1980s, she told her potential new managers, "These are the things that I know about global finance, and these are the things that I don't know." An in-depth understanding of foreign exchange was one of her areas of weakness. But she said, "I'm pretty certain I'm smart enough to grasp it. And so with appropriate learning opportunities, I'm sure I'll be just fine."

Shortly after she got into the job, however, the currency markets were liberalized, and Jennifer wasn't sufficiently advanced in her learning curve. As a result, the company sustained $175,000 in foreign currency losses. "Today, at that company, losing that amount probably isn't worth taking notice of," Jennifer explained, "but back then, it meant a lot to this company. And I got called on the carpet. It was a rather brutal opportunity for learning."

Still, Jennifer knew herself to be better than she had demonstrated. "I absolutely knew that I was smart enough to handle those issues," she continued. "I knew I had the experience. I knew what I knew, and I had told them what I didn't know. So the facts were out on the table." Still, she was accountable for the loss. She received a written comeuppance, and then wrote a response in which she said, "I know I'm better than this. And I'm going to show you that I am. If you and I decide to part ways, it won't be because you don't want me to stay. It will be because I have decided that this isn't a place where I can build my career."

By the following year, Jennifer was promoted. Her failure had become a terrific learning opportunity for her. "I had a lot of early career success, and I got a little heady," she explained. "Sometimes you need a really good whack in the head to make you stop and think about what you know and what you don't know and how good you are at regrouping. I got this chance to regroup. I was in an environment where the risks weren't quite so high, where the person I was working for said, 'Maybe you are better than you've been able to demonstrate thus far, so I'm willing to stick with you.'"

In the short period of ten months, the situation turned around completely, and Jennifer got the opportunity to be promoted and to build an outstanding career at the company. The fundamental element of her success, however, was knowing herself. It was her ability to draw from within and say, "I'm going to convince you. I'm going to show you that what you've seen isn't who I am."

"If you marry failure and self-knowledge, it's a terrific learning opportunity," Jennifer concluded. "But you have to have the ability to reflect on who you are, what skills you have, and what is your essence, so you can pull yourself out of difficult situations."

## "Create a Space" for Yourself

You can also use self-knowledge to "create a space" for yourself in your organization. When she was Vice President of Strategic Change at Kaiser Permanente, Linda Lewis explained to me how she did that. "Early on," she said, "my father used to tell me, 'You know, you're not very good in the chorus line. You've got to kick higher than the other people or have a bigger smile.' I didn't really internalize his advice then. But when I went on my very first interview—I was applying for a job with the State of California as a vocational counselor—the interviewer asked me, 'Why are you interested in this job?'

"'I really like to work with people,' I said.

"And the gentleman swiftly replied, 'So does a mortician.'

"And I thought: Now I've got it. My answers have to be different than the other person's answer. What am I doing that's going to differentiate me from the crowd?" In order to set yourself apart from other high performers, you have to be willing to dig deep within yourself to determine what specific skills you have that are above average and that you enjoy. Once you identify your strengths, you can effectively market and position yourself.

## Assess Your Own Motivations

Beth Sawi headed the electronic brokerage area at Charles Schwab when I spoke with her. She focused on the importance of understanding your motivations when you contemplate career advancement. "If you want to be an executive, there are a few questions you really need to ask," she explained. "The first is: 'Do I really want to become an executive and why?' If you can't answer that other than by saying, 'Because there's good money in it,' or 'I really think it would be prestigious,' or 'It would finally make my dad proud of me,' then I would reconsider." The motivations implicit in these answers are not sufficient to give you the fire you'll need to keep yourself going. Better responses might be, "I enjoy creating large-scale change," or, "I love leading people," or, "This work is really exciting—I have a passion for what I'm doing."

The second question many people neglect is: "Do I want to be an executive at *this organization?*" As Beth explained, just because Bank of America or Procter & Gamble gives you a job, that doesn't mean you're going to love it and thrive in it. "You need to ask yourself, 'Is this a company and a product line that I am so passionate about that I want to put in the necessary hours to make it happen?'" If you can't answer "yes" to that question, you're not going to win the extended fight, no matter what your other motivations are.

## Do You Have the Fortitude It Takes?

Work and corporate life can sometimes become quite difficult. You have to persevere if you want to succeed. Paul Brands, CEO of American Management Systems, explained that some people just don't want to make the commitment and the necessary tradeoffs. "There's no free lunch," he told me. "If you're talking about managing an operating unit, sometimes you've got a lot of unpleasant problems to deal with." There can be internal staff issues. Or you may get into some heavy lifting and negotiating and even combat in client situations. "Some people may not want to do that, so they may be ineffective (which means they probably can't deliver), or they may do it a few times and say, 'This is just too hard for me. I don't want to do it anymore.'" These individuals are unwilling to make the necessary tradeoffs or to endure the emotional challenges that go with corporate responsibility. So they may take themselves out of the game.

A caveat here: It's fine to take yourself out of the game, if that is what you choose to do. I urge you, however, to reflect on your own needs and what motivates you before you select out. By knowing yourself and deciding what's right for you, you can determine whether you want to play the game to its fullest. Giving it your all can be a great deal of fun—if you know that is what you want to do and if you feel you have the strength to tolerate the inevitable ups and downs.

## Are You Aiming High Enough?

According to Alan Buckwalter, CEO of Chase Bank of Texas, when women first came into the corporate environment, they didn't think of themselves as being able to aspire to the highest executive positions. "If ten years ago, you interviewed the top fifty MBA graduates (twenty-five women and twenty-five men) from the best business schools in the country, I'll bet you wouldn't get twenty-five women saying they wanted to be CEO of a public company. But I'll bet at least twenty-four of the twenty-five men would say that," Alan claimed.

AIM HIGHER: *If you ask a class of business school graduates if they aspire to CEO positions, perhaps twenty-four of twenty-five men will say yes. Most women will say no. In the past, women have not aimed high enough. Just remember, it can take twenty-five to thirty years of business experience to reach the level of CEO.*

In the past, some women have not aimed high enough. Even today, there are mid-career women who may feel, "If I've gotten to this level, that's pretty darn good. In fact, I've had to work like a dog to get where I am. The next level would mean burnout, and I'm not willing to pay that price. The sacrifices are too great." Perhaps they lacked advisers and role models to let them know that it is possible to aim higher—and that the initial learning phase may be the most difficult part of any promotion. Subtle cultural issues can also interfere. Maybe as young girls, we didn't want to appear "better" than the boys because we wanted them to like us. So we held back and didn't beat them at dodge ball or in chemistry class. Many of us have been socialized to let the guys take the lead.

As Alan Buckwalter explained, "I do recall, as a young person, that kind of issue with young women. Girls were told, 'Don't beat the boys, or be more delicate, and don't be too forceful. Let the boys win, not just in a sporting event, but in any area.' The boys would talk quite differently. In almost all cases, they wanted to win at all costs. And they would celebrate winning braggadociously. Men's egos are more fragile. They're crushed when they don't win." But that's not the way our kids are growing up. Today we teach our daughters they can do anything the boys can do. We don't expect them to play second fiddle and let the boys win.

Think about your own career aspirations. Are you aiming for the middle ground, or can you set your sights on a more senior position? Have you let subtle cultural conditioning or more overt pressure from your parents, peers, or spouse keep you from aspiring to the senior executive ranks? What do you really want to do? These are important questions to clarify whether or not you want to move forward in your career. And you will have a chance to explore them in more depth as you delve into the issues presented throughout the book.

## Are You a Perfectionist?

As counterintuitive as it may seem, the pursuit of perfection is a career-limiting move. Indeed, perfectionism is at the heart of many difficulties that women face at work. We often tie our self-worth and self-image to how others perceive us, and we fear being wrong or being seen as inadequate. In interview after interview, I have heard up-and-coming women lament that they have to do twice as much to be regarded as half as good. And so they strive for perfection.

One mid-level manager told me, "I think it all boils down to the fact that I feel I've got to be perfect at absolutely everything I do. If I'm not, I'm going to get dinged. I stick out because I'm the only woman at my level. The highest nail typically gets the hammer, so I sit back and don't speak up at meetings. I'm afraid I might say something that isn't quite right, that isn't quite perfect, so I say nothing."

The impulse toward perfectionism can come from unconscious sources—perhaps, as a child, the only way you would receive positive attention from a demanding parent was to produce flawless report cards. As an adult, you may think you must look perfect and act perfectly because you believe others are constantly evaluating and looking up to you. You may feel the need to be accepted and to fit into the business world. The higher you move in your career, the fewer the women—you do stick out, so it becomes even a greater challenge to fit in.

You know that you need to produce excellent results; however, perfectionism can actually impede your ability to produce and can infringe on your career trajectory in a variety of ways:

- If you are too demanding of yourself, you may become indecisive and may fail to complete projects in a timely manner. Your work is never good enough in your own eyes; you're constantly second-guessing yourself and you become frozen.

- Similarly, if you judge yourself as inadequate, you may never see yourself as others perceive you—a competent, high achiever—and they may wonder why you denigrate yourself and your output. Such self-deprecation can seem oddly coy or even come across as arrogant if misperceived by others.

- You believe no one can do the job as well as you, so you don't delegate enough. You end up micro-managing and, as a consequence, have little time left to take on all-important strategic, big-picture responsibilities.

- Perfectionism can also stop you from taking strategic risks. If you fear making mistakes, you may never venture beyond your comfort zone.

- Perfectionism is linked to isolation. The more perfectionistic you become, the more you separate yourself from others. You may push them away because you don't know how much you can share without revealing your imperfections. You fear getting too close, and that can interfere with vital working alliances.

As you grapple with ways to handle any issues you may have with perfectionism, you still need to keep your eye on the big-picture issues. In fact, it's important to structure time for strategic thinking and long-range career planning.

As you think about what you've done well in your life as compared to the mistakes you've made, ask yourself where the majority of your learning comes from. For me, it's usually from debriefing with other people about where I went wrong. There is great value in imperfection.

One senior executive shared her struggle with perfectionism. "Early on in my career," she explained, "I was very, very focused on not making any mistakes. That led to a lack of risk-taking and also a lot of concern about whether other people thought I was making a mistake or what the 'right answer' was. And I learned, through some tough experiences, that it's better to trust your judgment and plow forward. I'm happy to say, at this point in my career, I feel that I'm right a lot of the time, but everybody makes mistakes. It's part of life."

Of course, it's not unusual for people who are hard on themselves to be hard on others too. Liz Flynn, Executive Vice President at Chase Manhattan Bank, is in her late thirties, and she learned that valuable lesson about perfectionism early in her career. Because she had been such a perfectionist, she tended to set the bar extremely high in everything she did, including expectations of performance by her employees. Because her expectations were so high, her staff sometimes became more frustrated than motivated. Liz learned that her perfectionism disempowered them. She also learned that if she set the bar at 80 percent of what a perfectionist hopes to achieve, her employees receive a realistic challenge along with a sense of possibility and hope and opportunity for growth.

Liz's experience can help you. You want to stretch your direct reports, but not to the degree that they feel they will never attain an unrealistic goal that you've set. You do yourself a disservice when you disempower your own people! Most women who make it into senior management are high achievers. The higher you go, the more of an achiever you must be. But what may feel like a stretch to you can be torture to someone else.

Do your colleagues and staff a favor, and give them a break. And try to comprehend the roots of your own perfectionism—it will give you the capacity to deal with the impulse and overcome it. Rather than perfection, think about striving for excellence.

In the executive coaching that I do with senior women, I've noticed a shift in attitude about the need to be perfect. These very senior women are beginning to realize that it's not only what they produce and what they achieve but rather *who they are* that's ultimately important. Although we all know this on some level, it becomes more evident as these executive women reach midlife. They are still driven, but they perform at excellent levels with more grace and concern for others than they did earlier in their careers.

## Become an Expert on Your Environment

The senior executive women with whom I have spoken acknowledge that introspection is only the beginning. You also need to intimately understand the unwritten rules of your corporation and what is expected of you. Up-and-coming mid-level manager Patricia Martin told me how she regularly engages in what she calls "environmental scanning" to get a sense of what is expected of her.

> END PERFECTIONISM: *As counterintuitive as it may seem, the pursuit of perfection is a career-limiting move. It is at the heart of many difficulties that women face in the workplace. You know that you need to produce excellent results, yet perfectionism can impede that ability.*

"Environmental scanning is the ability to know what is going on around you: what the drivers of the environment are—whether it is your customers, peers, the people who work for you, your boss, or your boss's boss. It is having the skills to interpret situations and understand the atmosphere. Some of that is really intuitive, big-picture stuff. You do that by keeping yourself educated or through the nuances of talking to people and building relationships. People get blindsided. 'I just had no idea this was going on,' they'll say." If you don't understand your environment, it's more difficult to succeed because you're less apt to get results in the long run. You won't know what you don't know.

An excellent way to gain that knowledge is by seeking the advice of others who have been around long enough to know how the game is played. How do you learn the ropes? According to Karen Rose, Group Vice President and Chief Financial Officer at Clorox, "The biggest piece of advice I can give to anybody is to find out how to talk to senior management in your company. Every company has different habits and practices, different ways to get to the top. What you want to know is how you communicate with them. You're never going to have impact unless you know how they make decisions and how they take in the information on which to base those decisions."

You need to know the formal and informal lines of communication. Can you call up the CEO directly, or do you have to go through indirect channels? What are those channels? Do you have to pre-sell ideas? Or is this a company where you go in cold, make your presentation, and let everybody around the room hear it for the first time? If it's an environment where you have to pre-sell ideas, where the CEO isn't going to say "yes" unless certain key individuals are sitting there nodding, it's important to know who those individuals are and that they've bought into your idea, so they will in fact be nodding around the table and agreeing with you.

How do you acquire this insider information? First, ask yourself whether you know how to navigate in the corporate environment. You may need to seek the counsel of confidants who have more experience or exposure to top management, people who have had success in getting things done at your company. In Chapter 8, you will learn a great deal about advisers and supporters, and in Chapter 13, you will find a complete set of questions to ask your boss or other supporter, which will help you determine the steps you need to take along your career path.

SEEK THE COUNSEL OF CONFIDANTS: *Those who have had more exposure to top management can help you navigate the corporate environment.*

## Understand What Your Job Entails

Learning the ropes also means understanding the parameters of your job. When I interviewed her, Nancy Hobbs was Executive Vice President and General Manager of AirTouch Cellular. Her division alone managed $1 billion in revenue. Her career trajectory provides a helpful illustration of the importance of understanding what your job entails.

At the dawn of her career, Nancy was studying to be a teacher. Tired of the student's life and needing a breather, she decided to take a year off to earn enough money for a three-month trip to Europe. She found a job at the phone company, supervising a group of women who were from ten to twenty years older than she. "I had this boss who was incapable of coaching," she told me. "For the first six months, I remember just hating it, feeling like if I can only last for the year, I'll be so glad when it's over. I would go home at night and cry. Here I was, a 3.8 GPA person who had always been successful at everything I did, and I was totally frustrated and upset at this job."

But then, at about six months, something clicked for Nancy. Suddenly she started enjoying her job. "I found out little things that would help my life. I learned how to get my arms around the job. Then, even before the twelfth month, I had the chance to work on a team that was going to cut over the first electronic switching system in the San Francisco Bay Area. They were going to send me away for training, and it sounded really interesting. That was it! I took that job, and I was a new person. It was in that period that I said, 'You know what? This is fun. I like it, and I want to advance in the business.'"

The job got into Nancy's blood, and she decided this is what she really wanted to do. Mostly it was out of a sense of curiosity—she loved to learn. She began to tap into what was really important to her, the environment she was in, what it took for her to succeed. She mastered the situation by asking the right questions to understand the lay of the land. Because she had a better grasp of what was expected of her, she felt as if she fit in, and she began to produce the results that were needed. She also began to relax and to focus on what was important.

Once you understand the playing field and what's expected of you, you can choose if this is what you really want to do with your life. If so, you can analyze what you need to do to get ahead.

Evie Byrnes, Vice President at American Management Systems and a former executive at AT&T, spoke of the importance of really understanding the person or business issue you are trying to influence and understanding yourself as well. "They moved me all around AT&T," she explained, "and I frequently had a whole new set of people to deal with below, beside, and above me. Each time I moved, I would always go into my potential new manager and ask about what was important. I'd really draw the manager out, not only about the stated goals or the strategy of this organization, but also about his personal aspirations."

Evie wanted to understand what was driving him, what was making him come to work every day. And she used that same opportunity to negotiate and gain more latitude for her own success. "I then blended what was important to him and what was important to me so that they became one in his mind. I was working on making him successful and myself successful at the same time. We synched up, and that kept us from being at odds with one another. But I always went to those initial sessions with my head screwed on such that if we couldn't find something that meshed, I would be willing to walk away, to decline the job, no matter what it looked like as an opportunity."

## Assessing Yourself

I urge you to learn a lesson from the executive women whom I've interviewed. The majority of them set aside time to explore their own needs, capacities, and motivations. You too may find this helpful. Take a few moments to assess your motivations and preparation to move up, and your current understanding of your work environment. Bear in mind that as you progress professionally, your answers to the following questions might evolve with your deepening understanding of yourself and your career path. This is only natural, and you may want to refer back to these questions at different stages of your career.

Ask yourself the following questions. Record your answers in a notebook or other place where you can refer to them and amend them as you discover more about yourself and your career. As you consider these questions, just keep in mind that people aren't only driven by business goals; they're also driven by what's really important to them as human beings.

- Who am I really? What do I want for my life? What do I value?

- What am I capable of doing? What is it that I want to do?

- Am I aiming high enough?

- What distinguishes me from everyone else? What are my innate strengths? How can I build on them? What are my innate weaknesses? How can I offset them?

- What are my short-term and long-term career goals?

- Do I want to move up to the senior ranks, or are other issues more important to me?

- Do I really want to move up in my career and why? Do I want to move up in this organization? Is this a company and a product line that I am so passionate about that I want to put the hours in to make it happen?

- What are some of the fears that may impede my success?

- Am I strong enough to tolerate the difficult situations that can arise in the corporate environment?

- Do I have perfectionistic tendencies? If so, where do they come from? How do I express my perfectionism? Am I demanding of others too? Has it helped or hurt me to be a perfectionist?

- How can I use my desire for excellence to move me forward in my career?

- Am I pursuing a career for myself or to prove myself to my parents, siblings, partner, or others?

- Do I carve out time for strategic thinking? What is the big picture of my environment?

- Do I recognize and understand the unwritten rules at my company? To whom can I turn for advice?

- Do I understand the parameters of my job?

- How do I stay true to myself while doing what I must to advance in my career?

- How do I maintain balance in my life? Which tradeoffs are worth making and which are not?

- Am I willing to move to another city, state, or country for the sake of my career?

- Do I enjoy the intense complexities of the business world?

- Do I want to devote my energies to help my company succeed? Do I want to influence the impact my company can have on society?

- What do I think the mission or purpose of my life is? What legacy do I want to leave?

# PART II

# SIX LESSONS FOR SUCCESS: SHATTERING THE MYTHS

# 3 | Focus on the Big Picture:
## *Results Are Only Part of the Story*

Like many women in mid-management, I always thought that results speak for themselves. That is, if you're producing results, you'll eventually make it into the senior executive ranks. But as I began interviewing senior executive women, I realized that many of them had a different perspective: Advancement wasn't just about results. In fact, as one executive told me, "My biggest failure came because I believed that results are the most important—or in my case, that a project which took account of the market facts and customers and was designed to make a profit was going to win out over the CEO's pet project. Call it political naivete. When egos are involved, the right answer doesn't always count!"

I decided to investigate a bit further.

The mantra at Intel is "No nonsense results." I figured if anybody was going to be able to validate that only results really matter, it would probably be Craig Barrett, the computer giant's CEO. So one day I asked him about it. He looked at me with a straight face and said, "Carol, that's not what it's all about."

"Well, what else is it?" I probed.

"Let me tell you something," he replied. "If you produce a great deal of results, and you alienate and isolate people on the way up, do you really think a CEO is going to want you as part of his or her respected executive team?"

He had a good point. In fact, some other CEOs with whom I've spoken noted that certain women employees become so focused on the work in front of them and the details that they miss the big picture altogether. One CEO, for instance, shared a story in which a bright, aspiring female employee corrected him while he was giving a presentation to the board of directors. He had mistakenly noted a profit of 25 percent, rather than 20 percent. This woman needed to be right at all costs—and lost sight of the fact that she had embarrassed her boss. She was correct, but ultimately her misjudgment in front of her boss and a roomful of potential supporters hurt her chances for advancement.

> RESULTS MATTER, BUT THEY'RE NOT ALL THAT MATTERS: *"What have you done for me lately?" is not the only question bosses ask when they're considering managers for a promotion.*

## Winning the Battle but Losing the Client

Let's not kid ourselves. Results do matter—but "What have you done for me lately?" is not the only question bosses ask when they're considering managers for a promotion. Indeed, you can derail your career if you focus only on results, to the detriment of everything else. The senior executive women whom I have interviewed told me that keeping an eye on the "big picture" is far more important than outcomes alone.

Unfortunately, Pamela, a thirty-one-year-old district sales manager for a software company, never learned this lesson. She was enthusiastic about her job—a real go-getter. Because she had just been promoted into this position, Pam felt she had something to prove. She worked day and night to increase the sales in her territory and expected her staff to do the same. She wanted to demonstrate to her boss that she could turn her newly acquired sales territory around—especially since she knew that "results speak for themselves."

But after putting in two months of caffeine-powered, sixteen-hour days and goading her sales force to aggressively market their products and services, Pam was physically, mentally, and emotionally exhausted. Not only that, but in her enthusiasm to get the job done, she had alienated her staff by pushing them so hard. Although her district's sales numbers had increased, her staff was rebellious and ready to change territories or even companies.

Pam had accomplished the "result" she had wanted to achieve (she increased her sales numbers) but in the long run she had hurt herself by caring more about the numbers than the people with whom she was working. Even the customers felt pressured and minimized, and began to question her motives. And in her single-mindedness to increase sales, she ignored many of her other management responsibilities.

Interestingly, in the short run, Pam's superiors were impressed with her diligent efforts and results. This, of course, served to reinforce Pam's view that only the results matter. But when her subordinates and peers began to complain about her behavior, her manager knew things must change. Not only had Pam alienated her subordinates, peers, boss, and clients, but she was so focused on achieving the result, she also ran herself dry. Sick and exhausted, she had the choice to relinquish her position or rebuild damaged relationships and start anew.

## Seeing the Big Picture

It's easy to get bogged down in the details of your job and, like Pam, forget where you and your company are ultimately headed. According to Linda LoRe, former CEO of Giorgio, Beverly Hills, and currently CEO of Frederick's of Hollywood, women tend to focus on short-term goals, instead of what's right for the long-term success of the business. "If you can be really clear on what the business needs are and then put your personality into that, you have a much greater chance of delivering your message and of succeeding," she explained. Women moving up in an organization need to take a broader view. When you step back and look at the big picture, your perspective changes, and your decisions are more reflective of creating a sustainable future for your company and therefore for your career.

For instance, some of the CEOs whom I interviewed complained that women focus too much on career advancement and not enough on their current responsibilities. When that happens, the corporation's interests can take a backseat. You can derail if you don't align the corporate interest with your self-interest. For instance, if your boss is suffering from information overload or is on a tight deadline, he or she may not want to be interrupted. If you persist in presenting an idea—even if it's a great one—it's gong to be a tough sell, and you even run the risk of alienating your superior. Timing is critical. Sometimes just waiting one day to present an idea can make all the difference in the world. For great ideas to turn into great solutions, they have to fall on ears that are ready to hear them. Keeping your own agenda in harmony with other demands around you is an important key to advancing in your career.

> TIMING IS CRITICAL: *Sometimes just waiting one day to present an idea can make all the difference in the world. For great ideas to turn into great solutions, they have to fall on ears that are ready to hear them.*

How do you grasp the big picture? First, as I've emphasized in the previous chapter, you must know yourself. Second, understand your customers and their desires. Third, discern what your boss and your company value. (The exercises in Chapter 13, "Constructing Your Road Map," will help you do this.) Determining where you and your company fit or don't fit is imperative in understanding the big picture and being able to make seasoned judgments. And that's of vital importance. According to the Executive Success Profile, an assessment tool developed by the worldwide consulting firm Personnel Decisions International, CEOs and senior executives rate "seasoned judgment" as the number one skill they use to determine whether to promote someone.

Moreover, as the CEO of Harley Davidson once said, "It's not identifying the businesses you want to be in, but figuring out the businesses you don't want to be in that's important." You need to keep those issues clear in your mind if you want to be successful.

Sometimes seeing the big picture also means stepping back and entertaining a smaller vision that you can execute well. Rick Belluzzo, Group Vice President of Consumer and Commerce at Microsoft, told me that some of the biggest mistakes he made occurred when he tried to do a task that was theoretically correct, "theoretically pure and clear," as he put it, but unworkable because the infrastructure of people and the ability to execute didn't exist.

Rick felt that focusing on a smaller vision can lead to more growth and success. "Less is often more. It's a weird principle that people struggle with more than anything in business," he told me. "It's counterintuitive, and I think that makes it hard for people to grasp. You might think, 'If I do five things, I could have a bigger opportunity than if I just do two.' But, in fact, if you only do two, you might have a bigger share of a smaller market. And that could be a much better situation than having a small share of a huge market."

## The Four Critical Success Factors

In order to be successful, many businesspeople tend to compartmentalize the projects that they're working on and, for that matter, their lives. Although the ability to compartmentalize can be beneficial and somewhat healthy in the short run, when you take it to the extreme, you can fail to remember how all of the elements of success work together, and you can lose sight of the big picture. As Pam painfully learned, *results matter, but they are not all that matter.* In fact, in the interviews I conducted with senior executive women, four characteristics consistently emerged as imperative for advancement into the top executive ranks.

I have found that adherence to these four *critical success factors* determine whether women managers move up, get stuck beneath the glass ceiling, or derail. These are what I call the "C.O.R.E." characteristics that influence a woman's career advancement:

- **C**ompetence
- **O**utcomes
- **R**elationships
- **E**ndurance

In fact, some executive women admitted to me that they would not have gone very far had they not developed and nurtured these C.O.R.E. qualities. Let's take a closer look at them.

## Competence

Some years ago, when I was a sales representative at IBM, the CEO at the time was John Akers. He distributed a memo that said, "We've got to move away from the water coolers and get busy." An IBM branch manager went to one of the sales representatives who had been there for twenty-five years, and said, "Pat, what do you think about that memo from John Akers about how we'd better move away from the water coolers and get busy?"

Pat looked at the branch manager straight-faced and said, "Well, then, we'd better get rid of the water coolers!"

In those days, there *were* some empty suits walking around—folks who weren't terribly competent but had the right connections. And they were consistently promoted. In today's business environment, however, given the fast pace of change, how innovative companies are compelled to be, and how savvy a person must be to lead, an incompetent person will rarely make it into an executive position of a successful company.

Competence is the sum total of your experience, skills, and talents: your understanding of how things get done; your leadership, sales, and financial acumen, to name a few. Intelligence, ability, and expertise—these are givens for any woman who has set her sights on advancement. For some, it's the ability to take a broad view. Karen O'Shea, in her role as Vice President of Communications and Public Relations at Lennox Industries, told me, "I'm a conceptual thinker. Even at a lower level in the organization, it was probably evident to other people that I was able to see the bigger picture and very quickly understand some unpopular decisions—even to embrace them."

When I asked Shirley Buccieri, Senior Vice President at Transamerica Corporation, to enumerate the keys to her success, she said, "Hard work, enthusiasm, perseverance, credentials (things like graduating from Purdue, being superintendent of engineering at General Motors), being able to process information quickly, being able to get on top of a situation faster than the average person." These are all elements of competence.

In most industries, business is so tough and competition for high-level promotions so fierce that any manager who doesn't consistently demonstrate competence stands little chance of making it into the upper tiers. Those empty suits may make it for a while, but they can't sustain the ruse and are found out eventually. You need to ask yourself: What types of information should I acquire to stay intellectually current in my industry and in my field of expertise (business books, trade publications, journals, additional academic training, conferences/seminars, professional organizations, board experience, and so on)? A realistic knowledge of what your competitors are doing, what the market can tolerate, and how you can scale an idea to make it profitable for your company are also all part of being competent.

### Scaling an Idea

The ability to scale an idea is an important aspect of competence. It involves a fundamental grasp of the "big picture": what will and won't work based on competing demands, trends, and situations. You demonstrate competence when you take a small idea and turn it into a viable product or service that your company can use and profit from. Senior executive women routinely assess new concepts to see if they might convert them into successful endeavors. They may ask, "This is a great idea, but can I get our R&D and manufacturing departments behind it? Will it sell?" They are attuned to the consumer as well as to upper management.

SCALE YOUR IDEAS: *You need a fundamental grasp of what will and won't work based on competing demands, trends, and situations.*

This sort of environmental scanning requires that you know your consumer base, understand your market, and recognize whether the environment can actually support the idea. This requires visioning and seeing the big picture.

## Credentials and Experience

These days, academic credentials may be a must, whether it's an MBA or another advanced degree in a specialized field—scientific, legal, engineering, or anthropology. Linda Lewis, formerly at Kaiser Permanente and now Senior Vice President of Learning and Training at Charles Schwab and Company, told me, "I needed to amass all the credentials that I could along the way because no one ever takes your credentials away from you. I really encourage up-and-coming women to get all of those degrees, to get all of the certifications that they can along the way. They're always yours no matter what job you're doing."

Only two of the senior executive women with whom I spoke made it into the executive ranks without a college degree, and only 25 percent made it without an advanced degree. In fact, one woman who did not have a college degree talked about the difficulty the lack of education had created in her life.

"It's an enormous burden not to have finished college," she confided. "Obviously, I never lie about it, but I never bring it up. There are people who assume that I have an MBA, and I just let them assume it. It's a big deal when you try to get a job; it's an entry hurdle. If you don't have that credential, you spend your entire career positioning yourself so that you don't talk about it. And there are things I don't know. I have plenty of work experience and reading to fill in the gaps, but it's the credential that's the issue."

A credential is not sufficient, however. Advancing into the executive levels requires the integration of education *and* experience. In fact, many of the executive women whom I interviewed did a good deal of on-the-job learning as they widened their areas of expertise.

Denice Gibson, in her late thirties, is another executive woman whose reputation for competence is well deserved and well rewarded. She began her career as a file clerk! As the Senior Vice President of Silicon Graphics (SGI), she reported directly to the CEO. Denice holds five college degrees, including a doctorate, and has become well known for turning around ailing companies. "I've worked in almost every part of an organization," she told me. "I've been in manufacturing; I've been in engineering; I've been in customer support; I've been in information technology. I've been just about everywhere in order to round out my background and be more effective at the chief operating officer or general management level."

Because of her wide-ranging experience, Denice has an excellent understanding of engineering, organizational design, and the different types of management structures and systems that make high-tech companies profitable. She also has expertise in marketing, sales, and finance. Because of her well-rounded competence, she has been able to make previously profitable but struggling companies profitable again. And because of the value she adds to organizations, she's in great demand. She's paid generously, based on the successful turnaround of the corporation, and has spent the last decade focusing solely on turnarounds.

Denice is an amazing person. She requires only a few hours of sleep a night and frequently hopscotches the world—she's probably not someone we can all emulate. But I share her story with you because of her commitment to developing broad-based competencies and the rewards associated with that strategy. On the continuum of what's possible, she's on the extraordinary end.

The truth is, most successful executive women don't stop learning once they are out of school. They continually expand and update their understanding of business and technology. For instance, Kathleen Alexander, Senior Vice President of Human Resources for Marriott's Information Resources, alluded to the importance of growth and learning when she told me about some of her dearest friends, who are in their nineties. "What inspires me is that these people are so much older than I, and they're still learning," she said. "People who move into the first tier are people who are continuously learning, who still get excited about what they do. You need a lot of passion to keep up. I think every executive who is worth her salt requires that level of excitement because it takes so much energy to do everything that has to be done."

Studies have shown that executives' biggest fear is that they will be revealed as inept "imposters." The best defense against the "imposter syndrome"—and hitting a career ceiling—is for you to continually improve your competency. Your sense of competency grows as you take on challenges and become more confident and assertive. Once you have confidence in what you know, you no longer see yourself as an imposter. You're free to be an independent thinker; you're able to stand up for what you believe is right.

As important as they are, however, raw competence and expertise alone are insufficient to propel you up the promotion ladder. The statistics speak for themselves. In 1987, one person in twenty was promoted to top management. In 2001, the ratio is expected to be one in fifty. And, even if you're still making your way into the management ranks, these C.O.R.E. skills can enhance and accelerate your success. Survival of the fittest is the corporate rule; to move ahead, you have to couple competence with clearly achieved objectives and results. And that's the second C.O.R.E. characteristic.

## Outcomes

Outcomes are even more important than sheer proficiency in determining who wins and who loses in the corporate game. The global economy and deregulation have rendered many corporations lean and mean. They are judged on their revenues and profits, and their executives are too. As universities turn out increasing numbers of business graduates while large corporations cut mid- and upper-management jobs, an enormous pool of talented, promotable managers vie for ascendancy in a dwindling market.

Managers who are most likely to stand out are high performers who can be counted on, time and time again, to achieve the corporation's goals. They understand which outcomes are important in their company and do whatever it takes to deliver them—without, however, injuring their work relationships with other employees. Along with the other critical success factors, you absolutely have to produce.

The male and female CEOs with whom I have spoken have

BE RELIABLE: *Managers who stand out are high performers who can be counted on, time and again, to achieve the corporation's goals.*

reached the corporate pinnacle because they were able to get the re-sults required of them. As Tom Engibous, CEO of Texas Instru-ments, told me, "Being in the right spot is very important, but perhaps more important is demonstrating results. You can be elo-quent, you can show great slides, but, in the end, if you're a circuit designer, your circuit has to work time after time. Producing consis-tent results is what matters."

Tom worked in high tech, and he provided an example of how this key success factor operated in his life. As a young engineer at Texas Instruments, he designed computer chips. "When the chip came out, you put your initials on it in metal. It was yours; there was no hiding. Everybody knew if it worked or it didn't. What we called 'first-pass success' was the measure of acceptance. That meant, if the chip came out and worked on the first pass, you were okay. 'Last-pass success' meant you had to go through many iterations before the chip would work. First-pass success required paying attention to the details and being thorough while you were meeting a schedule."

Tom believed first-pass successes jumpstarted his career. "My designs, by luck probably more than by skill, tended to work. One day my manager said, 'I've got a high-visibility design for IBM,' which was our biggest customer at the time, 'and they don't want to get in trouble. They want the first team on the field.' So if you were the one who demonstrated first-pass success very quickly, maybe just in one or two designs, you were suddenly put on the first team. And then you got to play on the field every play, and it's much easier to be noticed by those above you."

For Tom, first-pass success meant doing whatever it took to make the part work. "I wanted my mom and my boss and everyone else to be proud of me and what I was doing," he told me. "There were many engineers who would work hard, but there was another group that I fit into at the time—we did whatever it took."

If you focus on the job and the people for whom you're respon-sible, and if you understand how you can make your organization the best it can be, and if your organization values your achievements, you will be rewarded for your performance. Denice Gibson at SGI exemplified this ability to produce results. She was able to get the management of a struggling company to understand the different functions within the organization and then to make those functions work together extremely well. In fact, as a result of her efforts, she often increased the visibility of the company to the outside world—the financial community and stockholders. She produced measurable outcomes (the value of the company's stock increased because of her efforts) as well as implicit ones, such as creating an environment in which the employees communicated and worked well together. People respected her, and they wanted to work with her.

Gale Duff-Bloom, President of Company Communications and Corporate Image at J. C. Penney, spoke with me about her need to effect positive outcomes. "I get a lot of self-fulfillment out of achieving things," she told me. "That's what drives me and makes me happy. I'm at my best—I'm happiest—when I'm stretched. I love to start a program (or have people I'm working with start a program) and be persistent enough to see it happen. I feel good when the results are terrific. And I rarely take 'no' for an answer. One of my bosses told me, 'I think you're the most persistent person I've ever met in my life.' If I really believe in something, I just go for it. My dad always told me, 'Don't let the little things get in the way of the big things. If you get bogged down in the little things, you'll get nowhere.' From the time I was a little kid, I never let petty things get in my way."

One senior executive woman who participated as a panelist in one of my workshops was so committed to achieving a certain outcome that she would strategically position herself outside the elevator door, knowing that the person with whom she needed to speak came through it at a certain time each day. She would walk with him to his office and discuss the specific issue on the way. She even spoke of being at the train station at a certain time so she could sit next to someone she needed to talk to during the long ride home in the evening. "Walk with someone after a meeting to get that person's perspective on what went on during the meeting," she counseled. "You have to plan these things to be effective and achieve what you want."

## Relationships

I had always assumed that women were better at developing relationships than men. But then, some years ago, I read an interview with Secretary of Energy Hazel O'Leary that surprised me. In essence, the journalist asked Secretary O'Leary, "If you were to look back over your life and think of things that perhaps you haven't done very well, what would you change or do differently?"

And she replied, "I wish I had gone to lunch more."

"What do you mean?" the writer had asked her, "Didn't you do lunch?"

"No, I put my head down," she answered. "I did my job—there were things I had to get done. And there were many times that someone would come and say, 'Hey, you want to go to lunch?' and I would say, 'No, I don't have time.' I didn't realize that's where the decisions were being made. That's where people were beginning to really understand what was going on. That's where others helped you get your job done." Secretary O'Leary didn't realize that outside the office is where some of the most important professional relationships develop.

While competence and outcomes might once have been sufficient to guarantee a promotion in an organization, they no longer are. The ability to develop relationships is imperative in crossing the threshold to the next level. In fact, competency and results are assumed once you reach mid-management. It is the quality of your professional relationships that propels you forward. Even to be considered for advancement, you must form and maintain strong professional relationships—they are essential to corporate success.

Most senior women have built coalitions both inside and outside their organizations that support their advancement at all levels—this will be discussed in detail in Chapter 4. In fact, many concur that the higher you go in your organization, the more vital your professional relationships become. Factors like visibility, credibility, integrity, and interpersonal skills also become key. Those in power select those who can replace them—and they tend to choose people with whom they have a high degree of comfort and trust. As one executive woman explained, "On a scale of one to ten, I would give relationships a ten. That makes it sound as if they're the most important thing, and I don't think they are. But relationships are a ten in that I don't think you can get ahead without them. They are among a handful of things that are necessary."

Carol Bartz, CEO of Autodesk, revealed that she would never have been named chief executive of her company without the widespread business relationships that she had forged over the years. When the directors of Autodesk were considering her, they talked to people she had worked with on other boards, in previous companies, and in the community. It was in part because of her relationships and reputation that she was offered the CEO position.

> **DEVELOP SUBSTANTIVE RELATIONSHIPS:** *The quality of your professional relationships propels you forward. Good working relationships are the hallmark of a successful manager.*

Other executive women believe that relationships were important for their advancement too. At the beginning of one woman's career, like many mid-level employees, she thought the only thing that mattered was how competent she was, what she knew, or what she could contribute. "What I didn't realize," she explained, "is that you don't get to show people those things and contribute those things if they don't have some sense of who you are—and if they are uncomfortable with who you are, they don't give you the time of day. And so I recognize now how important relationships are. I just didn't understand that twenty-five years ago."

Relationships are also vital for meeting the company's goals (which, of course, in the long run can enhance your career advancement). You can't survive in business if you can't form professional relationships. You can't get teams to work or accomplish any of your goals unless you have people who are willing to follow your leadership. Good working relationships are the hallmark of a successful manager.

A vice president at a manufacturing concern understood this well. "I don't have a marketing degree or background," she confided. "I'm very much a self-starter kind of person, and this company hasn't done a great job of providing training. Everything is very much on-the-job training here. I would put my ability to develop good relationships as certainly one reason why I'm successful within this company. I can get things done because people enjoy working with me and are happy to do things for me. The people who work with me realize that I'm very supportive of them, and I care about them. They are willing to go out on a limb and work long hours. In fact, I've seen a number of people come into this company at a senior level and fail because they haven't immediately established relationships."

The majority of executive women possess many important interpersonal skills. Such skills can include the ability to communicate, to listen, to truly engage another person in something you both care about, be it family or work.

Not only is the quality of relationships important, but sometimes the frequency of contact is too. Several of the senior executive women with whom I spoke found it important to check in with certain people every six months or so. As one woman told me, "There are a few people, maybe ten, who I absolutely make a point to have lunch with twice a year—not because I want to, but because I need to have that relationship. It's very conscious, very deliberate. Years ago, I had lunch with whoever I wanted to, and I didn't have these sorts of relationships that I cultivate today." She was being quite strategic in the way she developed and nurtured her professional relationships.

Given the deluge of information we handle every day and the fast pace of change in the business environment, people tend to reach out to the last person they've seen or spoken to. The more connected and visible you are, the more access you may have to be selected for unique opportunities when they come across the desk of a busy executive.

Men tend to play more with each other, be it on the tennis court or on the golf course, whereas women, much like Secretary O'Leary, tend to put their heads down and work. Women even have a penchant for totally separating the worlds of work and play. But, in fact, it is vital to get out and develop professional friendships. Liz Fetter of NorthPoint Communications used some creative ways to break the ice at an earlier stage in her career. "I really feel strongly about creating events for people so they can self-select to be there and have fun," she told me. "A lot of people I interact with at work and in other professional contexts aren't close enough relationships that I would call them and say, 'Hey, why don't you stop by on Saturday night?' Yet I still want to keep those relationships intact. So I create a reason to get together—a Christmas tree–trimming party or a house-remodeling party. I was halfway through remodeling my house so I had a 'Don't-Use-the-Bathroom Party.' And then people feel free to come or not. Once they're there, you have an immediate icebreaker."

You may avoid getting too close with coworkers because of the pain that can be caused if you need to correct or even fire a friend (see Chapter 4). To counteract that, you may err on the side of aloofness. Unfortunately, others can view that as standoffish and feel uncomfortable around you. Also, like Secretary O'Leary, you may feel that taking the time to develop relationships impinges on your time to get your work done, especially if you have many responsibilities at home. These are valid and common issues.

Yet, while executive women often keep their personal and professional lives separate, that doesn't stop them from developing some "friends" at work. One executive found a way around this problem. "There is only so much time in the day, and there's only so much you can spread yourself around, so you need to choose with whom you spend the most time. I tend to pick out certain groups of people who I think I can have an impact on and be helpful to and maybe they can help me as well. There's a group of women I have lunch with on a regular basis. We're personal friends but professional friends too. *But they clearly don't work for me.*"

In addition, be careful not to limit your contact to other women alone. Recently I did some consulting for a high-technology company. Management asked me to help their mid-level women in their career and leadership development. I talked with these up-and-coming

---

**DRAW A DISTINCTION BETWEEN PERSONAL AND INTIMATE RELATIONSHIPS:** *It's important to be warm and caring about the people with whom you work. But don't confuse personal relationships with intimate ones. Senior executive women keep their deepest concerns close to the chest and, for support, find relationships outside their immediate colleagues.*

women about the biggest challenges they faced. Many didn't feel as well connected within the company as their male counterparts. "The guys keep getting all the good assignments," they complained.

The women wanted to create an all-woman's group as a way to counteract what they saw as an "old boys" network. That seemed counterproductive to me. It's important to connect and relate to other women, but that shouldn't exclude building solid relationships with men as well. In fact, many of the executive women whom I interviewed told me that the majority of their professional relationships were with men, since there were so few other women at their level.

Moreover, one male CEO stressed the importance of women learning how to interact with their male counterparts at work and in social situations. "Females need to be comfortable mixing with men," he told me. "If they're uncomfortable, they're going to get left behind, and that's a mistake." Men also need to make an effort to professionally connect with women; however, unfortunately, the onus is usually on the women to make the initial connection. Women have more at stake. You'll read much more about forming those all-important alliances in Chapter 4.

To get ahead, you must develop relationships at all organizational levels, and it is extremely important that there is a high frequency of contact with superiors and key decision-makers. Unfortunately, increasing the frequency of contact can be problematic too. Many women tend to think along the lines of all-or-nothing. That is, if they stop by someone's office to talk, they're afraid they'll be in there for half an hour. Since they just don't have time to do that, they don't make contact at all. But the successful women with whom I spoke make it a point to stop by a co-worker or boss's office and have a three-minute chat. "Hi. How are you? How was your weekend? How did your daughter's recital go?" is all it takes. They connect more frequently but for shorter periods of time. Ten three-minute conversations are more productive than one thirty-minute gabfest because you spread out the "face time."

As a further extension of the all-or-nothing syndrome, I have also found that women tend to keep silent if they believe they don't know *everything* about a subject. This manifestation of perfectionism can also be counterproductive. As a person gets to know you, he or she learns who you are and what your strengths and weaknesses are. By

> FREQUENT FACE TIME IS IMPORTANT: *Ten three-minute conversations are more productive than one thirty-minute discussion.*

building relationships based on honesty, you begin to develop credibility. Indeed, it is during open discussions and interactions that credibility and trust develop. This can even occur outside work. I have learned more about a coworker while playing on a basketball team with him than from working side by side with him for a year. His personality comes out in these more casual situations—if he plays fair, takes responsibility, or has temper tantrums, I know about it.

Everything we do is a reflection of who we are, even if it has nothing to do with work.

## Endurance

Bryan Dyson, the former CEO of Coca-Cola, explained that he feels we juggle five different balls in our lives: a health ball, a family ball, a friends ball, a work ball, and a spirituality ball. As we're juggling them, imagine that four of those five are made of crystal. If we drop them, they're going to shatter. Only one ball is made of rubber and bounces back: the work ball. I thought what he had to say was quite true. The work ball is the most resilient. If you let go of your job for a while and focus on other concerns, your career can repair itself and rebound.

You can be extremely competent, you can produce the results, you can develop the relationships, but if you are mentally or physically unhealthy, it's difficult to maintain the fast pace over the long haul. It takes time and hard work to make it to the upper levels. Endurance has a lot to do with success. Having good health, both mental and physical, is important. As you move up the corporate ladder, your job can become very demanding. If you want to spend time on the business and people issues, you have to invest an incredible amount of time. So you have to have incredible endurance to keep up the pace.

The executive women whom I studied had that kind of endurance. On average, it took them eleven and a half years to attain their high-level positions. And during those eleven and a half years, many worked at least sixty hours a week—consistently subordinating private time, family life, and personal interests to the demands of their careers. Women who have reached the executive suite understand the enormous, often overwhelming commitment it takes to get there. As Carol Hochman, President and CEO of Danskin, put it, "I gave a lot. I worked weekends. I worked nights. I'd spend five weeks in South America if I needed to. I made sure my bosses always knew that I was willing to do whatever it took to get the job done."

To sustain the fast pace of executive life over the long term, make sure that a mind, body, and spirit connection balances your life.

## Intellectual Endurance

Intellectual endurance requires you to ask yourself, "What do I need to read, what do I need to think about in order to stay intellectually prepared?" It means keeping abreast of the latest developments in your company and industry as well as new technology, knowledge, and trends. For example, if you work in a financial capacity, you'll want to subscribe to magazines and newspapers that give up-to-the-minute information about what's happening in the financial world. If you work in information technology, you will want to keep abreast of the newest technologies so you can always stay aware of the technological possibilities for your company as well as know the latest technological advances of your competitors.

If you want to succeed at your company, observe what the executives are reading—which publications are strewn about the executive lobby or in their offices. It's a sign of your organization's culture. If possible, ask your CEO or other higher-ups to recommend favorite business books or television programs. You can also derive a good deal of information from videos, the Internet, professional meetings, and talking with people inside and outside your organization about their latest news.

If your company is publicly traded, follow the movement of its stock and the news surrounding that movement. Even if you're not in a financial function, it's important to apprise yourself of your company's and its competitors' financial and market positions so you can better understand their corporate drivers. These forces will influence decisions and behaviors within a company. You also want to ensure that you appropriately time the releases of your products and services based on current market information. You want to understand the playing field and be aware of who else is out there and what they're doing. That becomes even more critical the higher you go.

Indeed, in the earlier stages of your career, most likely you've been concerned with getting your job done. But as you move up, management needs to know that you really have a grasp of the big picture and your place in it. You need an understanding of the playing field, which includes your company's position and the competition.

Carlene Ellis is a Vice President at Intel. The shelf life of technology is about three months, so if she doesn't keep current, she will fall behind. Carlene voraciously reads everything she can get her hands on about new technological advances as well as developments in the Internet. That's one way she maintains her intellectual endurance.

## Emotional Endurance

So much of endurance really has to do with emotional endurance— your ability to hold your own, to understand yourself and your emotions well enough so that you can successfully handle difficult situations as they arise. Successful women have the fortitude and resilience to bounce back from a mistake. They ask, "What do I need to do to take care of my essence and understand what I'm feeling? To take care of my heart?" They can tune into their emotions in a split second and choose whether they want to deal with their feelings in the moment or not. In fact, they don't let their emotions control their behaviors. They are pragmatic and strategic in how they handle them. For instance, one senior executive woman told me, "If somebody is head of a budget office, and I don't like him, it's kind of tough. But if I want any favors, I'd better have a good relationship with him, or I'm not going to get a damned thing done." She manages to keep her emotions in check for the sake of being able to produce and enhance her career.

Senior executive women have learned not to take failures or criticism too personally. This includes the capacity not to take themselves too seriously. They feel okay with who they are and can separate a person's behavior from who the person is. By understanding that attacks are not personal (but address a business or behavioral issue and perhaps might be based on the other person's anxieties), they can stay more grounded and stronger.

Emotional endurance also requires resiliency—the tenacity and fortitude to not retreat when the going gets tough. Sue Swenson, in her role as CEO of Cellular One, explained its importance to me. "It's crucial to be resilient to failure and disappointments. In fact, resilience means being able to rise above the chatter and the negative energy that can get created in an organization when things aren't going well. Just being able to see above it all is a really important characteristic."

The truth is that the more successful you are, the more you put yourself out there, and, consequently, the more mistakes you're going to make. It's a given, for instance, that if you invest in the stock market, at some point you're going to lose money on some of your stocks. But you learn to cut your losses and keep the stocks that are doing well. Everyone makes mistakes. In fact, the more often you make mistakes, the more comfortable you become with taking risks.

Similarly, in your career climb, you're not always going to get a "yes." You need to be emotionally strong enough to be able to endure the ups and downs, the wins and losses that occur within every project, every decision. To be able to cut your losses early is important too. People get into trouble when they let problems go on and on with the hope that they'll correct themselves. Typically they don't—they only get worse.

Regina fell into that trap. She was a mid-level manager planning her first marketing seminar. She had put much time, energy, and thought into the event, but two weeks before it was to occur, only two people had signed up for it—ten attendees were the minimum. She found herself caught in the dilemma of telling her boss or hoping the problem would correct itself. Not wanting to alarm her superior, she opted for the second alternative, but that was a mistake. On the day of the meeting six people showed up.

"Why didn't you tell me what was going on?" her boss asked.

"I thought I could handle it," Regina replied. "I worked so hard at drumming up support. I thought I could pull this off—and I didn't want to worry you."

"All you needed to do was keep me updated. Just tell me the truth," her boss persisted. "I could have pooled other resources to help you."

By not admitting to a looming failure, Regina allowed a small problem to grow into a fiasco. When you take a loss early, confront a problem, and publicly admit a mistake, it saves you from a larger loss later.

This can go against your psyche. It seems counterintuitive to admit to a small failure when it hasn't become visible. No one wants to acknowledge a "failure"—no matter how small it is. It may not seem to make sense to publicly take responsibility for a mistake, but that often defuses a potentially larger problem. Understanding that some of your decisions are bound to have negative results is the key to becoming comfortable with active risk-taking.

> **BE PROACTIVE:** *Take responsibility for small failures and reveal potential problems as soon as they become apparent.*

Some of the prerequisites for being able to develop emotional endurance include maintaining a positive attitude and being realistic about the magnitude of problems that arise—putting crisis in its place. It's important not to personalize difficulties. Keep your problems in perspective by realizing that no one is imposing this adversity on you; it's just business as usual.

Sometimes emotional resilience is a matter of genetics, family history, and upbringing. If you find you're having trouble bouncing back from the crises that are likely to come your way, you might want to seek professional or personal coaching.

### Physical Endurance

Executives ask themselves, "I'm not good to anyone if I'm sick. What personal regimen must I establish to stay physically healthy?" Your physical health is important—if you have a healthy body you're more apt to have a healthy mind. Or, as the Romans used to say, *mens sana in corpore sanem*. Typically, when you're overstressed, the body is the first thing to go—you catch cold or become more seriously ill if your immune system is run-down. While we may notice intellectual or emotional deficits, we're apt to let slide our physical well-being. But in the long run, the physical is extremely important. It is, therefore, vital to take care of medical problems before they escalate into crises and to take some proactive and/or preventative steps to provide the stamina you'll need.

Unfortunately, time allotted for physical activity is one of the first things women relinquish as they climb the corporate ladder. This was often the case for my interviewees, and it is a mistake. It is important for you to find the space for regular exercise. Sue Swenson and Nancy Hobbs, Executive Vice President and General Manager at AirTouch Communications, set aside an hour or so every week to jog with each other along the beach. They discuss the challenges of their demanding jobs and seek each other's counsel. They not only have an opportunity to reconnect, but they are also reducing stress and releasing endorphins, the body's natural painkillers.

Exercising with others is a great way to get to know them in a relaxed atmosphere, and it helps accomplish two goals at once. The activity doesn't have to be competitive. Walking, hiking, or playing golf are relaxed ways to develop a professional relationship, especially with all the travel required in higher-level jobs. If you're at a conference where you have to spend the night, use the hotel's exercise facilities. Spending time alone when bicycling or running (even on an indoor treadmill) can also provide the quiet time to sort through problems and think of creative solutions.

Other lifestyle issues are equally important in helping the body work at optimal levels. It can be difficult to eat healthfully in business situations, but the computer terminology "garbage in, garbage out" also applies to food intake. From my personal experience and observations of others, I've found that we can be in such a hurry that we subconsciously look for food that will slide down fast, without chewing—and that's not the healthiest of approaches. Our bodies need a balanced diet in order to operate at peak levels of performance. Be sure to drink plenty of water, especially when you're flying, since air travel can be dehydrating. (But make sure you get an aisle seat!) It's also important to limit alcohol consumption and to get sufficient sleep.

Part of being active is also enjoying yourself. Senior executive women understand the importance of having fun. Sue Swenson told me that when she sees employees laughing and joking at work, she knows they are having a good time at what they do, and they typically produce more. Fun adds a sense of levity to the work environment, and it builds good relationships. People get to know you as a human being and feel free to joke with you. That creates honesty and increases their comfort level with you. It allows others to come to you when they have a problem because they have a sense of familiarity, which creates a safe environment for them.

Jokes that are discriminatory, however, are a no-no. A suggestive joke can be okay if done in good taste, but something extremely rude, crass, or on the gross side is inappropriate. You need to be prudent and decide what kind of language and joke-telling is acceptable and not overstep that boundary. For instance, when a senior executive at a large accounting firm made it clear to her male cohorts that she could wield a curse word as needed, they immediately embraced her as one of the team. She knew she had fit in when she saw their response to her language. Another executive told me, "You want to make sure that you don't create an environment where men think it's okay to say whatever they want to. But you can still create a comfortable environment where they don't feel that they have to walk on eggshells."

This doesn't mean that everyone should use bad language. Rely on your good judgment and what feels right to you. Tap into your own sense of values and morals and what you're comfortable with.

## Spiritual Endurance

It is a struggle to separate what we do for a living from who we are. The objective is to keep your identity intact, even if you lose your job or encounter a career setback. Executives ask themselves, "How can I be in touch with my own sense of spirituality?"

Spirituality doesn't necessarily mean that these women attend religious services weekly. Linda LoRe, CEO of Frederick's of Hollywood, explained to me, "The spiritual level to me is not necessarily religious, the way religious is defined in our society. It's a feeling of enlightenment; it's a light versus a dark spot. It touches the soul." However, many executives do have a sense of a "higher power" and are very in tune with who they are and their value system. They feel a sense of purpose in their lives. For instance, Liz Fetter of North-Point Communications explained, "I feel a big part of my mission is making a contribution to other women's lives. It all gets back to my life's purpose. I'm here to do a job. Everyone's here to do a job in life, to contribute in some way."

People who have a sense of spirituality, who trust and are loyal to a higher power, are perceived as more trustworthy and loyal. They also exhibit a higher degree of well-roundedness and calm, which is quite attractive. The business world can be extremely hectic and fast-paced, and many are inherently in search of that kind of grounded-ness. They tend to follow leaders who exude that sense of wholeness.

Being a spiritual person means believing in something bigger than yourself. Because you are less focused on yourself and more focused on the external, your ego diminishes. Indeed, everything begins to fall into place when you get yourself out of the way. You know you're doing what you're supposed to be doing when you listen to your inner voice and follow the path of your intuition. Sometimes we're the first to ignore our intuition because we think it's invalid. We believe that what others say is more convincing than what we truly know within ourselves. We have to guard against tuning out our own intuition. Spirituality, although often not discussed, is a powerful force.

Linda LoRe has always been a spiritual person. In her talk with me, she outlined the four points that she believes are the basis of success:

"The first one is love what you do and do what you love.

"The second is adopt a positive can-do and will-do attitude. That doesn't mean that you are going to keep hitting your head against the wall; it means that you figure out ways to achieve a goal.

"The third one is learn how to communicate effectively, whether it's an audience of one or an audience of millions. If you're not communicating effectively, you're not listening. And if you're not listening, you're not learning.

"And the last one is—we all have a power inside us, and none of us really realizes how strong it is. We have to reach inside and make that fulfill us, whatever we do. It's a spiritual power and it's an intellectual power. It's that adrenaline that makes people successful."

## Assess Your Own C.O.R.E.

By answering the following questions, you will assess where you stand vis-à-vis the four critical success factors and your readiness to embrace the "big picture." You may want to write down your answers so you can refer to them as you progress through the book. Once they complete this assessment, many mid-level women find that they are well ahead of where they thought they would be.

### Competence

- How prepared am I? Are my credentials up to par?

- Do I have the skills and competencies that are necessary to get ahead in my field? Do these translate to other fields as well?

- How strong is my knowledge base? Am I a quick study?

- What experiences should I gain?

- Do I have the capacity to scale an idea?

- Have I been keeping up with advances in my industry?

- What must I do to prepare myself even better?

### Outcomes

- What outcomes have I produced that demonstrate my abilities?

- What outcomes do I need to produce in order to move to the next level?

- What outcome could I produce that would make the biggest contribution to the overall success of my company?

- Do I have the wherewithal to produce these outcomes?

### Relationships

- Which relationships have helped me to get to where I am?

- Which new relationships should I develop to help me along my career path?

- Am I able to build and maintain relationships even if I disagree with the person?

- Am I able to see the other person for who he or she really is and not just for what he or she can do for me?


## Endurance

- Do I have the resilience, stamina, and endurance that it will take to further advance in my career?

- Do I have enough support at home?

- How can I take better care of myself intellectually? What do I need to read and think about in order to stay intellectually prepared?

- How can I take better care of myself emotionally? What do I need to do to take care of my essence and understand what I'm feeling?

- How can I take better care of myself physically? How about my diet and exercise routine? What personal regimen must I establish to stay healthy?

- How can I take better care of myself spiritually? How can I be in closer touch with my own sense of purpose and spirituality?


## The Next Steps

- What are the next steps required of me in terms of my C.O.R.E. characteristics? Is this where I really want to go in my career?

- Do I have the drive to maximize my C.O.R.E. characteristics?

- Am I able to manage the intense complexities of the business world?

# 4 | Create Alliances:
## *Networking Is Not a Requirement for Success*

Contrary to popular belief, successful executive women don't use networking to get ahead—they use what I've come to call *alliancing*. This became clear to me during the very first interview I conducted—an hour-long discussion with Linda Lewis, when she was Vice President of Strategic Change at Kaiser Permanente, the largest HMO in California. Linda reported directly to the CEO.

Linda has short, black hair and kind, generous eyes, and she is deliberate in her manner. She gives the impression that she doesn't want to waste anyone's time—including her own. Even now, when she sends me voice-mails, her messages are short, informative, and to the point, as if she has thought them through in advance. Linda had an academic style about her; in fact, she had been a professor of adult development at a university before she jumped into the corporate world seven years later.

At Kaiser Permanente, Linda occupied a corner office that overlooked the magnificent San Francisco Bay, with the lush, green Oakland hills in the distance. On the day I met with her, her workspace was decorated with just a few hand-selected, meaningful, and exquisite items. A hand-blown multi-colored glass inkwell with a matching glass pen lying across it were the only objects adorning her desk. This told me that Linda paid attention to detail.

As with all of my interviewees, I had sent Linda the questions I was researching prior to our meeting, so she could think about her answers. I had barely settled into my seat across her elegant desk when Linda said, "Carol, before we get started, I have to ask you a question. Is this going to be a study on networking?"

I picked up a negative vibe. And, having been a successful sales rep, I knew to answer a question with a question, so I replied, "Why do you ask?"

"I have to be honest with you," she continued. "If you want me to tell you that networking played a useful role in my career, I'm sorry, but I have nothing to say."

My stomach sank. The whole study was predicated on networking! For years, books and magazines had focused on those bulging Rolodexes and the need for female managers to glad-hand their way to the top. Like many mid-level women, I was convinced that networking was the way others had climbed into the executive ranks. "Now what?" I thought, my mind racing. "Maybe I ought to be researching something else." Trying to hide my consternation, I paused, swallowed hard, and asked, "What do you mean?"

"Well, networking doesn't resonate with me," Linda replied, settling back into her comfortable chair as she warmed to the subject. "When we talk about networking, for me it carries the connotation of a superficial relationship or a device used to achieve a goal. I don't network. Rather I develop close professional relationships with just a few people. My relationships have much more depth, but it's narrowed and focused in terms of numbers of people."

There was no judgment in her voice. But she let me know that if networking was what I wanted to talk about, she wasn't a good fit for my study. She wanted to be honest about that, since she didn't want to waste my time or hers.

I was taken aback by Linda's statement, but decided to shift gears. "Everyone gets into the executive ranks through either a promotion or because they're hired in from the outside," I stated. "So people are important in your career. Instead of networking, why don't we talk about those deeper professional relationships you have." We did, and our interview turned out to yield considerable insights and to be a great start for an incredible research journey.

Since then, I have discovered that Linda was quite right. For executive women, networking connotes pressing the flesh, handing out business cards, and developing relatively superficial relationships at social functions and "networking" gatherings. And Linda was far from the last woman business leader to give me that feedback. In fact, of the initial seventy women I interviewed for my doctoral research, *nearly all scorned this approach.* Most admitted that they were not all that good at it. Besides, they didn't have time for it, and they didn't enjoy it!

The women I interviewed made it clear that it's not just who you know, but the nature of the relationship and how well you know your contacts that will dictate the importance they play in your career and the amount of assistance they give you.

## What's Wrong with Networking?

Why is traditional networking an ineffective route to advancement? The senior women told me that it is often a time-consuming waste of energy. Although you may meet hundreds of people by attending conferences, membership functions, and breakfast forums, the relationships you form there are often too shallow to be meaningful or even helpful. Moreover, the people you connect with are frequently miles away from the critical promotion path for your career. Besides, how well can someone get to know you in three minutes, while you're balancing a glass of wine and a plateful of dainty canapés in one hand and a stack of business cards in the other?

Indeed, a mid-level manager I interviewed at a large insurance company was beginning to understand that networking was not as helpful as she had once thought. "I used to believe that the people who are up there are the ones who are out networking and making sure they attend all of the right functions and all the right parties," she admitted. "But I'm not seeing that as much as their attaching themselves to the right people. I don't place as much importance on networking anymore—and that used to be a biggie for me."

This mid-level manager's observations are right on the money. Rather than taking the time to develop superficial relationships with thousands of people, the senior executive women with whom I spoke nurture more substantive relationships or *alliances* with fewer people. More than 80 percent of the women in my study neither enjoyed networking nor engaged in it on an ongoing basis. More than 90 percent said that their professional relationships did not come from networking but rather from collaborative work on tasks and projects. By getting to know others in an authentic way through situations that test and reveal their character (rather than by simply exchanging social pleasantries), the executive women developed meaningful and productive "real-ationships," based on shared experiences. And it is these substantive alliances that propelled them forward in their careers. Indeed, they allowed the executives to influence policy even without the formal authority to do so.

This sort of activity is so important in career advancement that I have coined the term "alliancing" to describe it.

## Alliancing for Personal and Professional Development

Over the years, substantive alliancing relationships have provided senior executive women with both self-development and career advancement. They learned and grew from them, and they helped provide the confidence, trust, and connections they needed to move ahead.

The Senior Vice President of Human Resources at an aerospace company told me, "I had always been nonchalant about my capabilities, but when I came into this company, it changed my life. I had been a thirty-five-year-old homemaker and part-time editor, and the men I worked for were very helpful to me. I kept knocking their socks off with the project I was working on for them, and they praised me highly and pushed and motivated me."

Lora Colflesh, as Vice President of Human Resource Operations at Sun Microsystems, elaborated on the same theme. "I'm an introvert, so it's not easy for me to get out and network. I don't find myself going to a lot of association meetings and things like that, but I have maintained a network of colleagues that I count on. I have built strong relationships with a few people. These are either colleagues or consultants with whom I've gone through a project. We have created something together, we've produced results together, we've built some trust. And, through our work together, we've found that we have the same values, the same beliefs, the same passions about what's important for a company, and what's important for employees at a company. And through that, we know we can count on each other for business advice as well as personal support."

Engendering trust is also important in your career advancement within your company. In order for you to get ahead, your superiors and peers need to trust and believe in you; they need to know you

well enough that they will recommend you to others. They're putting their reputations on the line for you, and a good reputation is
critical in the business world. They may be unwilling to risk that unless they know you relatively well and believe in you.

To this point, one woman, the Vice President of Operations at a
pharmacuetical company, told me, "If there is a crisis in the company,
I have to have the CEO believe me and trust me when I say, 'We
need to do this.' He has to trust me from a competency level but also
on a personal level. I think relationships are extremely important
with superiors, with peers, and with people who work for you!"

Trust is often developed by working together with people as part
of a group. A person's true identity often emerges when you work on
tasks with others. In fact, a project with a tight deadline can create a
crisis mode, and that's a stellar opportunity for you to demonstrate
your ability to handle adversity. Your boss and other higher-ups can
learn the following things about you when you're under duress:

- How do you react in emergency situations? Can you keep
  your cool under pressure?

- Can you maintain sustainable results?

- How well do you work with others?

- Do you have a tendency to take responsibility or blame
  others?

- Do you praise others and give them credit?

- Are you willing to hold up your end of the deal?

- Just how caring, loyal, and committed to the team are you?

- Are you trustworthy?

- Do you play by the rules, and are you honest?

- How well do you treat people in all parts of the company and
  outside the company?

- Can you effectively and quickly scan the environment to understand your competition and customers?

- Can you demonstrate your competencies and creativity, even when you're working under tight deadlines?

By working on a group project, you not only build alliances with others by getting to know them on a deeper level and by their getting to know you, but you can also create synergies to accomplish tasks more effectively and efficiently.

How can you get involved in such a group project? You can either volunteer, or tell your boss that you're interested in working with various people in special projects. Let others know you're open to opportunities, and they may come your way too.

NETWORKING ISN'T ALL IT'S CRACKED UP TO BE: *Senior women agree that networking is often a time-consuming waste of energy. Substantive relationships and alliances based on trust and shared tasks and projects are the key to building authentic connections and furthering career advancement.*

## Using Alliances to Get Things Done

Many of the senior executive women with whom I spoke explained how they used the alliances they'd formed to do their jobs. For instance, Kathi Burke, in her role as Vice Chairman of Corporate Human Resources at Bank of America, told me, "When I think of the term 'professional relationships,' networking comes to mind, and that can appear to be outside the scope of my job. But I realize that professional relationships are crucial, because you don't get anything done effectively without working with and through other people. Because of that, my preference is to work as a member of a team."

Kathleen Alexander, Senior Vice President of Human Resources for Marriott's Information Resources, was even more explicit. About midway through her career, she was given responsibilities for exploring a daycare center at her company. She worked on the proposal from feasibility through opening the operation. She did it all and worked very closely with the finance department, the architect, people in construction and operations, and the manager of the daycare center. She put together the marketing and operating budgets and finally opened the place.

"There were some people whom I relied on heavily and who worked well together," she explained. "One is the architect. The other is a Vice President, Finance. We have remained steadfast friends. They have helped me accomplish my goals and, in turn, I have also helped them, so it has been a mutually beneficial relationship."

Alliancing also allows you to influence policy without formal authority to do so. One of the best ways to affect a decision when you don't have sufficient clout is to gather supporters in various parts of the organization who have more formal authority in the situation. Rallying their support may help you get a decision to go your way. For instance, if you volunteer to help a colleague with a project she's struggling with, she may be more willing to pitch in and speak up on your behalf when you need support at a later time. I experienced this recently when one of my colleagues asked me to introduce him to a senior executive woman I know. I was more than willing to do so because he had always graciously answered my numerous questions about administrative details and had helped me on my projects.

Don't try to form these alliances only when you need them, however. Be proactive and develop them throughout the organization on an ongoing basis. Then, whenever you need to call in one of your chits, your supporters will already be in place. It's important to build alliances in "peacetime," not when you're ready to go to war.

## Cast a Wide Net of Professional Ties

You need good professional relationships at all levels to get ahead. Women need to cultivate strong professional relationships inside and outside their corporations—people who can be counted on to advise, advocate for, and support them when promotions become available. The executive women in my study almost universally agreed that their bosses, peers, and direct reports—and even outside professional relationships—had made a dramatic contribution to their success, often by opening up windows of opportunity, pushing them up from below, pulling them through from above, or redirecting them to different, more accessible points of entry. "I prefer to say that there is no glass ceiling," explained Linda LoRe of Frederick's of Hollywood. "Instead, the corporate hierarchy is like a web. One of the best ways to get through the web is through relationships."

In fact, in preparing for their participation in my Windows in the Glass Ceiling seminars, mid-level management women are asked to interview their managers, who typically tell them that they need broad-based experience. They need to understand what's going on in the other parts of the organization, if they want to move up and have more responsibility. Alliancing is the means to accomplish this goal.

Alliancing involves developing strategically important business relationships or allies at all levels, both inside and outside your company. When I talked to Carol Bartz, CEO of Autodesk, about her career success, she told me that she had professional alliances with about twenty to thirty key people. "It's important to have relationships with all different types of people," she explained, "especially people who have a tendency to speak well of you in the right circles." These were individuals with whom Carol felt she had made a good impression.

When I analyzed the results of my interviews, I discovered that half of my interviewees' professional relationships were outside their company and half were within; only 10 percent of the latter were in their own business units. Senior executive women's alliances are remarkably far-reaching.

## Internal Alliances

Of course, it's extremely important to develop and maintain good professional relationships within your organization. They help grease the skids so you can get your job done. Why not start at the top? It's important to be introduced to your company's CEO and senior executives and begin developing at least name-and-face recognition, if not a more substantive rapport. If it's not an interruption, you might venture a "Hi! How are you?" in the hallway or elevator without taking too much of the senior executive's time. That gives him or her the opportunity to ask, "So what are you up to these days?" This initial overture provides the senior executive an opening to be receptive to further conversation later.

> **GET TO KNOW YOUR SENIOR EXECUTIVES:** *It's important to be introduced to the CEO and the most senior executives in your company and begin developing name-and-face recognition, if not a more substantive rapport.*

In making such an approach, you should always have something positive to say. Congratulate the executive on some aspect of the business—the previous quarter's financial results, profit margins, marketing visibility and so on. A quick "thank you" or a word of praise also works. If the executive wants to continue the conversation, he or she will. Your brief interaction can engender positive feelings toward you because of your concern for him or her and the company. It will also demonstrate that you are aware of and knowledgeable about the health of the company. However, be careful not to overstep the boundaries. Your boss and division or group head are probably the people to spend the most time with, and they also can create situations for you to meet the CEO and other senior executives.

If you interact with the assistants to the top executives in your firm, know that they are the gatekeepers to their calendars and the information they receive. Therefore, it can also be important to get to know these assistants and to have fun with them. But be sure your behavior is genuine. Gatekeepers are astute—they wouldn't have attained their power positions if they weren't—and will quickly recognize if you're trying to butter them up or if you have ulterior motives. They certainly won't appreciate that! Treat them with a good deal of respect. And if you are honest in your desire to nurture a relationship, you can build a reciprocal and productive connection.

Many of the senior executive women spoke of their strong relationships with their immediate bosses. These individuals can make or break your career. For instance, Terri Dial, President of Wells Fargo Bank, saw many of her bosses in an advisory capacity. "They developed me beyond my job," she confided. And another executive woman told me, "The people I worked for and with gave me the opportunities and were instrumental in leveraging me. They helped me progress as far as I could go."

Alliances with your cohort—the team of people who are at your level in the various departments and functions within your company—are vital too. We often forget about this group, but these individuals have a big influence on your career. They typically have the ear of senior management.

Your peers can recommend you to higher-ups in a non-threatening way with statements such as, "She's really good; I've seen her work and she does a great job," or "I needed to work with her organization, and she was very helpful in getting me all the information and assistance I needed." They can say nice things about you authentically without your having to toot your own horn. I recently benefited from such an alliance. I connected a colleague with one of my executive friends who ran a company with whom we wanted to do business. The client liked what we had to offer and decided to do business with us. When my colleague went back to his management team, he praised me tremendously for the work I'd done, the relationship, and ultimately the sale. If I had gone to senior management and told them the same story, it would not have had the same credibility and influence as my colleague's recommendation did.

Since only 10 percent of the senior executive women's alliances were with people inside their departments, it may also be important for you to develop such meaningful relationships with others who work at your company but are not in your functional area. There are many benefits to doing so. For instance, you can find out about larger strategic issues such as:

- Budget cuts

- Corporate initiatives that are not yet affecting your group

- Who's in and who's out

- Customer responses to new products

The goal of these relationships is to have people know and trust you and to develop alliances with those who can help you and vice versa. Donna Callejon, as Senior Vice President of Single Family Marketing at Fannie Mae, explained to me, "My favorite group of people are the ones who work in the same company, the same business, but whose work doesn't really intersect much with mine. I learn a lot from those people because there's no dynamic about who's-doing-what-to-whom or people stepping on each other's toes. You can just talk and share information. The one thing you have in common is your professional life."

How might you apply Donna's experience to your situation? If you are in an accounting function, for instance, consider expanding your reach. If there are five individuals with whom you have rapport within your business unit, think about fifty others outside your department whom you might include in your circle of alliances. Who do you interface with in operations? What about in marketing or sales? Or human resources?

To get to know them, you might buy a table at a fundraising dinner or conference or tickets to the theater or a sporting event and invite one or a group of these individuals to join you. Once you have become professional friends through these informal contacts, you can have lunch with them and talk about your various experiences with a new system or your reactions to an upcoming initiative. You will all profit from your interactions, and your organization benefits too. If you want to move up in your career, you have to do what's best for your organization. Working and playing well with others creates cohesion and camaraderie within the company. Indeed, the more senior you are, the more important these connections become to your career advancement.

You can also create these all-important alliances by joining or volunteering to head up a team that's working on a special project, just as Kathleen Alexander of Marriott and the others have done. Or you might seek out a position that helps you make these kinds of broad connections. Carleen Burgess, in her position as Director of Aviation at Entergy, told me that, early in her career, her function as a quality-assurance auditor made all the difference. "I was able to meet a lot of people and not just one group," she explained. "I got an understanding of the operation of the whole company that way, and I was exposed to upper management very early."

> **DEVELOP ALLIANCES WITH COWORKERS OUTSIDE YOUR FUNCTIONAL AREA:** *If there are five individuals with whom you have a rapport within your business area, think about fifty others outside your department whom you might include in your circle of alliances.*

It would be a mistake, however, to just look to your superiors and peers for alliances. You also need to have good working relationships with people who are assistants or at lower organizational levels than you. This became clear to me when I heard the story of a woman who was in the running for CEO at a large multinational corporation. There were eight candidates for the job, and this woman, we'll call her Sharon, was a viable contender. The search committee did a 360-degree feedback on her—they interviewed her bosses, the people she had worked with, and the people who worked for her.

Sharon had outstanding ratings with her superiors and her counterparts, but the people who worked for her were quite negative. They felt she had treated them like steppingstones ("like dirt" is closer to how they put it) because she was so hell-bent on moving up in *her* career. They felt they were instrumental to her—she only cared about them for what they produced for her. Sharon wanted to make CEO so badly she didn't care what she did to get there, and ultimately it cost her the job.

Sharon would have been better off had she developed Carleen Burgess's attitude. "I love people," Carleen told me. "I can understand how people feel. People are our biggest asset, and my people can only be as good as I allow them to be. I love developing people. We have to be a team," she continued. "All through my career, my highest rankings on performance appraisals have been on teamwork and developing the people who work for me."

Interestingly, several senior women spoke of what they had learned from their relationships with individuals who performed even menial tasks at their organizations. Linda LoRe, for instance, told me, "I think everybody has a different purpose or a different influence on my life. I can learn from the guy who sits at the security desk and carries my bag out to my car every evening because that makes him feel important. That's a relationship that you have to build. To get someone to love where they work, to do the best job they can do—I learn from those kinds of things. And the guys who come in and empty the trash. I smile and say, 'Thank you very much.' If they weren't there, what kind of an environment would I be working in?"

Kathleen Alexander had a similar point of view. "There are a lot of folks I genuinely like," she told me. "There is a lot of professionalism, even in the people who clean the rooms. My test as to whether I'm accessible and whether I keep a proper perspective is if the secretaries and maintenance people can come to my office just to say, 'Can I talk to you?' And they do. When those conversations cease, I have either gotten out of touch or something is wrong."

## External Alliances

Paul Brands, CEO of American Management Systems, told me he believes that women tend to do a better job building relationships internally rather than externally. "Perhaps women have less of an understanding of the value and the necessity of building an external network," he explained. "There may be a bit more reluctance to independently go to external meetings." That hesitancy may stem from discomfort. "In a lot of business situations," he continued, "it's ten percent women and ninety percent men."

Paul's observations may well be correct. The women I interviewed who had made it into the executive ranks had extensive external alliances. They found that the more you mix with others and create external alliances, the easier it becomes. Because your internal connections are vital to getting your job done, sometimes it's easy to forget the importance of relationships *outside* your company. This is a mistake. It's amazing what you can learn from people at other companies.

One example of such an executive with numerous external alliances was Dorothy, Vice President of Corporate Planning at a large manufacturing firm. Dorothy attained her first corporate officer position at a Fortune 500 company by the age of twenty-eight. In her mid-thirties when I met her, Dorothy had assembled an astonishing network of alliances—she spoke of literally hundreds of professional relationships that extended well beyond the reach of her employer.

Dorothy sat on four corporate boards and a number of civic boards. She had professional relationships with consultants and academics with whom she had worked on a variety of projects for her company and other activities; people in government; people with whom she has worked in prior jobs; people who have gotten to know her because of her career but whom she would put in the category of mentors or sponsors; other businesspeople who have never worked in the same company with her; many people who participate in the same kinds of community activities—professionals, lawyers, accountants, doctors, and so on.

"I have an extraordinary network, which I've naturally acquired over the course of my life. It's truly hundreds of people," Dorothy told me. Perhaps even more extraordinary, only about 3 to 5 percent of her external network were fellow employees in the same industry.

Dorothy actively cultivated this enormous group of alliances. When she started practicing law, she immediately joined the Chamber of Commerce board and became a member of the United Way cabinet. "Part of my idea of how I interact in my life and in my job is that I form relationships with people," she explained. "I seek out people simply because it makes my life more interesting, and I think it helps me be a better contributor. My external network literally dates back to my undergraduate days. There are still people I know

well and have worked with on projects—professors from undergraduate school. I think it's part of the reason why I moved up so
rapidly."

Dorothy also looked for opportunities to be inclusive rather
than exclusive. "Sunday I had a party," she said. "If I can have ten
people over, I'll have forty. I will mix people up. I didn't have any coworkers but I had friends from childhood, neighbors, colleagues in
the external network with whom I've worked, people who I want to
get to know better. A lot of the people are also inclined to keep relationships going, so it's not as if I'm carrying the burden myself."

Dorothy used her vast network of alliances to her advantage.
She was always asking herself, "What expertise do I need to solve a
problem or undertake a project? Who would know something about
this? Who could I ask?" By reconnecting with people who could
shed some light on her problems, she was able to keep the relationships strong and current. "I'm more convinced than ever that being
thoughtful about professional relationships and nurturing them is a
very important component of how I go about solving business problems," she contended.

Debra Engel, as 3Com's Senior Vice President of Corporate Services (which, for her company, included human resources, facilities,
real estate, community relations, and management information systems), was a bit more circumspect in her alliances. But she did interact with numerous corporate executives outside her company,
initially by giving speeches. She felt it important to get the views and
perspectives of these other executives about how they solved problems. "In my position, I must be able to paint a picture of the future of our organization—how it will operate and how each and
every person will engage with one another and the whole to achieve
mutual success," she explained. "It is this picture that I choose to
test on various audiences. It is important to understand what cap-
tures their imagination and what doesn't, when people easily grasp
the concepts and when they don't. This response to my thoughts is
the best preparation I have found for leading my own organization."

Debra was then able to bring that external perspective back to
3Com. In fact, she acted the way a consultant might to help increase
productivity and profitability inside the company. "I learn through

relationships," she confided. "I paint a picture, I listen a lot, and it feeds the way I learn. It also feeds my credibility. When my executives are pushing back on something I've proposed, I can say with confidence, 'Such-and-so from this company and that company have all adopted this approach.' They think I'm a real resource, because I understand how things are being done outside. I've tapped into a wealth of information." Debra's external alliances give her the ability to think outside the box.

Jackie Boyden, in her role as Vice Dean of Administration and Finance at the University of California, San Francisco, used the alliances she created from participation in professional organizations in a similar capacity. She found that knowing people at like institutions increased her store of useful information. "Whenever we talk about doing anything new here, the first thing that comes out of everybody's mouth is, 'What is everyone else doing?'" she explained. "For example, tenure is a big issue at the university—what does it mean? What are your rights? The first thing my colleagues want to know is, 'What's everyone else doing about it?' If we do away with tenure, and Harvard doesn't, then all of our folks are going to go to Harvard! It's handy for me to know who's got my job at Johns Hopkins, who's got my job at Georgetown, who's got my job at Harvard. I can just pick up the phone and ask, 'What are you guys doing about this or that?'"

She then told me about a colleague at a public university in the South who had contacted her for information about the percentage of her budget that comes from state funds. Within twenty-four hours, he was able to come up with statistics from ten good public universities across the nation. He could do it because he had those relationships. And, of course, it's always reciprocal.

DEVELOP EXTERNAL ALLIANCES: *They enrich your contributions to your organization and can aid in your eventual promotion.*

There's another important reason for cultivating outside professional relationships. As you move up to the very highest levels, your external reputation has the lion's share of influence over whether you're promoted. If a company is looking for a new CEO, they want someone with contacts, someone who can influence the community. For women coming up, it's even more important to have that credibility beyond the resume.

As Karen Elliott House, in her role as President of International at Dow Jones, explained, "I find it hard to see how you would make a good CEO if you really don't want to know people or don't know very many people. Part of what you have to do running any company is have some sense of what else is out there and how your company relates to it. I don't see how you can do that in a vacuum."

## Alliancing on Boards

The higher up you go, the more important it is to be diligent and conscious about the quality of the relationships you develop. When you become an officer in a company, you have a fiduciary responsibility to that company. Therefore, the company needs to feel confident that you are trustworthy, responsible, and honest if they plan to hire or promote you into a senior executive position. A good way to demonstrate those qualities is through the creation of alliances on boards.

Dorothy spoke of her involvement on numerous corporate and nonprofit boards. I have found that many women business leaders are engaged in these community-related activities as an adjunct to their jobs, especially as they become more senior. Serving on and creating alliances within these boards fulfill several objectives with a single activity: They are a way for you to meet individuals important to getting your job done and vital to your eventual advancement. Just as with a team project at work, often there are deadlines to be met and crises that occur while serving on a board. Your personality and competencies emerge during these times, and that enables others to truly get to know you.

The fact of the matter is that your professional relationships are apt to become more broadly based as you move up the corporate ladder. In fact, the more your influence grows within your company, the more you need to expand your sphere. When you're starting your career, your affiliations most often reflect the specific tasks you must accomplish. But the higher you go in your organization, the more you need broader-based business skills. You have to look outside your immediate environment and understand how your company fits within the industry and how your industry fits within the general economy. Serving on nonprofit and community boards is a great way to make the outside connections that can give you that perspective.

Gale Duff-Bloom at J. C. Penney described to me several positive experiences she had had while serving on such nonprofit boards. "We have a seat on the North Texas Commission," she told me, "and our chairman asked me if I would replace him on their 'active list.' So I went to these big meetings, but I didn't have much to contribute. Then, all of a sudden, the president left, and they put together a search committee. The chancellor of North Texas University headed it up, and he was fabulous. There were six of us on that committee, and all were unbelievable people. It was a wonderful experience choosing a new president, and we all became good friends. We have a great deal of respect for one another. They're all CEOs of their companies from different walks of life, and they're just as down to earth as they could be. When you get into a smaller group, you really get to know them.

"Now the other members of the committee call me on certain things they're trying to do in their companies that we've already done. Recently I was at a luncheon, and a senior executive at a major bank was there. He came barreling across the room. 'Hi, Gale,' he bellowed. 'Come meet my people!' He was as proud as if I'd been his very best friend. He especially introduced me to the women in his company, and they were all saying, 'Tom came back every time from those search committee meetings talking about the talent.'"

Gale is Vice Chairman of the National Better Business Bureau, so she has established strong professional relationships there. She's also on the board of the National Alliance of Business and two independent paid boards. She believes joining a board is a real advantage for women, even in the earlier stages of their careers. "I think people should volunteer because nonprofit boards need them," she told me. And she has learned a lot about different management styles from these boards. "You bring it back home," she explained. "Sometimes I wish I had started doing this years ago. So now I'm trying to get my people involved at a much lower level. It's great to have that experience before you move into senior management. You grow from it. There's so much that applies to what's going on in your job, and you are so much better prepared for advancement with that kind of experience."

Some senior women chose their board involvements strategically and intentionally. For instance, one corporate executive did volunteer work predominantly in nonprofits. "I choose those so that I'm involved with people in organizations that are different from mine," she explained. "I specifically joined one volunteer group because they've got some people who are heads of advertising agencies. They're key officers in line positions, and I needed to get to know them better."

Sometimes the connections are unintentional—people in your social life or your religious institution. That's a way to get to know others on a personal level, outside the work environment. It's amazing how often those are the individuals who end up having the most influence as you move higher in your career. For instance, in the case of Carol Bartz, the people she knew at church and other organizations gave her the positive references she needed to land the CEO position at Autodesk.

Indeed, joining a nonprofit board is also a way to become part of the "good ol' boy" system. When a corporate search committee is looking for a new executive to run a portion of their company, almost all of its members are extremely well connected. Rather than contacting references listed on the resume, they may pick up the phone and call their buddies. "What do you know about Sally Lane?" they may ask. Even if they know you only through your religious affiliation, volunteer associations, or board memberships, this informal grapevine can play a big role in the decision to advance you.

## Too Close for Comfort?

Alliances are professional relationships that are not overly personal. (The reverse is also true. Typically, senior executive women don't talk business with strictly personal friends.) They are more intimate than just knowing a person's name, face, and occupation. It's a relationship versus an acquaintance. However, although these work-related alliances are substantive, they're not necessarily intimate. Your professional relationships need not know your deepest, darkest secrets, but they can know you well enough to ask, "So how are the kids?" Or, "How's your father's recuperation coming along?"

All of the executive women I studied were exceptionally good at forming strong professional relationships at all levels, inside and outside their organizations. Most, however, did not mix their professional and personal lives. Overwhelmingly, the women in my study made a very clear distinction—and drew very clear boundaries—between their professional and personal relationships. They generally did not socialize after work or on weekends with others in their company. "My professional relationships are not social," one executive woman told me. "They are strictly professional—the relationships I need to get my job done." Wells Fargo Bank's Terri Dial concurred. "I have a real big division between my personal life and my business life. I definitely separate the two."

In fact, if you think of relationships on a scale of one to ten, one being that you know very little about the person and ten meaning you confide your deepest, darkest secrets—there's nothing you don't share—my interviewees reported that only 10 percent of their professional relationships fell above a six. These women play their cards relatively close to the vest. They open up just enough so that others get to know them and realize that they're sensitive and caring human beings.

Professional relationships are a hybrid. They're not overly personal, but they are personal-professional. You may talk about compensation plans or share office buzz such as, "Did you hear about our new corporate travel policy?" or "Have you ever worked with Pat in marketing?" You're not necessarily relating to one another about something you need for a particular project, but you're also not sharing the details of what you did over the weekend.

One senior woman told me, "I learned early on to make the distinction between family and business, between friends and colleagues. It doesn't mean that I care for those folks less than I did before I figured that out, but it does mean that I've kept the perspective and more distance. I finally realized that my company wasn't my family."

Indeed, most senior executive women wouldn't dream of sharing their deepest fears or their hopes and dreams, or even much about what's going on in their home lives. For instance, Gale Duff-Bloom at J. C. Penney told me, "I just don't bring too many personal things to work. I never have. I'm married; they know that. They all know my husband. But I don't talk too much about my personal life. I love the others, and I used to be out there in the field. I had much closer relationships with many of the managers when I was on district staff and then with the district managers when I was on regional staff. But the higher up you go, the tougher it is to manage the information you share with those close professional relationships. Then you move much further toward non-disclosure. It's a whole different feeling—not quite as relaxed."

This separation of the personal from the professional is one of the most perplexing issues in every coaching session or workshop I give. Mid-level women are always asking me why senior executive women must make this distinction when senior men seem not to have to. Indeed, my research indicated that while male executives enjoyed one big personal-professional circle of relationships, women seem to have two separate, but somewhat overlapping, personal and professional circles.

There may be several reasons for this dichotomy. The first may simply have to do with the need to set limits when boundaries are blurred. Although lower and mid-level women (like Gale early in her career) don't seem to have trouble melding the personal with the professional, once these women become executives, they know intuitively that they shouldn't do so.

> **DRAW CLEAR BOUNDARIES IN YOUR PERSONAL AND PRO-FESSIONAL RELATIONSHIPS:** *Whereas male executives may enjoy one big personal-professional circle of relationships, women seem to have two separate, but somewhat overlapping, personal and professional circles.*

The truth is, they needed those relationships earlier in their careers, but now they are required to hold certain pieces of information in confidence. Indeed, you should be alert to the fact that the level of intimacy you share with others when you are moving up in your career may diminish once you attain more senior levels. And since executive women are reluctant to share too much of themselves with another person at work, they can get caught in an all-or-nothing struggle. They naturally want to deeply connect, but find it difficult to find the right balance. Either they put up a shield to keep distance between themselves and others, or they bond at a deep level—which can feel too close for comfort.

I recently asked Dawn Lepore, the Chief Information Officer at Charles Schwab, how she managed her professional relationships. "Carol, it's tough," she replied with candor. "Over the years I have gotten more comfortable having friendships with people in my organization, but I am always very sensitive to perceptions of favoritism." These executives struggle with how much they can really share without playing favorites, without letting others know their weaknesses, without getting too close. Besides, having favorites can undermine their credibility.

Then there's the issue of privacy. As one senior executive woman told me, "I don't think you can or should pour your guts out to people who you work for or who work for you. I don't think I'm secretive, but I think most people judge you." Indeed, because they keep so much to themselves, secrets become a big problem for these women. Terri Dial of Wells Fargo told me, "There is no such thing as 'confidential' confiding. I have learned to accept it. In the beginning, you think you can get away with it, and then you realize that you can't. I would get very angry with the people I felt betrayed my confidences, but then I came to realize that most people didn't do it intentionally. And even if they did it intentionally, they usually did it with good intentions, not bad ones. So now I just figure that if I'm confiding in one person, I'm actually telling seven different people, and I'd better be willing to do that. If you don't want everyone to know, don't tell anyone!" she cautioned.

Ironically, even if that one person never actually divulges the secret, it's most likely the confidence will seep out, through his or her actions and body language, to a larger group anyway. For instance,

Frances, a senior-level manager, told me a story about the time she shared sensitive information regarding a coworker's performance with Dana, a colleague with whom she had worked closely for twenty years. Frances was mortified when, at a company picnic, one of their teammates approached Dana to ask precisely about this issue. Dana quickly turned red. Though she responded, "I don't know anything about that," her blushing gave her away. She had inadvertently answered their teammate's question.

> MAINTAIN CONFIDENTIALITY: *There is no such thing as "confidential" confiding. Exercise prudence in determining the information you share with others.*

Other senior women were also wary of the personal information they shared with coworkers. "I confide in my friends, not in my professional relationships," one executive in the banking industry told me, "and I confide in my advisers but I don't necessarily socialize with them." Another female executive remarked that she turned increasingly reticent as her career progressed. "I've become more guarded," she said, "because I've learned that people talk. You have to work under the assumption that anything you tell one person will get to somebody else, and a lot has changed since I've taken on more responsibility. I've had to adjust to being the boss, which has not been comfortable in some cases. There are a couple of people who work in my group whom I used to work for. Our relationships and the information I can share have changed because of this new reporting structure."

Organizations are becoming flatter, and departments are being urged to communicate with each other. If you don't share, it looks as if you're hoarding information, but sometimes that's a burden that must be borne. As many as a third of my interviewees explained that one of the worst things they've ever had to do as an executive was fire a close friend. This is a strong deterrent to developing extremely close friendships with people at work. A senior human resources executive explained her dilemma. "People think that if you're in human resources, you know everything that's going on—you control who goes, who stays, how much they get paid. So I'm always a little on guard with people pumping me for information. They just walk in and ask, 'So what's happening with so-and-so?' I can't tell them. And sometimes you're in a relationship with someone who's a friend, and you want to tell them that they're about to get fired. It's hard to say, 'I'm not going to tell you. I can't share that with you.' But being in the position you're in, you can't divulge that information."

Sharing with your peers some personal information and the challenges you face can be very healthy; however, the lesson to be learned from executive women is to be selective in the information you disclose. As you move up in your career and gain increasing levels of responsibility and access to information, you need to be extremely conscious of the sensitivity of that information, and the impact it and you can have on people's careers and lives. You must be strategic in what you divulge.

I have also found that women keep their personal and professional worlds separate because when they're at home, they want to be able to relax and enjoy their friends and family; they want to detach and decompress. Indeed, they often prefer that their friends not know what they do for a living. I have found that this level of privacy is true of senior executives, but not of up-and-coming managers, who tend to openly discuss every detail that is going on at work.

## Sharing with Your Partner

Do you relate your travails to your significant other? That is, of course, a personal decision. Some executive women want someone they can confide in—but they don't want advice on how to fix their work-related problems. Some appreciate that their partners are in business and can relate to the issues they're coping with, while others prefer that they're not—they need a break.

Many senior executives are making decisions all day, and they're exhausted by the time evening rolls around. One woman said to me, "When I get home, I want my partner to make all the decisions for me and all the arrangements—where we go or what we'll have for dinner, what tickets we get, who we'll see. I'm tired of being responsible." And another, whose spouse was a teacher, said, "The good news is, when I go home, I don't have to talk about business. If I were married to someone who was a businessperson, that would be the topic. So he keeps me more genuine and refreshed."

It is important, however, that if you don't share your work experiences with your partner, you have a healthy outlet for talking through your professional frustrations or dilemmas. Both Nancy Hobbs, Executive Vice President at AirTouch Cellular, and Sue Swenson, President of Leap Wireless International, have husbands who are not in the business world. Since Nancy and Sue have similar career backgrounds, they have found it quite beneficial to share their frustrations and successes with each other. They have an outlet for their work discussions so that they can each focus on and more deeply connect with their respective spouses when they are together.

Others find it difficult when their partners don't work in the same industry—or even in business. They find it easier to connect with a significant other when they are intimately familiar with the challenges and demands of the business world. These women often don't want to spend the additional time and effort required to bring their partners up to speed or find it virtually impossible to do so. They may not share as much at home as they do with associates at work, or their many commitments can pull them away, and this can create jealousy and distance at home.

If you and your partner share similar careers, you may have an easier time communicating about both of your work experiences; however, you may also need to consciously turn off work discussions and connect at a different level to keep your relationship strong and fulfilling.

Perhaps the solution is to find someone with whom you can deeply connect who also understands the issues and demands you face. This requires that you also be supportive to your partner and make your relationship and family a priority. You'll find some helpful suggestions on balancing your work and family life in Chapters 9 and 10.

Whereas networking can be a time-consuming waste of energy, forming alliances is crucial to your career success. Let me summarize with a story that illustrates the importance of these "real-ationships." I was coaching the newly appointed treasurer of a large organization who felt her main focus was to effectively manage the financial department of her company—and from her point of view, that did not include developing and maintaining alliances with her colleagues and direct reports.

Rita's previous job had included crunching numbers. She was unaccustomed to building business relationships with her colleagues and frankly wasn't sure how to go about it. Her tendency was to put her head down and do her work. In her new position, her boss told her she needed to do a better job managing her relationships at all levels of the organization. Rita didn't think that was part of her job description, but she realized its importance when it came up as an area for development on a performance review.

"I just don't have the time for that stuff," Rita complained to me. The trouble was that she didn't think these alliances were all that important, so she had never learned to make the time for them. But, as with many women who advance in their careers, the skills and abilities that landed Rita her new position are not necessarily the ones that will help her succeed in it.

I coached Rita to allow time on her calendar for brief, friendly meetings with two colleagues each Monday morning. She was simply to ask them how their weekends had been. It wasn't long before Rita noticed a shift in her productivity and that of her colleagues. The department felt more cohesive, and, because of these minor adjustments, the team worked together better than they ever had before. It was just a small change in consciousness and behavior that made a big change in Rita's future.

# 5 | Help Others Be Successful:
## *You Don't Have to Be Ruthless to Succeed*

Recently I spoke with a mid-level manager who believed that in order to be an executive you need to yell at people to control them. When I asked her about what it takes to make it into the executive ranks, she replied, in part, "Most of them have quick tempers. The rest of us try to keep out of their way. We don't want to be on the receiving end of any of that. They will fly off the handle at a meeting. They may be sarcastic or put somebody down."

And the CEO of a large retail company recently remarked, "One of the women managers in my company told me, 'My perception of what it takes to make it into the senior ranks is you've got to be a bitch. That's what I see.' Is that belief really common?" he asked me, shaking his head.

Yes, it is. I hear that sort of reasoning all the time, and it works against your better interests. Yet, most often, it's what the media portrays in movies, such as the 1988 romantic comedy *Working Girl,* in which Sigourney Weaver coolly plays the heartless Boss from Hell. Although that movie was released some years ago, perceptions have not changed all that much. Much more recently, Darla Moore, the CEO of Rainwater Inc., an investment firm, was depicted in a *Fortune* article as a woman who eats nails for breakfast. The cover story about her was entitled "The Toughest Babe in Business." Described as a cross between the Terminator and Kim Basinger, she is quoted as saying, "I've harassed guys all my life."

Darla is married to Richard Rainwater. When she took over HBA, a health-care organization, she fired T. Boone Pickens and a couple of others and in the process was able to turn the company around. The article, however, didn't dwell on her business acumen. Instead it showed her as a hardnose and a dominatrix. In order to be an effective senior executive, you need to be decisive. But ruthless? That's just not often the case.

In fact, I have found exactly the opposite. My research shows that you have to be approachable and generous with praise, gratitude, and your time in order to succeed in the long run—a far cry from ruthlessness. Business is a very human interaction. At the top, decisions are based on relationships and trust. We've all seen the brightest stars burn out or get shelved because they can't get along with others. If people trust you—if you can lead, build a team, and get the job done without alienating others—higher-ups will think of you first for promotions. In business today, nobody's going to risk working with someone they can't trust.

In my research, I have found that the higher people rise in the corporate pyramid, the more their future promotions are based on relationships with superiors, colleagues, and subordinates. Linda Holsonback, former Vice President of Managed Care Operations and HMO Administration at Blue Shield, put it succinctly when she told me, "People get promoted because other people promote them. Those above you have to know that you're doing a good job, they have to know what your track record is, and they have to like you." Another executive told me, "I return almost every phone call. Sometimes it can only be a thirty-second call. I honor requests for visits. I often get calls from people who ask, 'How can I become more like you?' I always spend time talking to people—male or female—who have those questions."

> **BE NICE!** *You need to be approachable and generous with praise, gratitude, and your time in order to succeed in the long run—a far cry from ruthlessness.*

Indeed, the overwhelming majority of executives I studied were gracious, likable, generous, and friendly with a touch of lightheartedness—they were able to laugh at themselves and their foibles. They recognized that life is too short to take themselves too seriously, and they made a deliberate effort to avoid alienating others in their organizations. They were also extremely forthright and honest, since trustworthiness plays such an important role in career success.

## It Makes Perfect Sense

Jan Peters, President and CEO of MediaOne, lives by the saying, "Nice gals can finish first." She believes that the three most significant reasons for her promotions and the promotion of others include performance, credibility, and the highest integrity. With that comes trust and confidence. "You just can't violate trust," she told me. "It's the most important thing."

Think about it this way: If you were a CEO of a large company, would you want cruel manipulators as part of your senior executive management team? How would you be able to trust them to run your company if you're worried about whose back they were going to stab next—maybe even your own? The fact is that today no executive can be successful in the long run if she alienates and angers those with whom she works. In the previous chapter we saw that good relationships are of paramount importance. You need to cultivate strong professional ties inside and outside your organization—people who trust you and on whom you can count to advise, advocate for, and support you when promotions become available.

Let's look at the opposite extreme—someone who lacks the skill, the capacity, or the will to develop this all-important rapport with her coworkers. This woman lost her mid-level position (just shy of executivehood) shortly after I interviewed her. She had held that job for less than a year. "I have access to power by the very nature of my job and by virtue of the fact that people put confidence in me," she told me in the interview. "And if you can't get to the base of power you can get near the base of power, and that's me. I have access to the CEO. People will listen to me. They sometimes shouldn't, but they do!

"I am brutal on incompetent males and females. I basically would not continue the relationship. I just won't work for or with those people. And I have to be honest with you—I've crushed them before I've severed the relationship. I don't want them to be any-where near my organization. I get very protective. I can be brutal in how I sever the relationships. I walk away and refuse to participate in anything they do. I take opportunities—God, I sound so mean!—to publicly disgrace them. I distance myself physically as well as pro-fessionally."

Is there any question why this woman was fired? During her tenure at the company, she alienated just about everyone. Even her secretary hated working for her. Would CEOs want to move an up-per mid-level manager with this attitude into their senior executive team? Of course not. It makes perfect sense that they would rather promote people with whom they can communicate (and who make an effort to communicate with others), whom they understand, who are really part of the team, and who are able to help them. People willingly follow leaders who are generous, kind, thoughtful, and forthright, and who help others succeed.

In fact, from my experience and research, I've found that what's really important in getting ahead is to instill in others a desire for you to be successful. In order to do that, you need not thwart others but rather to help them achieve their goals. As Kathi Burke, in her role as Vice Chairman of Corporate Human Resources at the Bank of America, told me, "If I'm working for or with somebody, I see my job as helping them be successful. And I know the people I have worked for have been very supportive of me because of that. They have been willing to sponsor me to do different things within the or-ganization because of that."

Reflect on the bosses you've had in the past, the ones whom you really adored. What characteristics would you attribute to them? When I do this exercise, my thoughts drift back to Amal Johnson, my former boss at IBM. I really cared about her and wanted her to be extremely successful because she cared about me and wanted *me* to be successful. How can you be ruthless and care about others at the same time? These two attributes are simply incompatible.

## Some Important Lessons About Caring

Top women executives are tough, decisive, and effective while gen-uinely connecting with others. Any woman who is aiming toward the top must nurture relationships with others and instill in *them* a desire for *her* to be successful. It's reciprocal. If others feel heard and understood, they perform at their best.

God gave us two ears and one mouth for a reason! We need to listen to people and understand what's going on in their minds and hearts before we speak. Senior executives do that extremely well; they're great listeners. I also found that they seek to understand before being understood; they take the time to internalize what others are saying. My parents taught me "People don't care how much you know until they know how much you care." I found that senior executives tend to figuratively put their arms around you and ask, "What's really going on?" In so doing, they show their commitment and warmth, and that forms a substantive bond.

> BE A GREAT LISTENER FIRST: *God gave us two ears and one mouth for a reason! We need to listen to people and understand what's going on in their minds and hearts before we speak.*

Some people can get the message of caring across in a one-minute conversation when they simply ask, "Hi. How was your weekend?" In other circumstances, where issues are more complex, such as an employee's faltering performance, it might take a greater time commitment to draw out the other individual. In severe cases, you may have to roll up your sleeves and dig in to really get to know the person. This doesn't mean you must share everything about yourself. But a certain warmth and openness can help break through barriers to communication.

In her movie *Eddie*, Whoopie Goldberg teaches us these lessons through her own mistakes. Her character signs on as head coach of a hapless men's professional basketball team that is on a perpetual losing streak. At first, she tries to get her team to win by pushing them. She yells. She carries on. She criticizes them. She believes that the more she prods and cajoles, the better they will be. But it's all to no avail. They just keep losing, and it has nothing to do with her efforts or her attempts to motivate them.

Then one of her key players comes to her and asks, "Do you know what's really going on with this team?" He tells her that his teammates feel misunderstood.

"Do you know that one player is having marital problems? And another member of the team has drug problems?" He starts enumerating all of the personal issues that the basketball players were struggling with.

Whoopi gets the point. She understands that she needs to be committed to their success on and off the court. Taking this insight to heart, she seeks to understand their problems and initiates conversations with her players, one by one. They start opening up to her and begin to feel some connection with her. Soon they want to win for themselves and for her. Once the team believes that she understands and cares about their problems, they reach new heights and start winning. Because Whoopi wanted her team to be successful in their lives, they wanted her to be a successful coach. Her caring created a bond and a sense of connection that she and the team had lacked before.

---

GENUINELY CONNECT WITH OTHERS: *Each of us has an enormous need to feel cared about before we are willing to perform at our highest levels. Your purpose in drawing out your employees is to help them feel understood, part of a team, and valued as human beings.*

---

This dynamic is the same, whether you're a coach of a basketball team or overseeing a division in your company. Each of us has an enormous need and desire to be understood and cared about before we are willing to perform at our highest levels. Your purpose in drawing out your employees is to help them feel understood, part of a team, and valued as human beings. You're not just talking to them for the sake of talking. Your genuine interest will augment their motivation. Besides, it's hard for them to be productive if they're distracted by their personal lives. Such an attitude of caring has much to do with kindness—and nothing at all to do with ruthlessness.

## The Trust Factor

By definition, executives must inspire others to achieve their goals. The Center for Creative Leadership, based in Greensboro, North Carolina, has conducted decades of extensive research on the most common reasons why mid-level managers derail, why they are involuntarily demoted or plateau in their careers. One of the most frequent causes of career derailment is the failure or inability to develop the interpersonal skills necessary to maintain positive relationships. This was borne out in many of my interviews. You have to meet your goals without leaving bodies in your wake.

Often the development of trust means creating situations in which everyone wins. Nancy Hobbs of AirTouch Cellular explained to me, "You need to think ahead and consider the pros and cons of an issue. How can you make it a win-win for people?"

It's easy to become stuck in "I'm-right-you're-wrong" power struggles. But you have to think about the issues carefully and understand how to make your point of view more palatable for everyone. It's a bad idea to bring up big issues about which you have a strong opinion suddenly and unannounced in front of your boss at a staff meeting. One of the worst things you can do to undermine trust is to blindside a peer. It's much better to get the problem out on the table in advance. Then you know where the other person is coming from and what his or her issues are, and you won't be blindsided either.

AVOID POWER STRUGGLES: *Win-win situations help you create trust among coworkers and colleagues.*

## The Importance of Being Honest

Trust is predicated on such a show of honesty, and most senior executive women value the executive virtue of forthrightness in themselves and in others. Here is just a sampling of their responses:

- "Honesty and integrity are paramount to me, but that doesn't mean I want people to point out that I gained five pounds. I do want someone to say to me, 'Hey, are you really sure you want to do that?' if I'm headed in the wrong direction."

- "I don't really avoid anyone unless they are low on integrity. I don't have time for them."

- "I can't think of any relationship that I've consciously severed. Well, maybe once or twice, actually. And that would have been with someone who was doing something dishonest."

- "I have a real difficult time with dishonest people—like the back-stabbing—and people who would hurt other people needlessly. Dishonesty, meanness—I have a real problem with that."

- "People who have personal agendas as opposed to the organizational agenda and people who don't deal directly—about whom or from whom I hear indirectly—I wouldn't want to have professional relationships with them."

As mentioned earlier, you want to be careful about the amount of personal information you share with colleagues. However, if your performance may be impacted by a family crisis, it's important to be emotionally honest with your boss, to alert him or her to a potential slide in your usual levels of attainment. One woman told me how her candidness in face of an emotional trauma helped to cement her relationship with her superior. She and her husband were getting divorced after fifteen years of marriage. "This was the year from hell," she revealed. She had just become a vice president six months after their second child was born, and her husband "wigged out." The first person she went to was not her parents (who lived 500 miles away) or her best friend, but her boss.

"I'm an open book. So I told him, 'I want you to understand that I might appear irrational, crazy, or out of it over the next few months because the following things are happening . . .' and I told him the whole story. Then I said, 'Michael is in the first grade and Jenny has a nanny, so they'll be okay. I'm not going to punt through this. But it could get very messy because my husband is nuts. The whole thing might end up on the front page of the newspaper. I've never given you anything but one hundred percent, but I may not be sane on any given day. I'm not asking you for anything, but I just want you to understand what's going on.'

"My boss cried," she continued. "That's how much he cared. I was blown away, and truly felt supported by him."

## Be Humble, but Don't Apologize Up Front and Don't Give Away Your Power

Kindness and generosity presuppose a certain measure of humility. Jim Preston, retired CEO of Avon, cautions about watching out for arrogance. "Most everyone's got the same amount of gray matter," he told me. "Don't put yourself above other people by thinking that you're smarter or have a better memory. Also realize that you're going to do some really dumb things, and there are times when you'll have to say 'I'm sorry.'" It takes a sense of humility to know that you're human, just like everyone else. As another CEO put it, "It's important not to get too full of yourself along the way so that you start struttin' your stuff. I've seen situations where that can come back and get you. If you stumble, no one will be there to help you out."

In fact, some CEOs spoke of the necessity of being an easy person to be around. We all know individuals whose personalities and ways of doing business help us feel good about working with them, despite the difficulty of the task. And, of course, there are others whom we hope we never have to deal with again, even if the assignment is pleasant or exciting. You're probably going to run into most of those same people more than once or twice as you cycle in your career over the years, especially if you stay in the same company. As another CEO told me, "Some people don't understand that they may be in the power position only for the moment, and if they don't use some sensitivity and humility in how they deal with others, it could come back and bite them in the backside later."

But although it's important to be humble, make sure you don't go overboard and apologize for yourself up front. Alan Buckwalter, CEO of Chase Bank of Texas, advises women to be mindful of how they make their presentations. He observed that many management women come into a board meeting and immediately start their discussions with an apology. "I do think women tend to have a higher standard," he told me. "They'll come into a meeting and say, 'Let me apologize in advance because I wasn't able to gather this or that data. While this information is basically good, I don't have total confidence in it.' A man would never come in starting with an apology. I do believe that it's a macho thing, and men don't want to make excuses."

According to Alan, rather than admit they hadn't done their homework or didn't have all the facts, most men would just wing it. "I don't know very many women who wing it," he told me, "until they get to a pretty senior level and there's a lot more confidence. And then, of course, they realize that's what these clowns are doing."

The message here is: If you're asked a question that you don't know the answer to, tell the truth, but don't apologize. Start off strong. A savvy businesswoman would say, "I don't know. But my guess is . . ." Or, "Intuitively, I think it might be . . ." If others want the details, tell them you'll get back to them with further information after the meeting.

Moreover, just because you're kind, honest, generous, and thoughtful doesn't mean you have to give away your power. The CEOs whom I've interviewed have observed that when a male superior shoots down something a woman says, she often just walks away from it. If you think something is really important for the business, believe in what you're doing and figure out another way to present your case.

"This is a generalization," Linda LoRe of Frederick's of Hollywood told me, "but men tend to go through the back door with their plan if it's not accepted up front. And they lobby. That's how the political system works." Women haven't yet gotten that kind of informal corporate coaching. "We're just now learning that you need to form alliances," Linda continued. "If you have something you know is going to work, figure out a way to get it done. Don't ask for permission, but rather ask for forgiveness later, if you have to. When you allow somebody to shoot you down, you have given them power over you."

Don't back down when you know you're right. State your case in a factual and nonthreatening way—don't personalize your argument or make it an attack on anyone else. Gather supporters for your business case prior to presenting it to the decision-making group. Ellen Hancock, CEO of Exodus Communications and former Chief Technology Officer at Apple Computer, specifically recommended creating buy-in for an idea before presenting it to a group such as the executive management committee. She told me that she identifies two or three influential individuals who are willing to listen to her presentation and give her constructive feedback before she presents it. These individuals are then more likely to have a vested interest in the success of her presentation during the meeting. Remember that getting into a verbal fight will never serve your purpose. Your discussion needs to be a rational presentation of the facts and your business case.

> BE KIND, GENEROUS, AND HUMBLE: *But don't give away your power!*

## When Relationships Don't Work

How do senior executive women deal with relationships that are problematic? Unlike the manager who humiliated those with whom she disagreed, a good number of the senior executives with whom I spoke sought to confront the individual to clear the air, but they did so judiciously and in a way that was strategically sound. They were able to manage others' perceptions and understood the "rules of the game" in order to avoid career damage. Most didn't sever the relationships outright. Rather, they confronted the conflict and tried to work it through while leaving the other person's self-esteem intact.

Julie England, a Vice President at Texas Instruments, explained

her rationale for being careful with how she treated problematic relationships. "Very early in my job at the company, I learned there's
an unwritten rule that you never know who you'll be working for,"
she said. "It could be that, down the road, you'll be managing the
person you're working for today. That has actually happened to me.
So you never want to leave a bridge too burned as you cross it."

Bobbi Gutman, in her role as Corporate Vice President and Director of Global Diversity at Motorola, spoke to me about making
your points and handling conflict while preserving the other individual's self-esteem. She and her husband hold an annual party for
influential people. She has only one rule for her guests: No one is allowed to promote their products or services to other invitees at the
party. But toward the end of one of her soirees, she discovered that a
guest had violated the rule. While he was speaking with an executive
at the gathering, she overheard him trying to pitch one of his products.

Bobbi didn't confront this man immediately at the party but
pulled him aside the next day. "I'm sorry I have to do this," she told
him, "but you'll never be allowed to attend one of my social functions again."

When he begged her for a second chance, she said, "I gave you
one opportunity and that's it. I care about you. I really like you, but
I drew a line and you stepped across it."

In her communication to her erring guest, Bobbi had separated
her feelings for this man as an individual whom she liked (*"I care
about you"*) from her feelings about his behavior (*"I drew a line and
you stepped across it"*), of which she disapproved. Her key message to
me was, "You need to confront conflict and difficult situations
firmly, but remember to leave the other person's self-esteem intact."
Although this man was no longer welcome at her parties, she still
maintained her relationship with him.

Susan Weir, Vice President at McKesson, echoed the sentiment
that you don't need to end the relationship when conflicts arise. "I
really favor laying all your cards on the table and talking it out before I'd do something like severing a relationship," she said. "Sometimes you find out something that you didn't know. My style is more
to talk it out."

Others feel that to avoid making enemies, it's best to let troublesome relationships simply "die on the vine" instead of severing them directly. This approach allows all the individuals involved to preserve their dignity. The executive women may change the tone of the relationship and withdraw. Perhaps they don't personally return phone calls. As one senior woman told me, "I'm a really direct and frank person. But the difficulty of dealing with someone directly is that you rob them of a certain sort of face, and then you've created an enemy. You don't need to do that. I let it die gracefully."

And when you're in a larger organization, you need to retain relationships because you don't know when your paths will cross or what your next reporting relationship will be. You may report to them or they to you. A failure to maintain some sort of professional relationship makes it very difficult. In looking at the bigger picture, try to prevent your discomfort from interfering with the work that has to be done. It may be that you can't get close to someone because of something he or she did in the past; nevertheless, maintain professionalism about it. I have seen estranged colleagues revisit severed relationships several years later. People always want to start anew.

> **DON'T BURN BRIDGES:** *When you're in a larger organization, you never know when your paths will cross or what your next reporting relationship will be. You may find it helpful to let troublesome relationships simply die on the vine.*

## Maintaining a Sense of Humor

An important component of success for many senior executive women was their ability to maintain a sense of humor and even to nurture good cheer among their coworkers. One woman told me she calls others in her support network to share new jokes with them. This, of course, also flies in the face of ruthlessness.

Carlene Ellis of Intel told me, "I work hard and play hard. I know how to have a good time, and I think it has served me well because I stop and don't take myself seriously. It gives me a release.

Somebody said to me the other day, 'Don't you ever need to relax and have fun?'

"And I said, 'This is fun!' And our employees have a lot of fun going casual and wearing Halloween costumes on Halloween. You can't integrate work and fun much better than that!"

It takes a level of confidence to have fun at work—to laugh at your mistakes and poke fun at yourself. Most of the executive women I interviewed had a great sense of humor and a very quick wit. The interviews were typically quite jovial, while being highly productive at the same time.

## The "Ambitious Woman" Fallacy

The skills you may need to use to get into the executive level (and I'd be the first to admit you may have to be relatively aggressive) may not serve you well once you get there. After you become a member of the "team," you need to be a team player, and that requires a different set of behaviors. Indeed, managers—especially women, unfortunately—often antagonize others if they are perceived as overly ambitious or a threat. Although many of the women with whom I spoke admitted to being highly competitive, that didn't mean that they wore their ambitions on their sleeves. And some, it turned out, were more ambitious for their organizations than they were for themselves.

Rona Schmidt, in her role as Senior Vice President at the Fireman's Fund, spoke to me about the importance of not being a threat to anyone in the company—especially those who are above you. When I asked her why she believed she had made it into the executive ranks, she responded, "One of the key reasons for my success is that I'm not seen as threatening to my superiors. That helps people relax around me. I give them the time they need to become comfortable with me and my ideas." It's clear that if your superiors feel you are threatening their position, they will not promote you. They need to believe that you are on their side, a team player, and you're not out to get their job, but rather that you'd be an asset to the executive team.

Donna Callejon, as Senior Vice President at Fannie Mae, told me, "I'm a nice person; people like me. I didn't 'go after' any of it," she said, referring to her career advancement. "I wasn't overly ambitious in an overt way. Every job I've been in has been either because of mutual interest or because somebody else offered me the opportunity."

Indeed, Donna did not initially seek her current promotion. "I remember so clearly the day my boss told me he was leaving," she confided. "I went out to dinner with a group of friends that night and said, 'I'm not interested in his job.' And for two months, all I said to his superior was, 'I'd love to talk to you about the kind of person who I think would do well and what needs to be done to move this organization forward.' And then I saw who the candidates for the job were. I couldn't imagine that any one of them were more right for it than me. And so that's when I said, 'Look, let's talk. . . .' But I was still reluctant."

Donna seemed to place her organization before her own career advancement. And she is not alone in her sense of generosity. One senior executive woman admitted to me, "I care about my employees more than I necessarily care about myself in some ways." And Karen Rose, the Chief Financial Officer at Clorox, told me, "You want to be a teacher in your organization. Hoarding knowledge may make you feel as though you're indispensable, but it isn't the most valuable thing you can do for an organization—sharing information is. That's the most important piece of advice I can give you. I wish I had learned it a little bit earlier in my own career!"

---

**SHARE INFORMATION:** *Hoarding knowledge may make you feel indispensable, but it can get in the way of your advancement.*

---

I truly believe in the paradox: *You have to give and give and give until it becomes yours.* Often we don't think that way. We give cautiously, as if we're giving something away, but in truth the more we give, the more it all comes back to us. Although there may be times when you cannot disclose confidential information, it's important to impart knowledge that may help others solve problems and advance their careers. That kind of sharing implies a generosity and a trust that are antithetical to blind ambition.

## Is the "Queen Bee" a Dying Breed?

The ambitious woman brings to mind the "Queen Bee syndrome." This occurs when the first woman to reach a certain level tries to exclude other women from achieving the same status, as in "I've made it on my own, and, by God, so will you." That seemed to be the case in the movie *Working Girl*. But I have also found that it exists in real life too. During one of my earliest interviews, Carol Bartz, the CEO of Autodesk, described a situation in which she felt she was a casualty of this syndrome. Attending one of President Clinton's economic summits in Washington, D.C., she approached another female CEO of a large corporation, introduced herself, and said, "I've heard a lot about you." Her friendly overture was met with coldness. In fact, in Carol's words, the other woman "tossed me a piece of bread and basically said, 'Get lost!'"

The incident upset Carol, and she was curious if other senior executive women had had such an experience and why they thought it happened. So I told Carol's story to each of my successive interviewees and sought their opinion on this issue.

From their responses, I have come to believe that although the Queen Bee still exists, she is a dying breed these days. At one time, when only one woman made it into the executive circles, she was able to control who came close to power and who didn't. Now, however, as more and more women advance into the senior executive ranks, it's harder for such a woman to maintain her grasp.

Besides, many senior women understand the need to create teams and nurture strong relationships with their coworkers. Quite a few spoke of their commitment to fostering the careers of other women. And Christine Garvey, as Group Executive Vice President at Bank of America, told me that she believed in surrounding herself with people who challenge her. "I think it's really critical that we hire people who are very smart," she said. "As a manager, I feel that the smartest people, the people who will stand up and disagree with you, are the ones who can give the most to you in terms of success." This is not a Queen Bee attitude.

Nevertheless, because Queen Bee behavior is disturbing whenever one encounters it, some of the senior executive women ventured theories about why it arises. Several believed the Queen Bee attitude grows out of competitiveness. That is, if a woman has worked hard to become an executive and is often the first woman at such a lofty level in her company, she may feel that another female's presence threatens her uniqueness. Karen O'Shea, a Vice President at Lennox Industries, traced this behavior back to childhood patterns. "In my mind," she said, "it always boils down to that little girl thing of 'I want to be the center of attention; I want to be the A+ girl; I want to do the erasers; I want to be the beauty queen. And there's no room for anyone else.' It comes from jealousy or threat."

Competitiveness among women is a big issue, and numerous books have been written on the subject. I believe that people who have been involved in healthy competition (such as participation on sports teams) typically know how to compete more effectively than those who have not. They learn that winning is good, even though somebody else loses, so they're in the game to win, but not to crucify the other side. Moreover, they don't take losses so personally. And teammates really do want each other to get ahead. Just because one member of the team wins doesn't mean the whole team can't too.

Unfortunately, women tend to compete with each other because they often believe there are only going to be two women promoted to the executive level—as if there's some magic number. It becomes a case of every woman for herself, an unhealthy attitude when it comes to appreciating the big picture and what's good for the organization.

Other senior executives suggest that the Queen Bee attitude arises from insecurity. Karen Wegmann, in her role as an Executive Vice President of Corporate Communications at Wells Fargo Bank, proposed this rationale. "Some senior women say it's okay if I'm the most senior woman, and nobody else is," she speculated. "Then I can have great largesse for all the other women. But when they're senior too . . . watch out. The other phenomenon I've seen is the 'Bride of Dracula' syndrome," she continued. "Women whose talents I've been hoping would be recognized finally do get promoted and turn into witches overnight—power-mad, with smoke coming out of their ears. I just want to smack them and say, 'What happened to those talented team players that I so wanted to get promoted?' Maybe women behave in this way because it's so hard to 'get there.'"

Because of their recent entry into the corporate world, women can be much more insecure than men are. Or perhaps they are just less adept at hiding their insecurities. (Men have been learning how to mask their fears since childhood.) Part of the cat-fight mentality emerges from insecurity. Once some managerial women get a taste of power, they may be afraid to share or delegate it because they fear they're going to lose it, so they hold on. They stay aloof. They've never seen the rewards of sharing information and power. They don't understand that you only get stronger if you share.

While all of these theories have merit, I also believe that one of the reasons some executive women can seem ruthless, aggressive, or overly competitive is because they work under a great deal of pressure and can experience pent-up frustration that they can't communicate in the way they want to. They're starved to talk with other women in their position—it is indeed lonely at the top. Sometimes people who don't know them can view their behavior as overly aggressive. They even struggle with the appropriate levels of assertiveness—how forceful must I be to get my job done in face of the obstacles that may be thrown in my path? It's not until they connect with other senior executive women that they realize these are issues they all face.

From the Executive Women's Alliance Conferences I've organized, I have seen that once these executive women start to communicate with one another about the problems they all encounter, they immediately and visibly soften. They relax because they realize they're not alone. Others are struggling with similar issues.

What can you do when you encounter a Queen Bee? One of the best ways to effectively work with someone who "suffers" from this syndrome is to compliment her on her accomplishments and competence and allay any fears she may have of your being a threat to her by helping her become more successful. Another good way is to let her know that you respect her opinions and would be honored if she would be willing to help you with an issue that you are currently facing. These strategies might help defuse her insecurities.

But the need for such strategies may be waning. The fact that more women are really becoming a part of the fabric of the business is beginning to change the need for a woman to believe that she must be a Queen Bee. One senior executive embodied this new, more inclusive attitude. "Typically, I feel more comfortable dealing with women on a professional level than with men," she admitted. "I have things in common with them—a lot of shared experience and perspective. And each of us at this level is kind of unusual. It's just fun to connect. It's not that I feel uncomfortable with men, but it's easier for me to make a personal connection with women."

# 6 Take Risks:
## *Keeping Your Head Down Can Keep You Off the Fast Track*

I recently spoke with Renee, a fairly senior mid-level manager in a multibillion-dollar organization. Her role included the management of nine departments. All but one had stayed within budget, and she seemed pleased with that—but her manager wasn't.

"I was called into my boss's office last week because one of my departments is over budget," Renee told me. "I went into this year thinking that as long as the overall bottom line with all of my departments is okay, then I'm doing okay. But my boss threw a wrench in the game when he told me he wanted each department to be in budget. I knew they were not working as efficiently as they could be, but I had decided to let it go because it's my toughest, most volatile group, and I could make up for the shortfall in other departments. But my boss was making me deal with it."

Renee had tried all kinds of strategies with the troublesome department. Initially, she just left them alone, doing the minimum she had to because "it was so unpleasant to deal with them." She had eight other departments that were "nice" to work with, and she found herself ignoring the problems until they got too big to ignore. Renee believed that it was important to just keep her head down and hope that the problems would work themselves out. Unfortunately, they didn't.

"I've operated that way for quite some time, and it seems to keep me out of trouble," she told me. "My assistant, on the other hand, has taken the other strategy, and she's going to get a big promotion, so I guess there are things to say about that. From the day she got here, she became very visible; she seems to be in the middle of every discussion. She puts herself there. I, on the other hand, try to avoid difficult people and situations."

During our conversation, Renee identified assertiveness as one of the factors necessary for success. And she could clearly see that she needed to do some extra work in that area. "I view all of the people at the top as assertive," she said. "But I choose not to be assertive in a lot of situations. It seems to have worked; I got good ratings at my last review. But if I were to really strive for the executive levels, becoming more assertive would be something I would have to address in my own personality and my own style. That would be a development area that I would definitely have to work on. I'd probably have to increase my visibility with those above me instead of keeping my head down. I'd have to put myself out there in terms of volunteering to lead some big effort. I can maybe start to look at what kinds of big things can I pioneer. It's going to take some risk-taking."

It certainly is.

## Taking Calculated Risks

I can't tell you how often I've heard mid-level women espouse some version of Renee's belief, "If I just keep my head down, I'll be invisible so if I make a mistake, no one will know. If I want to get ahead, the wise thing to do is avoid taking risks." This is a myth. In reality, your very success may depend on your ability to take significant yet calculated risks and go beyond your "comfort zone." These risks will help you advance in your career and mature as a person.

Jack Parks, the CEO of Basic American Foods, told me, "You really need to try new things." And he lives his credo. He was a speech major in college and taught high school for several years before he joined Basic American Foods thirty years ago. Since his background was unrelated to business, there were occasions when he felt lost. But since he was sharp, people believed in him, and he prospered.

"There were many times that I had no idea what I was doing," Jack explained. "My boss would say, 'I want you to do a certain job,' and I would respond, 'If you think I can do it, then I will, because you know more than I do.'" Jack trusted his immediate boss and his own inherent ability, even though he didn't know what he was in for. The lesson for you in this: If you don't understand something, learn on the job. Don't think you have to have it all figured out before you begin.

Linda LoRe, CEO of Frederick's of Hollywood, explained that risk-taking *early* in your career helps build confidence and self-esteem, traits that are vital to career advancement. The more junior your position, the easier it is to start. "You've heard the sayings, 'No risks, no reward. No pain, no gain.' You will make mistakes, there's no doubt about it. But the risks aren't as great at a lower level and at a younger age."

When you're younger, you have more resilience to recover from a setback. If you make a big mistake and learn from it, it becomes part of your store of information to help you take the next calculated risk. Your experience builds cumulatively and becomes a positive growth cycle. The more risks you take, the more rewards you get. You'll also make more mistakes, but that's how you learn to forgive yourself and move on. But if you haven't taken strategic risks early in your career, it's never too late.

And when you do take risks, it's important to communicate your direction and motivate your employees. The likelihood of success increases when your staff and stakeholders are on board, and you're all moving in the same direction. But you do have to be willing to advance into your *discomfort* zone, particularly when it comes to addressing potentially controversial issues or creating possible conflict. And that means you've got to understand your business and the business case behind why you are taking the risks.

> GET YOUR STAFF AND STAKEHOLDERS ON BOARD: *When you take risks, communicate your direction to your employees and your superiors to get their buy-in.*

Indeed, risk-taking is a fact of life in the upper-echelon jobs, where executives must constantly make decisions involving enormous numbers of people and large sums of money with limited information. At progressive and fast-paced companies such as Intel, employees are rarely fired for taking a risk and trying to stay ahead of the curve, even if that risk is unsuccessful.

I talked with Carlene Ellis, Vice President at Intel, recently. "You know," I told her, "Intel seems to be a hard place to work. Like other companies, especially in the high-tech industry, if you mess up, there's somebody else waiting right behind you to take your place. It's a fast-paced, hard-charging environment. What if you *do* fail here? Is there a possibility for you to get fired?"

And Carlene said, "Carol, if you don't take a risk and get out there, you *will* get fired." It's almost reverse psychology. You've got to get out there, and you've got to try. If you fail, it's okay; you pick yourself up, dust yourself off, and try again. People who are extremely risk-averse, be they men or women, tend not to make it up into the senior ranks. Indeed, in my research I have found that women managers who are willing to change jobs or take on challenging new assignments demonstrate their ability to embrace risk and often find that they advance more rapidly into high-level positions. Sometimes it's simply a question of speaking up.

> TAKE RISKS: *So many women try to keep their heads down and avoid taking risks. In reality, success depends on your ability to take significant risks that go beyond your "comfort zone."*

Take the case of Leslie Altick, Executive Vice President of Consumer Checking at Wells Fargo Bank. She had started out as a securities analyst in a large trust department at Harris Bank, a major financial institution in Chicago. The first critical turning point of her career came when she left that job for one in strategic planning. "What you should read into 'strategic planning,'" she explained, "is that the job put me into very close contact with the highest levels of senior management at a very young age. And the important thing about that assignment was that I asked for it.

"I'd been a securities analyst for four years. It was great, but it was isolating, and I didn't like the isolation of the job, so I developed some critical relationships outside the trust department. One of my friends was controller of the company. I had helped him on a couple of projects that involved competitive industry analysis. I finally decided I'd just go to him and say, 'Look, if anything ever opens up in your area that involves this kind of project, please consider me.'

"Two weeks later, literally, he came in and asked me if I'd like to head strategic planning for him. Talk about being in the right place at the right time! But the important thing was that I'd asked. And if I hadn't asked, it's almost certain that I'd never have been considered for the job, because I was in the trust department, which wasn't really part of the bank."

As you will see, although "keep your head down" is regarded as the golden rule in many corporate cultures, virtually all of the executive women whom I have encountered reject it out of hand. Like Leslie Altick, they feel their success depended upon their ability to take calculated risks and venture far outside their areas of comfort, despite the potential for failure. In fact, some of them have learned to embrace failure because it enhances learning and growth.

## The Paradoxical Value of Failure

John McDonald, the CEO of McDonald-Douglas, has said, "Adversity is what introduces you to yourself." One of the consequences of risk-taking is the potential for failure. But, ironically, many times our failures hold the keys to our success because of the lessons they teach us. Despite our need for perfection, it's extremely important to go out on a limb, and sometimes to fail and "fail publicly," as Dawn Lepore, Chief Information Officer at Charles Schwab, put it. "You learn a lot more from failure than you do from successes," she told me. If you're not failing publicly, you're not going to succeed publicly. The trick is to learn to be resilient when you do miss the mark. Dawn's CEO at Schwab, David Pottruck, calls it failing smart. "Huge, spectacular, corporate-terminating failure is not a very great thing for anyone's career," he explained. "So we try to fail, but fail small and fail smart. Failing smart is understanding why did we fail? What can we learn from our failure? How do we find out how to stack the deck next time in our favor?"

Denice Gibson, as Senior Vice President at Silicon Graphics, provides a perfect example of that skill. When she was in her mid-twenties, a corporate president gave her a company to run. "We went off and built what we thought was a great plan," she told a Windows in the Glass Ceiling audience. "We were executing along that plan, but about eighteen months into it, we realized we weren't going to make it. It was one of my largest failures. The market consolidated much faster than we had estimated. Because we weren't paying attention to a list of assumptions we'd made, we didn't change our business plan in time to make the market window."

From this, Denice learned to always compile a list of assumptions and validate them periodically to make sure they're still sound. But, perhaps more importantly, the way she got through the experience and salvaged her career holds lessons for all of us. She actually stepped back from the fiasco and analyzed it as if she were a consultant. "I had to take all the names and faces out, put everybody in their roles, and step through the entire process to look at who did what to whom, where, when, and how. What did the board say? Who gave his advice and who didn't? When did we ask the right questions, and what questions did we fail to ask? That's part of the learning process.

"The culmination of the learning was going back in front of the board and presenting it to them. We brought in the entire management team, and we each had our own piece of what we learned and what we would do differently. As a result of that, I think we're all running companies today."

## Take That Flying Leap

The vast majority of the executive women with whom I spoke shared such stories of bravery and corporate derring-do as they pursued their career goals. For some, risk-taking grew out of need or desperation. A divorced mother of three and vice president at a pharmaceutical company told me, "I never thought about moving up the career ladder. When I got divorced, I was concerned about making enough money to feed the kids and not lose the house. It occurred to me after working for a while that I would be supporting myself and my children. I looked around at some of the guys I was working with and thought, 'I can do that. Never mind that I don't have a degree. I can do that.'"

Karen Rose, Group Vice President and CFO of the Clorox Company, also took risks out of need. She graduated from the University of Wisconsin with a bachelor's degree in history. "I was one of those classic cases of a woman who had avoided math," she explained, "I even took extra language courses so as not to have to take math. But I was desperate for a job, and there was an ad in the paper that said, 'Business Manager, will train.' I answered that ad, and here I am today!"

During her twenty years at Clorox, Karen has held seven or eight positions as she has moved through the corporate organization, all within the finance and accounting area. As CFO, she has direct responsibility for the array of activities that one might expect: all of the finance and accounting organization, as well as information services, corporate communication, investor relations, and corporate administration. "But more importantly," she said, beaming, "the most enjoyable part of my role is that I sit on the Executive Committee, which sets the strategic direction of the company. That's where I'm having the most fun!"

Karen spoke about being appropriately innovative within the position you hold. "You go into an assignment and things can be running very smoothly, but everything can benefit from improvement. Get under your belt very quickly what the actual job description might be, and do that well in a routine way. But then," she advised, "figure out how you're going to change the nature of the job so that yours is a value-adding position. And this can be done at any level and in any part of the organization.

"For instance, I used this strategy in my very first job where I went into a forecasting assignment. The end result was okay, but the team got there in such a chaotic manner that there were bodies lying on the ground each month as we got through with our job. My introducing a simple process changed the nature of the work coming out of there. As I moved up the organization, obviously the nature of the work that I could concentrate on took a broader, more strategic perspective. But you don't have to wait for those things to come to you. Look for them and define the job that you want to do, that you know needs to be done. Grab it and run with it."

For other women, the challenge was thrust upon them. Nancy Hobbs, Executive Vice President and General Manager of AirTouch Cellular, explained, "I've had periods in my career that have been difficult. They had put me into business sales. It was in a mid-management position. I had been there for a year. I had no knowledge of business sales. This was one of those things where people say, 'I like what you're doing over *here;* I think you could really make an impact over *there.*' So at first I was excited about it, and I took the job. They gave me a branch that was in the bottom quartile in sales, and in a year we made it to the top quartile. I was so excited about that and so proud of the people and what they were able to achieve."

At the end of the year, the same vice president who had taken Nancy from her previous job and put her in sales grabbed her and said, "I'm going to put you in this staff job." She was in charge of all of the product marketing for the business organization—all the data and business systems products. She had no background or experience whatsoever in this area, and there were some thorny issues associated with a number of the products. "I was three months into the job, and I remember thinking, 'This is terrible. This isn't going to work. I don't have the skills to do this job.'"

At one point Nancy asked to talk to her boss. "He's a great guy," she explained, "and I was worried that he had put me in this position of responsibility, and I was going to screw it up, and the business was going to be worse off. So I told him that. I said, 'You know, I really appreciate the confidence that you have in me, but I think this is not the right job for me, and I'm worried that I'm going to fail you and I'm going to fail the business.'

"He sat there quietly and took it all in. So then I volunteered, 'I'm under a lot of pressure.'

" 'How do you know that?' he asked me.

" 'Because my eye is twitching.'

" 'Which eye is twitching,' he wanted to know. 'Is it one or both?'

" 'No, it's just one.'

" 'Well, which one is it?' he asked.

" 'It's the right eye,' I told him.

" 'Why don't you come back and talk to me when the left eye

starts twitching too! I have confidence in you that you can do this job. Just don't be so hard on yourself.'

"I thought, 'Oh, my God! This guy is bright, but he has just made a bad personnel decision.' He called me about two months later. 'I just wanted to follow up on our conversation a couple of months ago,' he said. 'I'm wondering if you still think you're on a kamikaze mission.' Of course, by then I'd adjusted to my new position and things were going well!" Nancy was able to get her arms around what she needed to do to make her project successful, and she was off and running.

Nancy was fortunate in that her manager was supportive of her moving into uncharted (for her) territory. He had confidence in her abilities, and his faith in her paid off. But not every woman is so lucky in her corporate climb. Sue Swenson, President of Leap Wireless International, had a tougher time of it. A true believer in the importance of gaining a broad range of experience within a company to move ahead, Sue felt that she needed to learn operations after having been primarily in customer service and marketing at Pacific Bell. So she asked for a transfer. She had had in mind a cushy job in southern California, close to her home and people she knew. Instead, she was catapulted into a position 400 miles away and with an awful boss. "It was my choice to take on an assignment like that, but it was my supervisors' choice as to where. I said, 'I'm ready to go.' And they said, 'Okay. This is the one we found. Take it or leave it.'

"On the first day at this operations job, my new boss said, 'Tell me about your background,'" Sue continued. "It wasn't his choice that I was there; it was part of my development. When he heard I was new in this function, he said, 'Do you mean to tell me you've never been in operations before?'

"I said, 'No. But that really doesn't bother me. I've been around people who work there. It's the same. You're dealing with customers. You're dealing with employees. You're dealing with business process. There's probably some technical stuff I'll have to learn to understand the new environment, but I can do it."

" 'Well, you will never be successful here,' he told me.

"And I said, 'You know, this is day one. Could we wait a couple of weeks before you make that judgment?' "

It didn't end there. He continued to humiliate Sue and the people who worked for her. "Thank God, I was as tough as nails," she said, "because I don't think too many people could have survived that. In fact, I almost quit. It was probably the hardest thing I've ever done. My supervisors had sent me over there. They were saying, 'We know you can do it.' There was a lot of confidence in me that I could 'go in and turn the organization around.' But I had no peer support because I didn't know any of my colleagues. I was not my new boss's choice, and he certainly didn't say, 'Oh, sure. I will mentor this person.' Basically, I ended up getting together a group of people who were looking to win against this guy, and he was terminated from the company. It just shows how bad he was. But it was almost to the point of breaking me.

"I didn't know anything about the organization until I got there on the first day and found out how horrible it was. Then I decided that I was going to show them. I have that kind of attitude. 'I'm going to show them I can do this!' It became a personal goal to work through it and just ignore the negative environment. I grew up with a lot of change in my life. I was from a military family, and we moved every two years, so change was normal to me. But I think others would not have survived that; they would have quit. There's a point where people can make it so painful, it's not worth it. You look into yourself, and say, 'I thought I was pretty good, but I'm not so sure anymore.'"

But throwing herself into this painful situation had its rewards. It taught Sue a great deal about responsibility, commitment, her personal strength, and the process of growth. "I learned a lot there," she admitted. "I learned a lot about employee motivation. I learned a lot about employee commitment, even in really negative environments. So, at the end of the day, looking back on it, I have to say, it was good growth. I'm just glad I made it through so I can look back on it and enjoy it."

How did she survive? "You just get in and immerse yourself in it. Sure, it's hard. The learning curve is really steep, but you can do it. I think you have to be willing to go into areas that you're not perfect in and recognize that your breadth of experience will, over a relatively short period of time, enable you to do well in the job. But you have to feel confident that you will do that. And, let's face it, the various jobs in business are not really that different from each other. But they have little things that are unique to them. What fun! To get to learn something that you don't already know perfectly."

If it turns out that you must re-group because you cannot survive in your position or company, you will still have learned many important lessons about your interests, as well as your strengths and weaknesses. Always be mindful of what you can take away—even from the most difficult of circumstances.

## The Perils of Perfectionism

Sue Swenson makes an excellent point. The need for perfectionism has stopped many a mid-level woman in her career tracks. In fact, as I've interviewed CEOs of large companies and asked them what they feel are some of the real differences between men and women as they try to make it to the top, the one issue they all mention is that men are more willing to learn on the job. They may not necessarily know what they're doing, but they give it a try anyway! Many businesswomen, on the other hand, are more risk-averse. They understandably feel that they can't afford to make a career mistake that may be the final roadblock to their path to the executive levels. Consequently, they strive to understand everything about a job in advance before they say, "Okay, I'll take it." But often there's only a small window of opportunity that we miss because we don't say, "I'm not one hundred percent sure what I'm doing, but I'm going to do it anyway."

"Men figure if it doesn't work out, I'll just go do something else," Sue Swenson told me. "They have a much healthier attitude than women do about trying new things and being in a position where you aren't in total control. I think women just have to say, 'Hey! This is a great opportunity to learn something new, and I may have to spend a hell of a lot more time learning this than I did in the previous assignment.' But if you go in with that attitude and recognize that there are going to be tough times along the way, that it's not going to be easy, still, at the end of the day, you end up being a better person. You learn a lot about yourself in those kinds of situations."

Gale Duff-Bloom, President of Company Communications and

> Don't Be Afraid of Mistakes: *If you're not making wrong decisions, you're probably not making critical decisions, and you're not learning! Be mindful of what you can take away from a difficult situation.*

Corporate Image at J. C. Penney, embodies that kind of spunk. She never graduated from college, but that didn't stop her. "I was willing to take the risk and get into new areas," she told me. "I proved that I could do it and that I was willing to do it, even though it was out of my comfort zone." She had no financial experience, only a background in retail, when she said, "I want to work in the Investor Relations Department. I don't know what I'm doing, but I'm going to give that a shot." She was extremely successful at it because she brought a lot of talents to that position that other people didn't have. It wasn't investor-relations knowledge, but rather her ability to motivate people and create a team.

## Be Decisive

You need to display firmness when it's required. Sometimes when you manage, you do so through consensus, as you take into account different views. But sometimes, in urgent situations, you have to make a decision. You must say, "I'm the manager, and this is the way it's going to be," even if you're wrong.

Indeed, the CEOs and senior women whom I interviewed had much to say about the importance of decisiveness in career advancement. One corporate leader praised a woman executive with whom he had worked very closely just because of her take-charge attitude. "One reason I respect and like her so much is that she's a tough lady when she needs to be. I haven't seen her back away from difficult internal or external issues. But I have seen other folks, both male and female, back away." He really liked her style.

Another CEO explained, "In any kind of mid- and senior-level management jobs, you're going to face some tough issues. Just put them on the table and don't Mickey Mouse around. Don't try to be slippery or clever," he advised. Be straightforward even when it's difficult or when you're dealing with people who are not only business colleagues, but personal friends. Problems don't fade away when left unattended; they grow bigger. You have to address them early on.

Nancy Hobbs of AirTouch Cellular told me, "As a leader you've got to set the course. There are times when you're the only person who thinks that this is the right thing to do, and you've got to get everybody else on board. And, hopefully, most of the time, you're right. But sometimes you're going to make a mistake too. If it's a matter of changing the organization, then you've got to burn the boats. You've got to say, 'Okay, group. That's it. We're going. There's no more time for talk or debate. I'm going to make the decision. We're heading this way.'" Even if the direction might change, at least you're moving someplace.

That reminds me of what Steve Case, the CEO of America Online, said. One of the most important things that he'd ever done in his life, that has gotten him into the CEO position, was that he made a lot of *wrong* decisions. And Nancy agreed with that philosophy. "If you're not making wrong decisions, you're probably not making critical decisions, and you're not learning," she said. "More learning comes from the wrong decisions than from the right ones. When you miscalculate, you tend to spend time thinking, 'How did I screw that one up so badly?' You don't spend a lot of time diagnosing a right decision. You just do it." That sort of postmortem analysis sounds very much like what Denice Gibson of Silicon Graphics engaged in when her fledgling attempts to run a company failed.

In fact, Denice also described herself as "extremely decisive." "People need decisions," she said. "Someone just has to make a decision so that you can go forward. You can argue later, but just make a decision." Denice does that through what she calls "fear and fearlessness." She believes part of the reason she has been successful is that she's afraid to fail. And one way in which she overcomes that is to become fearless. "Even if I hesitate for one second to pick up that telephone to do something that might be confrontational, or something that might be very difficult to get through, I always tell myself, 'They're just as afraid as I am.' So I pick up the phone and make the call." Denice never lets herself take more than just a few seconds of being afraid. She takes action and moves forward. And that's part of what got her to where she is today.

Bear in mind that when your boss gives you the responsibility, that means he or she has confidence that you can lead the charge. Your seasoned judgments will be based on your experience and on information you've collected, but sometimes the specter of perfectionism can cause you to hesitate. You may fear making mistakes. But, as Paul Brands, CEO of American Management Systems, told me, "You can wait until you've got one hundred thirty percent of the data needed before you make a decision. Having ninety or a hundred percent is fine." You need to do enough data collection and analysis to feel that you have the right answer, so that it's not a gamble. You might miss now and then, but you're going to be right most of the time."

Another CEO felt that women can fall into the paralysis by analysis trap. One woman he worked with wanted to analyze everything first, and he became frustrated with her because she couldn't seem to get off the dime and make a decision. "There are certain windows of opportunity that you need to capitalize on," he told me, "and this woman is too slow and methodical."

You have to remember that you wouldn't be in a management position unless someone believed in you. As Gloria Everett, Senior Vice President at Globalstar, explained, "A boss once told me, 'You have a lot more responsibility than you think you have. So if you don't like the way something is being done, change it. Get your hand slapped if you go too far, but change it.'" Indeed, sometimes risk-taking requires that you do what you feel is right without asking permission. If you have a broad base of support, you can take calculated risks based on sound judgment and apologize later if you need to. This is another way for you to exert influence without having authority.

Although many CEOs felt that women tended to more deeply analyze a situation, they also felt that they were able to make tougher decisions faster than men. Alan Buckwalter, CEO of Chase Bank of Texas, told me, "In my experience, most women will pull the trigger faster than men do on a conflict resolution issue or a performance problem, whereas men tend to drag it on." He believed women were better able to depersonalize the problem, to look at the more positive aspect of it and say, "This is not the right answer for the business, and this is not the best outlet for this person, so we need to make some changes and move on."

Women may also feel a greater sense of urgency in making tough decisions when someone is not producing on their team, because of the negative impact it will have on their team's performance and their ultimate career advancement. They may believe, "I can't afford to have a laggard working for me because I am being so closely scrutinized since I'm a woman."

Interestingly, many of the CEOs felt decisiveness was one of their own areas of weakness—one that they advised others to be better at. For instance, one saw it as a personal flaw that he forgets to follow his intuition when making decisions. "Sometimes the best thought is the one that hits first," he told me. "Many times I feel that I knew the right direction but I didn't take it. I see that a lot in my company. It's the fear of jumping out in front of something. By definition, the sooner you jump out, the more often you'll be wrong. But when you're right, the result is much greater. Our culture—and I think this is a negative—is that we punish failure far more permanently than we reward success."

Another CEO told me that he wished he had spoken up more. "I'm not a confrontational person," he said, "I don't like conflict." Often he wouldn't disagree with people, even when he knew they were going down the wrong path. But his reticence created more problems in the long run. "I was trying to lessen the pain by not being confrontational because it didn't feel good, but that created more long-term pain," he explained. Speaking up sooner is more pleasurable than letting things go and watching bad decisions being made later. You need to be decisive and speak your mind, but remember, it's counterproductive to get into a power struggle.

---

BE DECISIVE: *Sometimes you've got to say, "Okay, group, that's it! We're heading this way." Even if the direction might change, at least you're moving someplace.*

## Act with Confidence

Recently I heard Jim Kouzas, coauthor of *The Leadership Challenge,* speak. He said, "You can't believe a leader if you don't know what the leader believes." If you keep your head down and don't take risks, how will your subordinates know what you believe in? In order to be a true leader and visionary, you've got to create a vision and point the way; you've got to go where no one has gone before. And when you do take those risks, you also need the courage to communicate your vision and the skills to build passion for it in others. In other words, you need to act with confidence.

What keeps women from being decisive? One senior woman believed that insecurity has much to do with it. "I watch myself and think insecurity is something that hurts women. I appear to be much more secure than I am inside," she confided.

Leaders aren't necessarily secure types. But, even though they may be feeling insecure, they're still willing to stick their necks out and maybe fail, despite their fears. In order to lead people, you've got to take a stand. You're probably going to get shot a few times, because you're at the head of the pack, but that's what it takes to ascend in your career. Or, as one senior woman said, "There is no other way of doing it. You have to pick yourself up by the bootstraps every day of your life to be able to survive."

Indeed, the vast majority of senior women with whom I spoke pointed to confidence as one of the keys to their success. Sometimes this comes from having the proper training and preparation—the C.O.R.E. characteristic of Competence. Christine Garvey, who is now in her fifties, managed 200 million square feet of commercial real estate space (worth about $7 billion) in forty countries for the Bank of America. "In any measure of success, you have to have professional confidence in your field of expertise," she told me. "Historically, real estate has not been an area of expertise for women— especially managing corporate real estate. But I think my legal background gave me credibility, especially when I was starting. When I went to law school, there were only three other women in my class!"

At other times, confidence grows from resilience—having had to face challenges and succeed—in adjusting either to a new position or to a difficult situation. Nancy Hobbs of AirTouch Cellular told me how she adapted when thrown into jobs she knew little about. "You have to be willing to stretch yourself and do things you've never done before. That builds confidence. It's really fun. It's addictive," she said, in explaining why she loved the challenge of trying out new positions. "The more you do it and the more you succeed, the more confidence you have. It's this happy circle. It just builds up your self-confidence, and then you do it again and again."

## "Strategic"—The Operative Word

While all of the executive women extolled the benefits of risk-taking, it's important to make a distinction between taking wildly impru-dent gambles and engaging in risks that are strategic and calculated. Successful risk-taking behavior is consonant with the executive virtue of being realistic. I found that senior executive women really understand the big picture. They have a clear sense of what will work and what won't. They are able to scale an idea to the point that they can tell if it will succeed, given competing trends, demands, and situations. They are also extremely realistic as to their own strengths and weaknesses. Demonstrating their resourcefulness, they develop teams around them that help offset any deficits they might have.

> BE STRATEGIC AND REALISTIC: *When taking risks, under-stand the big picture. Have a clear sense of what will work and what won't, given competing trends, demands, and sit-uations.*

Leslie Altick, Executive Vice President at Wells Fargo Bank, found that a second assignment turned out to be the springboard of her consulting career and for many of her functions as head of cor-porate communications and marketing. "I was happily situated as head of investor relations for Wells Fargo when my boss came to me and said, 'How would you like to work in a major line group and do strategic planning, like you did at Harris Bank?' It was an interesting task, but I really loved my job. He was asking me to take a job in the least progressive part of the bank, to tackle a Herculean task, and the probabilities of that task being resolved were very slim.

"But, despite everything, I decided I'd take the job because of its content and because it was probably the most exciting and visible area of the financial services industry at that time. Both this and my strategic planning job at Harris Bank relied on a particular skill. I was not an expert strategic planner when I took these jobs. But a former boss said, 'What you were able to do was take an impossible job, size it down to a series of doable tasks, and find the right people to get those steps accomplished.' And that's what made it possible for me to take these different jobs and pull them together and do them."

Sue Swenson equates strategic risk-taking with patience. "I'm willing to recognize that things take time," she explained. "So I'm not impatient. I don't get upset with people; I don't lose my temper. I have the ability to keep the longer-term vision in mind, so I am willing to wait the appropriate amount of time to let things play themselves out. I have a little saying: 'Trust the process.' And I do trust the process. I'm very tenacious about that.

"Patience and tenacity have been reinforced for me throughout my career. Even though a goal looks unattainable, with the right plan in place, the right focus on it, and the right kind of people, anything can be accomplished. You have a fundamental belief that anything can be accomplished if you're clear about what you want to do and have a plan to get there."

## Resiliency

You must be resilient in order to tolerate the potential failure that may come from taking strategic risks. Resiliency refers to your ability to bounce back after you make a mistake or encounter a failure. It also implies that you have the wherewithal and discipline to thrive in challenging situations. And it means the capacity to not take mistakes too personally—to realize that everyone fails. Failure is a fact of life.

Julie England, a Vice President at Texas Instruments, was highly resilient in salvaging her career when "world peace broke out," as she put it, and she believed she had lost a five-year investment in defense electronics. "That situation was completely out of my control," she explained. "No plan I could have ever made would have helped me through that. But every time I see a big disaster—a truck that's about to run me over—I like to visualize that I just start picking it apart one wheel at a time. I take the license plate off first, then the windshield wipers, then the steering wheel. There's no problem too big for any of us to tackle if we break it down into individual pieces. A lot of situations in business, especially market conditions, are outside our control. But that doesn't mean we can't do anything about it. It means we have to step back and break it into understandable and manageable chunks."

Julie took many steps to rectify her situation. First, she made it clear to management that she wanted to move out of operations. She transferred into program management and managed a group of six instead of eighty. She also decided that it was time to take advantage of the defense budget crunch. Her company had set up a senior management team that was looking at how to convert defense technology into commercial endeavors. She went to the vice president of her division and asked to be on that team. "I was giving up all management roles, and I was going to become a market researcher instead of an engineer, but I thought, 'This has got to turn into something different. This is not going back. I'm shutting the door on my past. This has to lead to something bigger and better.'" Her new role was highly visible.

The next thing she did was tap on the doors of some of the old relationships she had had in her prior semiconductor business. And the gutsiest thing she did was make cold calls on senior management in the old business unit where she thought there might be a growth opportunity. Basically she said, "I'm Julie England. You don't know me, but here are a couple of my competencies. If you ever need anyone with these types of competencies, please think of me." As a result of these actions, Julie survived the upheaval in her industry.

It's important to bounce back from failure. I have identified three steps that are crucial for resiliency:

- **Take an appropriate amount of responsibility—immediately.** Remember, forthrightness is a highly valued quality. If

you've made a mistake, admit it. Take 100 percent responsibility for your actions that led to the problem, and allow others to take 100 percent responsibility for their behaviors as
well. Owning your own mistakes and allowing others to own
their behaviors and inadequacies enables people to maintain a
healthy and responsible working relationship.

• **Don't generalize the problem or take it personally.** As in
*"I'm a failure at everything I do."* That will stop you from rem-
edying the situation. Recognize that everyone fails. As Gale
Duff-Bloom at J. C. Penney told me, "You have to distinguish
between losing a battle and losing the war. Sometimes when
things don't work out, you can't worry about it. It didn't work
out. You go on."

• **Learn from your mistakes.** You need the ability and the
courage to discuss your mistakes and failures with others so
that you can learn from them. Keep in mind Denice Gibson's
example. Analyze where a situation went wrong and what you
can glean from it. Make a commitment with yourself to do a
postmortem on significant mistakes or losses. It's in the honest reflection of these situations that true learning occurs. This
form of "double-loop learning" (in which you go back over
what went wrong) will enable you to internalize the key lessons and integrate them into your future behaviors.

Liz Fetter, President and Chief Operating Officer of NorthPoint
Communications, explained to me how she rebounded from a mistake, using these three guidelines. Some years ago, she had delegated
an important task—the development and design of a strategic planning framework—to a member of her staff. "It was supposed to go
out on a Monday," she explained. "It went to the CFO and controller, who I was working for, over the weekend for their final look.
The CFO hadn't seen it before, and frankly, I hadn't been that close
to it since I'd delegated it. I had confidence in the person who was
working on it.

"Well, I got an urgent call on Saturday night from the CFO.
'Liz,' he says, 'this is not what I expected. I'm very disappointed.
There is no way we can send this out. It's really pathetic.'"

Liz looked at it, and thought, "Oh, no. He's right." She went to see him Monday morning. He was busy, but she just barreled her way into his office, and said, "I want to apologize. I dropped the ball. I delegated this; I wasn't close enough to it. This was to be a learning experience for someone, and I didn't do my job. I'm going to redo it myself, and only if you're satisfied will it go out."

She cleared her calendar and rewrote the whole document from scratch in a day. After she rewrote it, the CFO looked at it and said, "This is light-years better. We can send it out now." He knew that Liz had completely redone in a day what it had taken a month to create. And he told her he had never had someone come in and say, "I'm not going to blame anyone else. It's me, and I will do whatever it takes to make it right."

"That was a really big turning point for me," Liz explained. "It went from being a disaster to a triumph. And that's why I think being accountable at every level is the best advice." Liz was highly effective in taking full responsibility for the debacle, not personally blaming others or herself, and learning from her mistakes. She turned a potentially career-limiting situation into a positive reflection of her character and ability to get things done.

## Curiosity and a High Appetite for Learning

Carlene Ellis, Vice President at Intel, said to me, "Carol, I have the best job because I get to play with computers all day long." Carlene absolutely loved that—she has a playful curiosity about her work. Karen Elliott House, President of International at Dow Jones, also views curiosity as an integral part of her work. "I still see myself as a journalist who happens to be a businessperson," she told me. "I think of myself as an acquirer of information. Sometimes I process it for Dow Jones, and sometimes I process it for readers. I try to figure out what do I need to know, who knows it, how do I get them to tell me, and then what do I make of it. I genuinely seek the truth. And that's fundamentally what you do in a business job. You can't delude yourself; you can't just believe what people tell you. You've got to ask a lot of questions; you've got to use your head."

The executive virtue of curiosity also implies a high appetite for learning that can lead to wonder and ultimately passion about your field. As you have seen, when engaged in the "learner's mind," you can make mistakes, but you will consider these as opportunities for increased understanding rather than failure.

The need for perfection can stifle this sort of inquisitiveness. On the other hand, a curiosity and willingness to take on new challenges and move into new positions enhance your career and your self-knowledge. Many senior executive women, like Karen Rose at Clorox and Gale Duff-Bloom at J. C. Penney, held numerous posts within one company. Others moved lithely from company to company in search of self-knowledge and corporate learning. Whatever the career trajectory, they all have a high appetite for learning. As Nancy Hobbs of AirTouch Cellular told me, "You hone your skills by taking on different challenges or moving from one group to another. You're always in a learning mode, but at the same time, you're also getting a sense of how to run an organization."

For instance, one senior woman tried her hand at many organizations to learn what she could about business and her own place in it. Often she seemed driven by her curiosity, asking herself questions such as, "What can I contribute here?" "How will I fare under these circumstances?" "What if I try this sort of organization?"

"I view my career journey as a self-learning opportunity," Traci explained. "I think it's important as you go through your career to extract the value you can from the experiences you get." Traci began her odyssey early. She got through college quickly, earned an MBA, and then loaded all of her worldly possessions into her car and drove across the country to seek her fortune. "I started my career at a big company at which I could take risks. I had the good fortune of working in an organization right away where people identified in me perhaps some drive, some inner capability. And so I was provided with opportunities to move around this big company and learn to do things that I could not have learned in a smaller company. I began to discover my own interests, relative to internal finance (the controller-type of role) or external finance."

Traci used the big company experience as a learning opportunity to hone some of her skills. She moved from the big company to a smaller one. And all those things she had learned at the big company were truly treasured by this smaller company. "I was bringing skills they did not have internal to their own organization, so I got a chance to have some early wins. I brought capabilities and experiences that demonstrated that I was giving to this company right away. And as you build a portfolio of early wins, then you get more opportunities within the company. So it was a different risk profile than in the larger organization, but I had a greater opportunity to contribute.

"Because of the possibility of 'getting rich quick,' I decided to go to an Internet start-up company. I said to myself, 'I'm going to see if I can add value to this very small enterprise. But I found out I didn't like a small company. Its success was much too oriented toward the personal whims of a few people. And so I said, 'This is a learning opportunity. I'm going to back out of it. I'm going into a bigger company,'" which she did. Traci regrouped and returned to the large company she had left before, but now she contributed at a different level and in a different division.

Traci's managers there said, "If you're going to stay at this company for the long term, you've got to be in operations." So she went to operations. She learned again. But then she realized she didn't like it. "You have to be willing to take the risk. Extract something from it that says, 'Do I like this? Do I not like this? Is this playing to my strong suit?' If it's not, regroup, and go down a different pathway."

Finally, in her early forties, Traci had been promoted to Executive Vice President. By that time, she had accumulated a pretty big portfolio of self-knowledge and was willing to sit back and reflect and use it.

Echoing other senior executive women (see Chapter 2), Traci advises mid-level managers to "look hard at your experience and learn something about yourself. Be honest with yourself about what you like and what you don't like. And then you will find the place where your true genius is allowed to be free. You'll know when it doesn't feel right and when it does. It's important to assess how you fit."

Karen O'Shea, Vice President of Communications and Public Relations at Lennox Industries, also described her career trajectory, which spanned many types of work. "It's a patchwork quilt," she told me. She started out as an English teacher, and then went into the wholesale clothing business. Later she owned a retail store with photographic supplies, cameras, and developing. She worked in editorial at the *Dallas Times Herald*. While she was there, she came across an ad in the paper. A company was looking for a person who could teach dealers how to run a business from the financial side, as well as someone with writing skills. "That's an odd combination," Karen explained, "but I had it right on. I knew when I saw the ad that if I wanted that job, I could have it. And that's how I came to work for Lennox."

Christiane Michaels, President of Waverly Lifestyle, has also taken a series of calculated, career-changing risks that have served her well. "First, I was an English teacher," she explains, "then a journalist, then a vice president of marketing, and then got into product design, management, and product development. Every five or six years, I look at my resume and say, 'Now what skills do I need to learn to get to the next level?' And I reinvent myself."

The great variety of career moves that these women engaged in is indicative of their desire and ability to be perpetual learners and leaders.

## Broaden Your Base with Profit and Loss

The most important job change a woman manager can make is from a staff assignment to a general management position. Although women have traditionally been herded into supporting assignments such as the "three P's"—personnel, purchasing, and public relations—the reality is that profit-and-loss (line) responsibility is often a prerequisite for the top jobs. To move forward in the corporate world, you have to work in the business side; you cannot work in a support function. By taking on risky, mettle-testing operations jobs, you may find that you have enhanced your opportunities to win recognition and advancement.

Many CEOs with whom I spoke felt it imperative for a woman to work in all parts of the business—especially to have profit-and-loss responsibility—in order to get ahead. This will help you gain a good feel for how the company functions. Your experience doesn't have to be within one corporation. Even if you jump from company to company, as the women above did, it's good to have a smattering of exposure in all areas. For instance, before he became CEO of Basic American Foods, Jack Parks worked in all aspects of his business: sales, the factory, human resources, production, engineering, and customer service. Acquiring such a broad range of experience may, of course, require risk-taking.

One CEO told me, "If you think about very senior people running the company, you've got to have people who have been in the operating roles. They've seen it all. That's just not true when you work on the staff side. If your goal is to get to the top of an organization, I believe the way you do it is through the operating end. There's a much, much higher probability of getting there when you have profit-and-loss responsibility."

Sue Swenson of Leap Wireless International also explained to me, "People are looking for your breadth of experience. To be a senior executive you don't really have to be an expert in every part of the field, but have you been close to it? Have you worked with people who are connected to all parts of the business, so that you at least have some working knowledge of that part of the business?" As early in your career as possible, try to get a broad range of experience so that you are not a one-discipline person. As you keep progressing in the business, that will give you the flexibility to be moved into different assignments. When Sue considers hiring a person, she asks, "How much breadth does this person have? How many spots can he or she fill in the company?" And to the degree that you limit your track, you're going to limit your options in terms of being given the opportunity to demonstrate yourself in a variety of positions in the business.

It's also important to stick with a position long enough to prove yourself and make a difference in the company. Jim Preston, retired CEO of Avon, explained, "You can't expect to become a CEO in three to five years. Women—or men—have to run a core business long enough to become proficient as executives." Be advised that although eleven years was the average length of time for the women in my study to attain their high levels of corporate success, it may take many more years to become CEO of a large company, if that's what you're aiming for.

It's not just having experience but having the right kinds of experience that counts. You have to be working in the right area. It has to be something that the company cares about, that's in the mainstream, that people will view as critical to the company's success. Everything you do must be associated with a value-added activity. That requires being aware of what matters to your company and leveraging your talents wisely.

Unfortunately, if you don't have profit-and-loss experience, you may be afraid to lead an operations group, because you don't know what you have to offer. You may feel you need to understand the job first before trying it. It can become a vicious cycle. The CEOs noted that such an attitude has slowed the career advancement of high-potential women.

For instance, one CEO told me about a female employee, I'll call her Marsha, whom he felt had limited her career based on choices she had made. Marsha heads the human resources department in her company, but she doesn't want to lead a manufacturing plant. "She has got to learn that she needs to muck around with it until she figures it out," this CEO said. "It's not that you have to know the job before you do it. You don't even have to do it well. Some people believe they can't make mistakes while they're learning. I say, get in there and flounder around a bit until you get it."

Moreover, the higher up you go, you may want to take on less risk because there's so much at stake. These are big jobs, and if you don't do well, it reflects on the whole company. "I'm mentoring a couple of women now and encouraging them to get into profit-and-loss positions," Sue Swenson explained. "When they move up a notch, people will say, 'Yeah. They've been in customer operations, they've been in finance, they've been in sales. They have a broad band of experience, and I think they're going to do well over here because they've got a more stable platform on which to build.'"

> TAKE ON PROFIT-AND-LOSS POSITIONS: *It's not just having experience but having the right kinds of experience that counts.*

Sometimes that means taking a job that may seem distasteful. "You have to determine where you are in your career," Sue continued, "And where the organization is. You may have to look at one of these operations jobs and say, 'I'm going to need to take this job because I have to show them what I'm made of, and it may be the breakthrough for me.'"

Nancy Hobbs of AirTouch Cellular adds her words of encouragement. "Obviously, there are going to be functional differences when you take on an operations job, but the leadership aspects of it are consistent across the different functions. If you're a good leader and you're a fairly bright penny, you can pick up all of the other 'stuff' you need to know about the function, enough to run it. And in some cases, I think you're better off not knowing as much detail as people who have grown up in it, because you don't take anything for granted. That can be a strength as opposed to a liability.

"I've seen women gravitate toward human resources or the professional roles, like legal, and less toward the operations side of the business. But if you are in a staff role and really want to move up, you've got to take a risk. I think the hardest thing is if you've stayed in the staff jobs too long and you've progressed up that ladder. And now, all of a sudden, you wake up and say, 'I want to be a senior executive, and I can't get there unless I have profit-and-loss experience.' But by then, not many people will be willing to take a risk and put you in charge of a large organization. If you've never run an organization and you don't have the functional experience either, you can be in deep trouble. You need a strong boss and someone who's really going to take a risk on you."

Overall, the consensus among senior executive women and CEOs seems to be: Just jump into a line position; you're going to learn on the job. Don't be afraid to learn from your mistakes. You probably know more than you think you do. Even though you don't have profit-and-loss experience, you bring other skills to the table. You may know how to manage and motivate people, communicate effectively, and possibly have financial skills. Value those other skills and know that in every job you're going to take, you'll have to learn something new.

JUMP INTO A LINE POSITION: *You will learn on the job, and you'll learn from your mistakes.*

## Risk-Taking: Corporate Responsibility

According to Alan Buckwalter, at Chase Bank of Texas, one of the biggest stumbling blocks in the advancement of women in corporations today is that they have not been groomed for success. "A large proportion of women are in nonprofits, running foundations, or professors at colleges or universities," he told me. "They're not CEOs of public companies. That's changing. Ten to twenty years from now, it will be totally different. But that's not the case today."

Sue Swenson has thought about this problem and found a solution that she believes works, based on her own life experience. "One of the things I've been trying to do," she explained, "is to put people into different assignments and, particularly, to stay ahead of what they think might be the next best move for them. My whole philosophy is to come up with where they need to go before they formulate it themselves. Normally, people come in and say, 'I've been in marketing; now I'd like to go to sales.' What I do is say, 'You know, Carol, I've been thinking about what you should really learn, and on Monday I'd like you to start in customer operations.' People take the safe route to where they want to go, but I want to move them out of their comfort zones. And, of course, that would be the furthest thing from their minds."

This type of out-of-the-box thinking provides many opportunities for growth, especially for women at lower levels in the organization when they find themselves thrust into operations. Sue advocates giving employees this experience of discomfort early in their careers, so if they don't do well immediately, it's not universally fatal. And she also recognizes that they will need support to get in there and learn the job. "Until I experienced jumping in with both feet myself, I didn't know what that felt like. And no one can tell you enough about it. You have to go through the pain and the suffering to develop new skills and confidence. And that's just all part of it."

Sue even believes that various departments should collaborate to create these stretch opportunities. "I get management support for this kind of move," she explained. "I might say, 'Okay, here are some people whom we believe want to have a career here. They're ambitious and want to learn new things. Peter and Joanne, I want you to think about how you can move this person over to this job, now.'" Sue does this with people whom she and her management team have identified as high potential, as well as with individuals who express an interest. "I figure if somebody raises her hand and says, 'I really want to learn all these different parts of the business,' then she should be part of your planning as well. She may surprise you, and work out to be the star performer."

I agree with Sue's approach, and I also believe companies should develop a high-potential list for their up-and-coming male and female employees. Management should know who is on the A-list, the B-list, and the C-list. In the consulting work I've done, I have found that some executives are fearful of developing such a high-potential list because they're afraid of its impact. They're concerned that it will give the A-list people a "big head" and they'll stop working so hard, and that it will disempower people who didn't make the top list—they'll just give up in frustration.

But my experience has been just the opposite. I can remember earlier in my career when I worked at Goldman Sachs, my superiors never told me how highly they thought of me. After a year with the company, I decided to leave. Only then did my boss inform me that she had slotted me to head up the department I had been working in. Had I known my superiors had that much confidence in me and my abilities, I would have thought differently of my skills and my position there, and I certainly would have reached out for coaching in areas that I felt needed attention. Because of that experience and by working with companies on their executive development, I'm a firm believer in being honest with people about where they fit. Often managers don't share positive or negative feedback, and their employees flounder because they don't know how they stack up.

People want to know where they stand. Once they do, they can make changes. If you make the A-list, for instance, you are aware that you're being watched. You're perceived as a highly valuable employee, so it empowers you to behave in a manner that is consistent with that image. And if you make the B-list, you know the specific areas you need to improve upon. (Making the B-list is nothing to be ashamed of. If you weren't valued, you would have been fired by now.) A "B" rating highlights the fact that management doesn't currently see you as an A-player. But that doesn't mean you'll stay there. Of course, if you make the A-list, it doesn't mean that you'll stay there either. You could move down to "C" if you stop performing. Indeed, these ratings provide nothing more than a snapshot in time.

Companies are often too covert about succession planning, or don't even have any sort of plan in place. It is only when people get both positive and constructive feedback that they can understand how they are perceived and what they need to do to improve.

Trying to develop people without such a rating system is like a company running its business without financial worksheets. Maybe the news isn't good—you're not making a profit that quarter—but it's better to have financial reports than to go along thinking you're doing fine when really you're losing money. We would never run a company that way, so why do we think we should run our human resource function blindly? If companies say that their human resources are their most important asset, then they need to start treating them just like they do their financial assets—they should consistently track and report them. I highly urge companies to maintain an employee balance sheet and communicate it with the executive team. Once high-potential women have been identified, they can be groomed to take leadership positions in their organizations.

Since they've identified these A-list people together, senior managers must work in unison. For instance, if high-potential employee Pat doesn't have operations responsibilities, I might recommend that you take her for a year, while I take on your employee from customer service. This orchestrated cross-pollination is important, because senior managers don't naturally trade employees on their own. They may have little to gain from this practice. They're bringing in someone who knows little about their business; it's a risky move for them. And they're losing one of their seasoned employees to another group. And employees may also be unmotivated because it forces them into a discomfort zone. Most people like to do things they're good at instead of taking on a new challenge that they don't know anything about.

But the interdepartmental exchange of employees can help high-potential women grow in many ways. Often people fresh out of school with MBAs join management training programs that put them on a rotation. In a two-year period, they may work in several different departments in the company, each assignment lasting two or three months. But if you have a high-potential mid-manager who hasn't benefited from one of these programs, the company should learn from Sue Swenson's approach and take responsibility for getting this person the proper cross-functional training and experience she needs to become a senior manager. This rotation needs to be made part of her succession plan.

## Just Go for It!

Carlene Ellis of Intel has that "just go for it" attitude that is so common among senior executive women. They refuse to be victimized or stopped by their fear of failure or by obstacles that may litter their path. Liz Fetter, President of NorthPoint Communications, articulated this point of view so well. Let her words be an inspiration to you:

> If you don't like your job, either start liking it or change. If you don't think you have enough education, go get that education. If you don't think you're doing something interesting, go do something else. Once you realize this is it, and you have control over your life and the choices you make—and know that everybody has unexpected stuff happen to them—then the way is clear. It's not the situation but what you do with the situation and with the hand that you're dealt that really determines your ultimate success and happiness.

# 7 | Be Yourself:
## The "Man's Game" Isn't the Only Game in Town

Despite the fact that countless books of a prior generation encourage aspiring corporate women to "learn the games your mother never taught you," in truth, you don't have to play golf or memorize football scores to be accepted into the male-dominated inner circles of corporations. In fact, many of the executives whom I interviewed stressed that you should not strive to be "one of the guys" if you want to move ahead in your career. Such a strategy can backfire. If "one of the guys" is not who you really are, you will come across as inauthentic, and that can undermine others' trust in you. Your colleagues and bosses won't give you credit for being genuine in business if they can't give you credit for being genuine as a person.

Carmen, an executive at a large chemical processing company, told me, "I don't chum around with my male colleagues; I don't know how to talk sports with them. I'm not like them. That doesn't mean that I can't get along with them. I may not be one of the guys, but I'm a perfectly acceptable guest!"

Carmen explained why she believed her male colleagues accepted her, despite the fact that she didn't "chum around" with them. "I'm a no-nonsense, practical person. I think they like that. Some of my predecessors were real jerks. All men. Their personalities were aggressive to the point of being abrasive. It made it difficult for them to work with the operations people. I think the company was reaching a point where they were much more interested in teamwork and solving problems together rather than mandating solutions. I was more that type."

BE YOURSELF: *You shouldn't strive to play "the man's game" if that's uncomfortable for you. You will come across as inauthentic, and that can undermine others' trust in you. Your colleagues and bosses won't give you credit for being genuine in business if they can't give you credit for being genuine in person.*

## The "Professional Trap"

Authenticity is the name of the game here. In fact, if you try to behave like a man, it can blow up in your face. One male CEO told me, "One of the biggest mistakes women make is when they try to adapt and change to live in a man's world, instead of really being true to themselves." He found that distressing. In fact, he told me about a woman he had really wanted to promote. Claire was serious at work—very "professional"—but she seemed to be somber all the time. Then one day this CEO caught a glimpse of her when she was out with friends. She was having a great time and seemed like an entirely different person. The disparity shocked and alarmed him.

"This conjured up in my mind that I'm not sure I really know who Claire is," he told me. "And because of that, I'm not sure I trust her. Unless I'm comfortable with knowing who a person is, I'm not ready to advance him or her into a senior position. I need people on my team who know who they are and whose behavior is consistent with that. I need people I can trust so I don't have to watch my back. I need to know that they're going to be there for me." The sad part of all of this is that Claire was probably behaving so seriously at work because that was how she thought she needed to act to get ahead.

For some women, playing the man's game can mean putting on a "professional" facade at the expense of their softer side. Alan Buckwalter, the CEO of Chase Bank of Texas, cautioned, "Some women try to act like someone they think they're supposed to be. It's this whole idea of being so professional, rather than just being a woman and letting your femininity and your personality come out. It's powerful and effective for a woman to be herself. I don't think you build relationships based on trying to act or be someone you're not or on acting like someone you think people want you to be. So be yourself—that's what's important."

You can establish a wonderful balance between being decisive and confident on the one hand, and warm and fun-loving on the other—you can be "nice" and "firm" simultaneously. In fact, most of the women I interviewed are what we would consider to be consistently "nice" much of the time. However, when they need to be "tough," they typically do so with sensitivity. It's much easier to maintain a healthy relationship with someone you need to discipline or correct when you have already established an effective and positive relationship with him or her.

> AVOID THE PROFESSIONAL TRAP: *You can't build genuine relationships based on what you think people want you to be. It's powerful and effective for a woman to be herself.*

## Get Real but Be Realistic

Being yourself entails engaging in behaviors and activities that you're comfortable with rather than trying to mold yourself into someone you think you're supposed to be. In her position as Senior Vice President of Utility Services at Atmos Energy in Dallas, Texas, Mary Lovell told me, "There are things that I just don't enjoy doing and probably won't ever do, like hunting or fishing. Certainly I would not do them very well." Since many of Mary's colleagues enjoyed hunting and fishing, she could spend more time with them if she joined them on their outings. But, rather than being inauthentic and doing something she didn't enjoy at all, she found other activities to do with them, like having them over for dinner and going to local events with them.

Having said that, however, I also firmly believe you need to be realistic and *strategic*. Try to put yourself in situations that could be conducive to conversations with other executives—and especially male executives. If you enjoy sports, by all means learn to play golf. It's a fabulous way to develop relationships with businessmen. You hold them hostage for four to five hours—long enough to play eighteen holes. You can communicate about personal and business issues during that time. Besides, everyone tends to be more relaxed outdoors as they walk the beautiful rolling hills of a golf course. People loosen up and become more informal when they're exercising. And you have the opportunity to develop more of a personal relationship with an important business contact than you would if you were merely sitting across the desk from one another in an office. In fact, when I worked at IBM, I sold more mainframes on the golf course than I ever did from my office.

Jack Parks of Basic American Foods told me he believed that women should participate in company activities at whatever level feels natural to them. They need to do this so they don't isolate themselves. "It's important to be a part of company recreational opportunities and not say, 'I'm not going!' if you don't like the activity. If there's a golf outing, you need to go, even if you just ride in the cart or if you play 'best ball' and shoot one or two. If there are tickets to a baseball game, go and enjoy the social aspects, even if you don't like the game or understand all its nuances. You need to be adaptive and create new ways to interact so you won't get left out." If you feel that your company should change its standard fare of activities, then work with your corporate executives to create more gender-neutral get-togethers.

Bottom line: Find your own way to participate that feels comfortable and authentic or change the activity.

## Finding an Appropriate Topic of Conversation

Whether or not you participate in a sport, it's important to connect with your male and female colleagues on issues that matter. According to the executives I interviewed, you have to find some way of making an authentic interpersonal connection with male and female colleagues. That usually means being yourself and finding real mutual interests or experiences that you can talk about. This may include a discussion on your organization's strategic focus or your shared interests and/or activities. A conversation about each person's previous or next vacation can be an enjoyable and "lite" topic through which you can get to know one another. The key is to connect genuinely and positively with your coworkers, thus creating an increased level of comfort and an ease in communication that will eventually segue into a more substantive business discussion.

Creating a positive connection is important in developing a lasting professional relationship. It's easy to fall into the trap of complaining about your commute or long hours, and it is often equally easy to get others to join you. However, in order to create a "positive" relationship, it is best to find a topic that leaves a good impression and feeling with the person rather than a negative one. This might include talking about the great movie you saw over the weekend or the wonderful new restaurant that just opened in town.

There are subjects that people will always have in common, such as major news events, politics, the stock market, the latest movies, the theater, pets, other outside activities, or even the weather. These seemingly banal conversations can reveal your values and show others how you think. And they are a little more personal than sticking strictly to business issues. As long as they're not all that you talk about, children can be a bonus in this regard; most people love to be drawn out about their kids.

Cindy Hawkins, in her role as Vice President and Controller of 3Com, uses conversations about her and her boss's children to create rapport with him. "Sometimes I try to chitchat with my boss on purpose because he's a very shy person," she told me. "He's like me in a way, because we're very serious and we're always working. But I want to build a relationship, so I try to build a bridge with him. He's very interested in sports, but I have no interest in sports. He's a runner, and I hate running. But the one tie we have is children. So I'll push the conversation toward children. I make a conscious effort to try to bring it to a personal level rather than just talking about work."

Be careful, however, that you don't talk with other women about children to the exclusion of all else. Often, professional women don't enjoy *only* talking about kids. Rather, they want to show they are not only mothers but also competent and successful business professionals.

CONNECT GENUINELY AND POSITIVELY WITH CO-
WORKERS: *This creates an increased level of comfort and
an ease in communication that will eventually segue into
a more substantive business discussion.*

Sometimes it's important to actually prepare business topics for
conversation with higher-ups so you can genuinely connect without
feeling flustered or embarrassed. Gloria Everett, Senior Vice President of Operations at Globalstar, an international satellite-based
phone service, advocated such an approach.

"Sometimes you have the opportunity to spend a little time with
some very important people in your company or individuals who
interface with your company," she said. "You're going to a luncheon
and just by chance, the CEO will be present. Or you're going to a
company meeting, and some of the key officers of the business will
be there. You know there's going to be an opportunity for interaction. Nothing is worse than sitting in a room or at a luncheon and
worrying, 'What am I going to say?' If you say nothing, nothing is
*zero.* If you're an introvert, it can be even more difficult because you
are worried about whether you will say the right thing."

Gloria recommended very strongly that you prepare. "I still do,"
she admitted. "I put together five questions, comments, or concerns
before I go to the event. They have to be at the level of the person
you want to approach. I rehearse my comments in front of the mirror. What words do I want to emphasize? What do I expect as a reply? Your comment has to leave the door open for a reply, and it has
to give the impression that you are adding value to your company."

Being so prepared also has the advantage of allowing you to
feel spontaneous and relaxed. In fact, the conversation may go so
well, you won't even need to use any of your rehearsed subjects. In
either case, you can be the best you can be, and you can take the opportunity to make the best impression you can make because now
you're letting your higher-ups see who you really are. Also, be sure
when you make the comment (this is also true in significant meet-

ings) that the people you want to reach with your message are attentive.

Some of the topics you might consider discussing include last quarter's profit margins, the company's stock price, or a recent merger or strategic alliance. You could also bring up a news item that might affect your industry, a recent article about your company, or the hiring of a new executive employee. Make sure that if you ask a question, you understand the terms you are using, so that you come across as genuine and truly engaged in the conversation.

## Talking Personally but Not Intimately Builds Trust

Talking about business to the exclusion of developing more personal relationships may be counterproductive. It can give the impression that you have little interest in your coworkers' lives—they may feel that they are simply instrumental for your own success (as in "What can you do for me?")—or that you are overly aggressive. In fact, the only way you can really build trust with someone is to enhance the human bond, and not keep communication just on a purely business level.

One female senior executive made it a point to find some common outside interest with male colleagues, so she could chat with them about something besides business. "If you don't have something that you can talk about as an icebreaker," Julia told me, "you can come off to male coworkers as being too abrupt. For me, talking personally is a necessary prelude with some men because I can come on too strong. If I just barge into their office and say, 'I've got your report. We need to talk about paragraph sixteen . . .' they seem offended, and taken aback, like they're wondering, 'Where is she coming from?' I don't want to fall into that 'aggressive woman' stereotype. So I try to be more social in the way I approach them."

Julia's boss has a house by the lake not far from hers, and she often begins conversations with him by asking about their mutual interests related to their vacation properties. " 'How has the fishing been lately?' I might ask or, 'Are you having the same dry rot problem with your deck that I'm having?' " she continued. "We need a warm-up like that to break the ice before we can get to the business conversation. The women with whom I have professional relationships seem to have no problem cutting immediately to business after a few pleasantries like, 'Hi. How are you?' But when there's time left at the end, we switch to a deeper social interaction. So I definitely notice gender differences there."

As I've mentioned in earlier chapters, there are multiple levels of sharing. Engaging in personal conversations doesn't mean that you should bare your soul and unburden yourself about your private life—all of your hopes, dreams, fears, and challenges. Rather, in these personal (but not intimate) interactions, you express your character, interests, and concerns on various subjects. And you become in the eyes of others a warm, caring human being and not a business automaton.

When you establish an appropriate level of personal sharing, others will know who you are and may more readily trust you. Most people enjoy coming in and talking with someone with whom they feel comfortable. It's difficult to chat with a person if he or she is an enigma. (Think back to all-work-no-play Claire and her surprised and ultimately disgruntled CEO.) The overall purpose in developing a relatively personal relationship is that others may feel at ease asking you a few questions. They enjoy working with you, and it's reciprocal. You can ask them questions, and they can ask you questions, instead of the relationship being purely one-sided. You begin to develop a more relaxed working relationship that flows better.

> **ESTABLISH AN APPROPRIATE LEVEL OF PERSONAL SHARING:** *That will clue others in to who you really are, and as a consequence, they may more readily trust you.*

As one executive woman told me, "Over time you can develop rapport, a little bit of the personal along with the professional. From that point of view, it's easier being a woman, because I'm a little different from what they're used to. And they're a little interested in what's going on in my head."

Indeed, trust is built on individuals connecting in a person-to-person way rather than in an instrumental way—that is, purely on a business level. In order for superiors to promote you, they must feel that they can trust you as a human being, that you're honest and faithful. In fact, one CEO emphatically told me that the lack of integrity is the only trait on which he will never give people a break. As he explained, "I'd give them a second chance publicly, but my mind is made up. I'm a bigot when it comes to that! And I never change. There are people here who have violated my trust, and after twenty years, if you put up a flashcard with their picture, that's what I think of first. I can't change it." This CEO may be nice to people who betrayed him, he may work with them, but he'll never promote them into the highest echelons because the risks are just too great.

## The Problem with Being "All Business"

When you focus on your own needs and goals and view a coworker as merely the means to fulfill your needs and accomplish your goals, you run into trouble. Paula, a mid-level manager, came to me for coaching. Her difficulties epitomize what can happen if you fall prey to this behavior. Although she had great relationships with her superiors, Paula felt she didn't have the support of her colleagues or subordinates in her organization. She was reaching out for help on how to develop better relationships with them.

Paula was in a high-stress job, running multiple projects and constantly dealing with emergency situations for a multimillion-dollar account. When a crisis would arise, she would typically, in her own words, "throw bodies at the problem" to fix it.

Interestingly, Paula failed to realize that even in the language she used, she was dehumanizing the people whom she was asking to help her. She would railroad somebody with the skills her client needed into repairing the breach, but with little regard for the personal sacrifices that employee would have to make in order to get the job done. She would strongly suggest (with statements such as, "If you know what's best for your career . . .") that people travel weekly to the client site to fix the problem, with no concern for the family life they left behind. Employees can tolerate this for a while, but when they are unsupported as people, they eventually feel objectified. No wonder Paula didn't have a good working relationship with her colleagues and subordinates.

I spoke with Paula about being realistic and authentic. Authenticity requires that you be conscious of what's going on around you, that you are aware of how you present yourself in general and in the moment. It's an important aspect of self-awareness. "If you talk to someone," I told her, "and somehow in your words or manner communicate that you don't care about them except for what they can do for you, you are using them for instrumental purposes rather than connecting with them as a human being. That's a behavior you'll need to be aware of and keep in check," I advised.

Sometimes we're so driven to accomplish results that, like Paula, we use others as a means to our cherished end. I suggested to Paula a simple exercise to help her better connect to others in the moment. You might try this too if you find that you tend to view your co-workers and employees as instruments of your success instead of fellow human beings with needs and wants all their own. The next time you talk to them, just notice the color of their eyes without judging their external facade or behavior. This will help you to see them as people, rather than looking past them or regarding them as skill-sets. You are trying to see their essence, who they are, and what's important to them.

You will then begin to connect with them as human beings and build trust and credibility, rather than seeing them only as a means to an end. It may even help to make working with others more enjoyable.

---

**TREAT YOUR EMPLOYEES WITH RESPECT:** *Be careful not to view them as simply a means to achieve your cherished goals.*

---

## Are You More Masculine or Feminine? Who Cares?

When I interviewed Ruth Handler, cofounder of Mattel and its CEO for nearly thirty years, she spoke of the importance of maintaining her femininity. "Of the few women in business whom I knew in the early days," she said, "there were some who were very mannish in the way they carried and handled themselves. They were unpleasantly unfeminine."

"Why, do you think?" I wondered.

"I guess it came from being in the business world, in a rough, tough business, and needing to be aggressive and to push your way through," she replied. "You did have to call on some pretty aggressive tendencies, perhaps masculine tendencies in some people's eyes. I tried to keep my femininity. One reason was that my husband wouldn't have liked me to act like a rough, tough person. The other reason is an incident that occurred rather early in my Mattel career. A man from another company came to my office for an appointment. He walked in and sat across from me at the desk. Then he looked at me and said, 'You're not at all like I expected.'

"'Oh. What did you expect?' I asked.

"'Well, I figured you'd have your feet up on the desk and a cigar in your mouth,' he said.

"'What?' I said, 'Is that what my reputation is?' That stuck with me. It really hit me, and it kind of scared me. We got into a conversation on this subject. And at that moment, I made the deliberate decision that I was going to somehow fight off these so-called 'masculine tendencies,' but I can be kind of tough. And if people didn't keep up, I might not have been too gentle with them."

I wondered whether men in Ruth's position would be any gentler. "Was this just an anomaly because you happened to be female?" I asked her.

"I think men might have been rougher than I was," Ruth replied. "The fact that I was a female performing these so-called 'male' things made me come across as 'masculine.'" Beneath her gruff exterior, I could tell that Ruth was a really kind, gentle soul, but that was a part of her she hadn't believed she could let out; for years she had struggled to balance being "tough" with being "feminine."

Ruth's experiences from many years ago are similar to the issues women face today, and they raise some interesting questions. One of the issues that feeds into the challenge of authenticity is the whole discussion of whether we are being masculine or feminine if we are assertive (Ruth's "rough and tough"), as compared to being nurturing. The fact is, I don't think it's a question of being masculine or feminine. I wish we would never use those two words again in a business context. They're so general and subjective that each of us interprets the words to mean different things. Rather than being masculine or feminine, I believe it's a question of being yourself.

Although we tend to categorize females and males as having certain characteristics, such stereotyping doesn't serve us well. If we think of men as being nurturing, warm, loving, and caring, and we pigeonhole them as having "feminine" characteristics, then we're saying, according to *Webster's Dictionary*, that they're "acting like a female." That's not right. They're being themselves as nurturing, caring, loving men. They're not like women; they're men who are empathetic and warm.

Liz Fetter, President and COO of NorthPoint Communications, benefited from her relationships with such men. "Some of the best bosses I've ever had were the guys who knew something was wrong the instant you walked into their office. They'd put their arm around you and say, 'What's going on?' They have that nurturing quality." And Linda LoRe, CEO of Frederick's of Hollywood, spoke of Jim Preston, retired CEO of Avon, in the same terms. "It's all about authenticity and genuineness," she told me. "Jim Preston is a perfect example. I wouldn't call him feminine; he's very much a man. He is a caring, nurturing individual, but he's still himself."

By the same token, if we characterize women who are assertive, decisive, and results-oriented as exhibiting traditionally "masculine traits," then we think because they're more "masculine," they lose some of their femininity. Often we judge women negatively who display "masculine" characteristics as not being "feminine" enough, but they are. They are females who are assertive, decisive, and results-oriented. Perhaps they are linear thinkers, like their male counterparts. But they are just as female as a woman who is less assertive, decisive, or linear. These sorts of stereotypes make it difficult for strong businesswomen to be themselves.

I urge women who are assertive in business to accept their confident, action-oriented, decisive side, and not classify those traits as masculine. By being comfortable with our more assertive selves, we also unconsciously accept the more nurturing, caring, loving side of men without judging them as being feminine. On the other hand, when we characterize those qualities as masculine or feminine, we have more difficulty in accepting them as part of who we are as male or female.

As Linda LoRe told me, "The word 'femininity' has a bad rap anyway because it evokes the feminist movement for some people, while others think it means being frilly with lace and ruffles. The fact of the matter is that, for me, being feminine doesn't mean anything more than just being who I am. It's really about being confident enough to be myself and still being tough enough to get things done. Lots of times I get into a work mode, and I don't even realize that I'm not being sweet and nice and kind. But I'm still being me. I'm saying, 'Okay, we need to do this and this and this and this and this.' You can say that with a smile. And then you can say, 'Okay, let's get it done.'"

Many businesswomen believe that if you're a kind, loving person, it leaves you susceptible to attack. But Linda found just the opposite to be true. "For me, the best armor I can have is to truly be loving," she explained. "I don't mean loving in the, 'Oh, I'll give you anything you want' way. I mean loving as in, 'We're going to do what's best, and we're all going to do it together.' Treat the other person like you would like to be treated. Some women think that if they don't put on their armadillo armor, they're going to lose themselves. But you've already lost yourself just by donning the armor."

> BECOME COMFORTABLE WITH YOUR MORE ASSERTIVE SELF: *As you accept yourself for who you are, you unconsciously give other people permission to do the same.*

I find it interesting that even an armadillo has a soft spot. When predators attack an armadillo, they immediately go for the most vulnerable area. Similarly, if someone gives the impression that they have a hard outer shell, his or her opponents will often look for the chink in the armor, so they can pounce. But if you give them your genuineness, where can they aim their strike? All they have is you. Besides, it can be so difficult and time-consuming keeping that shell intact that it prevents you from focusing on and accomplishing your larger goals.

## Common Traits

Whether they're men or women, I have found that people who move up into the senior level have many of the same characteristics. They're thoughtful; they're concise in what they say; they're straight-forward and direct. A conversation with Jim Preston, the retired CEO of Avon, brought that home to me. "I'm sure this is an over-generalization, but some women tend to consider more possibilities than men, and that can sometimes actually get in their way," Jim told me. "Because they're relatively global thinkers, they don't nec-essarily make a decision based on what's at hand," he explained, "but they tend to get a little bit too scattered. Some women also tend to verbalize more questions and thoughts than men do, and perhaps those questions and thoughts, at times, don't seem germane to the issue. Because of that, they're sometimes seen as less focused and not really tuned in to the real issue."

But when I asked Jim, "Do you feel that senior executive women have these characteristics?" he looked at me quizzically, and I could tell a light bulb went off in his head. "You know, you're right," he said. "They're not that way. The ones who make it are really much more lin-ear. They think clearly, and they don't bounce around the issue. They tend to go directly at the problem, in a straighter and more linear way."

So is it true that they think like a man? Or do they tend to be logical, linear women? Because successful men and women share many of the same character traits, I would like to introduce a differ-ent paradigm, with the full knowledge that our culture has created a dichotomy. Lovingness, assertiveness, logic, caring, and confidence are neither male nor female attributes but *human* characteristics that each of us experiences in varying degrees. These traits have developed in all of us and are dependent on our environment and experience.

Let's look at the issues of masculinity and femininity not as a fight, but as a way to open dialogue about our humanness. It is ben-eficial to be inclusive and nonjudgmental, acknowledging that these characteristics are innate and valuable in varying degrees. Besides, any of these traits, when exhibited in the extreme in either gender, can create problems in life as well as in career advancement. You need only think back to Carmen's male predecessors (who were aggressive to the point of abrasiveness) to appreciate that.

## Maintain Your Integrity

Linda LoRe told me an amusing story about how she maintained her integrity—with humor, I might add—in face of a good deal of subtle pressure. When Procter & Gamble acquired Giorgio, Beverly Hills, several years ago, she continued in her position as CEO and became a corporate officer at P&G. When she attended her first P&G national meeting, she committed what some might consider a faux pas, but she used this situation as a learning experience and also as a reinforcement for her own identity and values.

"I showed up at the first Procter & Gamble national meeting that I attended as an officer of the company dressed in fashion, because my business is fashion," Linda explained. "And I never felt like such a fish out of water! I had a really beautiful deep purple suede coat, and everyone else was wearing Burberry or London Fog trench coats, either beige or navy. There were all these conservative coats, and then there was this one gigantic purple thing hanging in the coat closet. Under the coat, I was wearing a Carl Lagerfeld designer suit, jewelry, the works.

"Because I come from the fashion industry and because fashion and beauty was our business, I looked totally different from anyone else at the meeting. But, instead of letting that get to me, I decided to use it. I think one of the biggest mistakes we make is we try to blend in. When we do, many of our best attributes can't emerge. Now, if I had gone overboard—if I had dyed my hair purple or something like that—it would have been a different story. But I was very well groomed and nicely dressed. I was just different from what the rest of the corporation was all about, and so was my business."

Linda's advice to other women: Don't sacrifice who you are because it won't come out genuinely. But remember the message and whom you're speaking to. "If I had it to do over again," she explained, "I might not have worn the purple coat. I wouldn't have blended in more, but it wouldn't have been quite so outstanding.

Still, for me, it worked. I had enough confidence in myself to be able to pull it off. I had already been CEO of Giorgio for five years at the time of that meeting. I was a newly acquired person, but I was coming in knowing my job and being pretty well versed in my industry."

One of the lessons in Linda's story is to understand the corporate culture you are going into. "The culture of a company can make or break a person," Linda explained. "If you don't fit with the corporate culture and the values and the way they are expressed, you can really lose yourself and then you cannot be as effective. If the corporate culture is strong—and often it is—and you can fit into it, great. If not, you may want to look somewhere else."

## Partner with Men to Overcome Barriers

You may encounter many different kinds of barriers during the course of your career. Some of the these obstacles can be organizational barriers. For instance, there are just so many vacancies at the top, and only a limited number of people will be able to enter those ranks. There may also be an expectation—stated or assumed—that you must stay in one position for a certain length of time before you are promoted. In some companies, it may be more difficult for women to enter into the operations side of the business. There are also personal barriers. If you've decided to have children early on in your career, does your company provide daycare facilities? What are the provisions for a sick child? Are you being asked to relocate, and will that create a hardship for your young family?

Some perceived barriers may be in your control and some may not. But there can also be gender-based barriers—ones in which your male counterparts don't recognize your value or contribution or in which you feel the deck is stacked against you. As one mid-manager told me, "We have a departmental off-site meeting once a year, and my boss really wants us to bond. But the way we 'bond' is to participate in the most macho, athletic activity so that all the men can show their strength and athletic prowess, and at the same time show just how team-oriented they are. I don't want to have to deal with that kind of macho stuff—it's so blatant! It's always athletic competitiveness, and I don't enjoy that."

The Vice President of Operations at a large manufacturing concern told me, "I sometimes feel that the guys at my company get a little uncomfortable with me. I'm female. I haven't been at this company for a long time. I sometimes come up with some very different ideas, which is what they say they hired me for. But sometimes I don't think they're terribly comfortable. They don't know what to do with someone who is different. I have watched these guys and other guys like them. They begin to squirm when someone who is different than they are talks openly."

These sorts of gender-based slights and unconscious behaviors can enrage you, but such a reaction is often counterproductive. As Linda LoRe explained to me, "I'm not angry at men. I have no anger toward them whatsoever. They are a little threatened by women coming into the top levels because we haven't been there before. They don't quite understand us. But if you make them your partner, they will be less threatened. You have to recognize that the reason there are more men at the top executive levels is because they have been in the game longer. We're getting there. The women who have resentment or hatred toward men are the ones who will never get very far. They may get to a certain level, but they won't go all the way." I might add that people who are cynical or tend to have hatred toward men or women will have a difficult time working with diverse groups of people, and therefore difficulty in making it into the executive ranks.

Linda Lewis of Charles Schwab told me a great story that illustrates the importance of partnering with men to accomplish your goals. Early in her career, Linda ran into a proverbial brick wall. She was the new faculty member in a university department comprised solely of tenured male professors. "I would go to those staff meetings and sit quietly until I got the lay of the land. After about the fourth month there, I decided to chime in, because I certainly have no trouble being assertive or having an idea.

"I would make a suggestion. Absolute silence around the table. Nothing. I was using my best language skills. I wouldn't apologize—for example, I would never begin a sentence by saying, 'If you don't mind . . .' or preface a remark with, 'You may not agree with me, but . . .'—but rather simply asserted my position. Still no response. No follow-up; no one coming in on my comment. I tried all kinds of interventions. Once one of the men made a point that I had made five minutes before, to which no one had responded. I simply confronted him in the meeting and said, 'I believe I made that same point earlier.' It didn't change a thing. I began wondering, What is happening here? What can I not overcome?"

Linda approached her department head and asked him for help, "Please," she said, "I'm starting to feel a little crazy. Could you please observe the dynamics of the meetings? This is what's happening to me."

Linda's chairman sat through the next meeting, and he saw exactly what she had described. "We went back and strategized about what we were going to do," she continued. "The next time I made a suggestion at a meeting, and there was no follow-up, he became my champion. He jumped in, saying, 'Didn't Linda just suggest that?' or 'I agree with Linda. Her suggestion is right on target.' And from the very first meeting that he did this, I never experienced this problem again. The dynamic changed, and I was on the team. However, I was never sure if what transpired was based on the fact that people had simply tuned me out before or that my credibility had to be sanctioned by the most respected among them.

"You have to figure out how to penetrate the system and keep persevering," Linda advised. "I believe you have to get at the root cause and partner with champions who can help. It may take a very long time, but once you do, you feel terribly victorious."

> **PARTNER WITH MEN TO SUCCEED:** *Women who have resentment or hatred toward men are the ones who won't get very far.*

## Maintain a Sense of Humor, or at Least a Sense of Perspective

Many senior executive women spoke to me about the importance of having a sense of humor. As we have seen, it is a vital factor in maintaining professional relationships and alliances, as well as an integral part of the C.O.R.E. attribute of Endurance. Your achievements and confidence will get you to a certain point in your career, but your success can also depend on how well you are accepted—whether your colleagues enjoy being with you. People tend to feel more comfortable if you can joke with them, if they believe you enjoy their company, and if you don't take them or yourself too seriously. A sense of humor can also help you defuse potentially uncomfortable situations with male coworkers.

Liz Fetter of NorthPoint Communications explained why she felt it's important for women, in particular, to have a good sense of humor and not get too bent out of shape. "When I was doing management consulting in Australia, which has an incredibly macho culture, and working with plant managers or in a manufacturing plant, the men would say things like, 'Liz, would you mind going up that ladder first?'

"And I would ask, 'Do you guys want to look up my skirt or what?'

"And they would say, 'Well, we've just been appreciating your legs . . .'

"A lot of women would be filing for sexual harassment suits, but instead I would just laugh at them and say, 'You guys are too much! Maybe next time.' And I'd always wear pants after that."

"Because of my response, those men would say to each other, 'Well, you know, she's really okay. And that was a lousy thing for us to do.' They were testing me to see if I was going to get upset." When she didn't, Liz was accepted as part of this more macho environment. It is important to stay true to your own personal values and boundaries, and to realize that a difficult situation or inappropriate remarks can often be handled more effectively when humor is introduced into the conversation.

Another senior executive woman mentioned that when she first started working in the utility industry, she encountered what others might consider sexual harassment. "When I first came into the business, the utilities in particular were incredibly nondiverse," she told me. "It was a closed community, especially where the rubber meets the road. The highest-valued people were male engineers. The whole utilities industry was comprised of white males coming back from World War II who stayed with the business until the day they retired.

But having almost all of my postgraduate experience in the South, which was not normally women-friendly, I learned you either go with the flow and tolerate certain things or you're not going to achieve any results, and life is going to get pretty difficult.

"In my career, I have worked with very caring and generous men, but often they just didn't know how to appropriately express themselves. If you didn't hear their words in the total context of their personality and environment, you could easily take things they were saying to be male chauvinistic and discriminatory. But I didn't sweat what I considered to be the small stuff. A manager in my early days might come up and say, 'Oh, you look so nice today!' Well, I'd just say, 'Thank you so much,' and go on because ninety percent of the time it was innocent. It was his way of connecting. He didn't know what else to talk about."

It can reach a point where there is a Machiavellian motive behind words—someone is purposefully being condescending or making inappropriate comments. Then you take a stand. If you become excited about the small stuff, you can lose your ability to discriminate between something that is seriously offensive, harassing, and intended to demean and a comment that's innocent and is simply intended to connect.

## Times Are Changing

Although there are still many challenges to women achieving executive status, especially in male-dominated industries, the necessity of living totally in "a man's world" is decreasing. In many companies, top management has fewer rigid male-oriented rules than it used to. For instance, Terri Dial, President at Wells Fargo Bank, told me, "It's not the way it was in the old days, when companies were run by a macho management team who all went hunting, fishing, and drinking together. In those days, you had to be like that to fit on the team, but that started to change in the early 1980s, although in some parts of the country it might still be true," she said. "Today there's a lot more tolerance in the executive suite for a diversity of personalities. It's not like it was in the old days where the relationship had to include attending the same school, belonging to the same clubs, going golfing together."

This sentiment is also shared by Jim Preston, the retired CEO of Avon. He also noticed that corporate cultures were beginning to change, and he accelerated this new, more enlightened reality by implementing innovative programs in his own organization. For example, when he joined Avon fifteen years ago, the company's reward system consisted of hunting or fishing trips, poker games, or tickets to hockey games. But he immediately changed that to be more gender-neutral. Today the reward system consists of tickets to the opera or theater, a weekend at a spa, dinner out—special activities that both genders can equally appreciate and enjoy.

Linda LoRe also believed that attitudes are changing. The "squirm factor"—men's discomfort with female executives—is decreasing. "As more of us get into the upper levels, there is more tolerance and less fear of women in management. We still have a long way to go, but I have to give credit to some of the corporations I've worked with, including P&G, who have put in place focus groups and training on how men and women can work together. These companies are finding that they're losing too many really capable women at lower- and middle-management levels. These women are not making it to the top ranks because they don't want to play the game. Or they don't fit. Or they're not accepted."

The biggest challenge companies will face in the upcoming decade is recruiting and retaining talented employees. If we stay true to our own values and do so with a sense of humor, we will continue to be highly valued contributors. The challenge is to listen without internal filters to your inner self, your intuition. If you think you're unhappy, chances are you are. If you think you don't fit, most likely you don't. Whatever is happening, you can be sure it will be evident to those around you. Either change your current environment or move to one that better supports who you are.

The best way to be yourself is to *know* yourself. That involves self-reflection and self-exploration. Are you making decisions based on fear or on pleasure? Fear means you're being controlled by something outside of you. And if your fear keeps you in an unsatisfying position, you can be sure you're in for a bumpy ride. Pleasure comes from knowing yourself and what you want. What better way to be yourself and be passionate about your career and your life?

# 8 Find Advocates:
## *One Mentor Won't Pave the Way for Your Career*

Surprising as it may seem, most of the senior executive women I studied had no such "golden bullet" mentor. Rather, they had encountered many advisers or supporters who helped them along the way at various stages in their careers. For instance, Terri Dial of Wells Fargo Bank told me, "I have never found this mentor that everybody talks about—the person you magically hook up with when you're twenty-seven and stay with until you're forty-five. There isn't one person who has played that role for me. Instead, I can name half a dozen people—I call them 'influencers'—who have been very important to me at different times in my career."

Liz Fetter noted that she had had "advisers, not mentors—people who promoted me and gave me as much responsibility as I could take as quickly as I could take it." Similarly, Kathi Burke, in her position as Vice Chairman of Corporate Human Resources at Bank of America, said, "I haven't really formed allegiances with any particular individual but rather with a very broad set of people with whom I work." And Ann Walthall, in her role as Chief Administration Officer for Providian Capital Management, told me, "I haven't had a mentor off to the side helping me. But there was this group—mostly bosses or ex-bosses—who acted as sort of mentors. These were supporters or advocates who would very often give me stern coaching—just very clear, direct advice."

It is apparent from their comments that these successful women relied more heavily on groups of "influencers" than they did on a single mentor. These influencers are individuals with whom they may or may not feel a close personal connection, but who have been interested and instrumental in their career development and in helping them become successful.

## What Influencers Do

Influencers, advisers, supporters, sponsors, advocates—whatever you might call them—are individuals who want you to succeed. They may recommend you for promotions and new positions, advise you on how to proceed, alert you to the company's (or industry's) unwritten rules, act as sounding boards for your innovative ideas, encourage others to take a positive view of you, and open doors that might have otherwise remained closed. They may even run a bit of defense for you and grease the skids, especially as you enter a new phase in your career and are working in unfamiliar territory. Their faith in your abilities and their eagerness to help you can add immeasurably to your career success.

Nancy Hobbs, Executive Vice President and General Manager of AirTouch Cellular, explained how her supporters helped her advancement. "At each turning point in my career, when I wanted to try something new, there has always been somebody above me who has had confidence that I could do it. It was often my saying 'I would like to do this.' And somebody in a position of authority responding, 'You know what? I think you could too, so let's give it a try.'"

When I asked Nancy whether she would call those people mentors or just champions of her career, she replied, "In some cases they were mentors. In some cases, they were champions for my career. It depended. One boss I had was definitely both a champion and a mentor. This guy is the first one who stands out in my mind as somebody from whom I learned a great deal and who was a sounding board for me."

Linda Holsonback, former Vice President of Managed Care Operations and HMO Administration at Blue Shield, believed that her supporters paved the way for her to do what she did best. "I like to solve problems," she told me, "I like to keep moving. I was always able to go into areas that were troubled and do cleanup. Then I like to move on after that. And that was honored. The people who mentored me (and I had some good mentors) allowed me to move on and to do other things. They encouraged me to do that. 'Here's an area with some problems,' they would say. 'Why don't you go in and fix it?' It was fun! I believe a lot of my success is due to these individuals. They are people whom I trusted and who trusted me."

Some women have a loose collection of advisers in addition to a formal mentor, and they also use a lot of peer-mentoring both inside and outside the company. They think out loud a good deal of the time, so they have people against whom they can bounce their new ideas. It's not as if they say, "I'm an empty vat; pour it in." Instead, they say to the people with whom they're working something along the lines of, "Here's my idea of what I'm planning to do. Let me bounce it off you."

They may try out their new ideas and then go back to those same people and ask:

- How do you think that worked?

- Is there anything else I should have been aware of or that I need to follow up?

- Where do you think we are now?

- Where do you see we're going as an organization?

- Are there any other questions I need to ask?

This is a type of environmental scanning—being able to know what's going on around you, what might be needed, and how to adjust. These same sorts of interactions with your coworkers and advisers can help you determine what you don't know—and may not even know to ask about.

## The Role of Role Models

Many of the executive women with whom I spoke used role models along with their influencers and supporters to help them move forward. A role model is a person who possesses some quality or qualities we wish to emulate, but we don't necessarily interact with him or her personally or frequently. We may even combine the valued characteristics of many different role models into one composite entity that we use to fashion our careers. Role models come and go, but they help us to shape our own values and behaviors at critical times in our lives and careers.

You might identify some role models within your organization. Indeed, most of the women in my study honed their skills and corporate style by carefully watching and emulating the behaviors of top executives whom they admired within their companies as well as at other companies. For instance, one senior executive in the apparel industry spoke of several role models she had encountered over the years. "Anita was the first president of my company. We worked together in the beginning, and she was brilliant. She has influenced me tremendously. Anita—her whole thought processes—her never accepting 'no,' her always knowing there was a way to get the job done if you wanted to do it. And Daniel, who was chairman of the International Division of a big department store chain, was just a whirlwind and brilliant to watch. Daniel was nontraditional in his approach to business and to life in general. He and Anita were constantly breaking the paradigm. And Kevin was the world's best seller—the best I've ever seen in my life. I was just awestruck by his handling of stores and accounts."

---

USE ROLE MODELS: *Carefully watch and emulate the behaviors of top executives whom you admire within your company as well as at other companies.*

---

Many senior executive women did not consider these role models "mentors" in the usual sense in that they did not approach them for advice or to "bounce off" ideas. In fact, they largely avoided linking themselves too closely with a single powerful individual and instead modeled themselves after different people as they progressed in their careers. Remember, this is not a formalized relationship, and often the object of your observations and admiration may not even know you or know that you hold him or her as an ideal.

You might also seek role models outside your company and your industry. When I was younger, my biggest role model was Elizabeth Dole. I admired her courage in taking on such enormous levels of responsibility such as being the U.S. Secretary of Transportation and later the President of the American Red Cross. She displayed confidence and competence, yet demonstrated a compassionate "human" side.

Of course, just because you admire someone in one area of his or her life doesn't mean that you must idolize him or her completely. Even if you dislike the behaviors of the whole person, you may choose to emulate particular attributes and characteristics that you hold valuable. For instance, you might respect an individual's courage and drive but not want to imitate the harshness or aggressiveness that comes with the package. Or you may see a person whose gentleness and sense of caring and compassion are laudable, but who lacks motivation. Although you might wish to model yourself after her softer side, you may not want to emulate her passivity or what you might interpret as a weak drive.

## The Trouble with Mentoring Programs

In the same way that successful executive women do not rely on a single mentor, I have found that formalized, company-sponsored mentoring programs are typically ineffective. Rather than growing organically from a meaningful partnership, they are imposed from without. Usually the corporation weds mentor to protégé based on what it believes would be a good skills/experience match. But often the mix of personalities doesn't mesh. Just like an awkward blind date without chemistry, the relationship is simply not going to be effective. Rapport can grow from common personal values, moral principles, a similar work ethic, and a sense of relatedness. When the chemistry is weak or absent, rather than being a stimulating and satisfying bond, mentoring interactions can become burdensome and unproductive for both parties.

Some companies have programs in which the protégé chooses the mentor. Unfortunately, as often as not the mentor doesn't want a formalized relationship with that person, so those relationships are ineffectual as well. Barbara Haas, former Group Vice President of NiSource, was adamant on this point. "You just can't say to someone, 'I choose you. You need to be my mentor,'" she said. "That isn't going to work. You can ask that person for advice, but that's a different relationship than working with someone who always wants you to succeed."

And sometimes the presence of a mentoring program can undermine your willingness to take charge of your own fate. You may begin to believe that without that "all-important" mentor, you may be stymied in your career advancement. And that can stop you. As one senior executive woman explained to me, "Twelve years ago, I thought I needed a mentor. And I thought I needed to find a way to create comfort levels for people in power to mentor me. When that didn't happen, I had to keep on going anyway." This courageous woman found her own way.

Claudia, a mid-level manager at a large financial institution, explained to my why she eschewed a formalized mentoring program. "The problem with those programs," she told me, "is that mentoring is not something that can be prescribed—'someone gets assigned to you.' You have to 'click' with that person. It has to be a relationship where, for whatever reason, that person takes an interest in you and believes you have potential. So I don't think you can *look for* mentors in that sense.

"You have to be able to share with your mentor. And if you can't trust your mentor implicitly, that's a very dangerous thing to do. I will probably continue to rely on my former boss (who has now left the company) for coaching because I trust her. And the funny thing is, now that she's not here anymore and not my boss, it's actually a little easier. I can bounce things off her at no risk. I can ask her questions like, 'What if I said this? How would you react?' That's very useful." And, of course, the same politics are not involved when a former boss no longer works at your company.

From my experience, the only formalized mentoring programs that work well are those that allow the mentor and protégé to choose one another. It's time-consuming—a matchmaking nightmare—but both parties must be attuned to one another in order for the relationship to be beneficial. Indeed, I have found that it's easier to allow those types of relationships to develop informally, and not to impose corporate structure on them.

I've also seen supportive relationships work well when an executive connects with a manager in a different company. The manager gets many of her questions and curiosities answered while the senior person develops a better understanding of the real issues that preoccupy the up-and-coming generation. Indeed, formal mentoring programs can even work against your career, especially if your mentor falls from power or if you are so strongly identified with him or her that the "sidekick effect" sets in.

## The Sidekick Effect

Top executives do not associate too closely with any one person in power so as not to put themselves at risk if that individual falls out of favor or leaves the company. If they do, they are in danger of falling victim to the sidekick effect—that is, being perceived as an extension of the more powerful individual rather than a force in their own right. And they may be shoved to the side if their mentor departs. Besides, relating intensely to a single individual can deprive you of opportunities to learn how to work well with others.

> AVOID A SINGLE MENTOR—LOOK FOR "INFLUENCERS" AND ROLE MODELS: *Although your boss may be a great adviser and supporter, it can be an ineffective strategy to limit yourself to just this one individual. Develop a broad range of supportive relationships.*

Lora Colflesh, Vice President of Human Resource Operations at Sun Microsystems, told me a hair-raising tale of what can happen when you become too closely identified with one individual. "Back in the late seventies and early eighties, when I first came into the industry, the only advice that women in management got was to get a male mentor," she explained. "It was important to find somebody who either was the decision-maker or somebody close to those who were making the decisions about positions and promotions. So I got a mentor. He was my only mentor, and he was also my boss."

Lora thought it was the right thing to do, and although her boss proved to be a great teacher and mentor, her peer relationships suffered. Her colleagues began to believe that her relationship with her mentor, rather than the results of her own work, got her jobs, whether they were lateral moves or promotions. As you can imagine, this made it difficult for her to work well with her peers and to influence other people. The others became resentful.

"The second problem was that my mentor/boss abruptly left the company," she explained. "That created a terrible dilemma for me. I began wondering, 'Am I next?' because I was too closely associated with this one person. I realized then that because I had not built multiple relationships with varied people, I had really blown it. Once he was gone, it felt pretty lonely because I had not developed the other business relationships I needed."

Because of her difficult experience, Lora advises up-and-coming women against over-reliance on only one or two individuals. Lora bounced back from this career debacle by slowly building a strong network. It took time and patience. First, she had to repair the relationships with her peers and the people she worked with daily. She needed to prove to them that it really was her good work that had moved her ahead, not just the relationship with her mentor—that he had not protected her along the way. Simultaneously, she also had to rebuild relationships with other senior executives. Eventually, she set her career back on course, but it was a life lesson she will never forget.

There are other pitfalls as well. What if you have only one mentor and don't agree with him or her? How do you proceed? And sometimes you can get caught in the crossfire. A mid-level manager in the insurance industry told me, "The biggest hurdle was when I transferred here. I ended up working for an older woman who didn't like her superior, the man whom I had worked for previously. She saw me as a spy and a threat, and that did a lot to hurt my self-confidence and my ability to perform. She had favorites—I wasn't the only one who wasn't part of that group. There were a lot of subtle things

where I wasn't invited to be part of something—a black-tie dinner—even if it was work-related. For a long time, it made me feel as
if I didn't have a chance, and my work suffered as a result."

If you feel that you may be in danger of walking in a mentor's
shadow, you need to begin developing your own positive image in
your company—achieving valued outcomes and receiving appropriate recognition for your own accomplishments. Mentors might help
to connect you to the right people and champion your career. But
remember, it is best to develop a broad range of supportive relationships rather than a limited number of intense ones.

## Using Your Bosses as Advisers

Many of my interviewees spoke of their bosses as being their best advisers and supporters. Your boss is a wonderful influencer to have. He
or she is the one person who can vouch for your productivity, competence, and proficiency in your position. Moreover, your boss will
probably have the greatest impact on whether you are promoted.

This is true, of course, if your boss wants to be supportive. Most
do, unless they are like Sue Swenson's former boss who didn't believe
she could do the job, or the mid-level manager whose boss saw her
as an enemy and spy. More commonly, bosses want the most out
of their employees, so they willingly champion their careers. They
want to take a chance on you, give you opportunities, bet on you.
Most senior executive women benefited from their relationships
with their bosses.

It's your responsibility to cultivate a good working relationship with your boss. Sometimes you're lucky enough to be in an
employee-manager relationship that clicks. Everything is going
great; you get good feedback; your boss treats you the way you want
to be treated; you get exciting opportunities to test your wings on
new projects. Unfortunately, I've also heard mid-level women complain about their managers, but in so doing they put the onus on the
manager to make the relationship work. The truth is that the responsibility is mutual. But if the relationship is in trouble you need
to take 100 percent responsibility for making it function, as well as
allowing your manager to take 100 percent responsibility.

As one senior executive woman explained, "Probably the worst boss I ever had gave me the best advice *once*—not continuously, but just once. Out of that year, I was able to take away one really good nugget. But even though I didn't like him, I nurtured the relationship. I think that's key, whether you have a good boss or a bad one."

And don't be afraid to ask your boss for help when you need it. First, you must be willing to say, "I need help," when you are floundering, or, "I don't know," when you're stumped. It's important to demonstrate the capacity and desire to continue to grow and learn. Sue Swenson spoke of an employee who had difficulty in this area. "What's surprising," she explained, "is that she creates the illusion that she has it all together. But the truth is, she doesn't have anything figured out! Unfortunately, when you create that kind of illusion, you're not getting the help that's out there for you." The fact that you won't let down and say, "How do I even approach this problem?" will get in the way of your career advancement. Indeed, an honest discussion with your boss may result in difficult feedback such as, "You shouldn't have said that at the meeting. What were you trying to prove?" Responding openly to that kind of input without becoming defensive or hostile is a hallmark of humility and can help to advance your career.

Because your boss can have so much influence on your life, Sue also cautioned up-and-coming women to be careful about whom they choose. You may be distracted by superiors who you think are well-intentioned but who really aren't interested in your career. They may see that you can bring talent to the organization, but, at the end of the day, they're not out advocating your advancement. They're really doing it for their own self-interest.

Your boss must also be a person worthy of your trust. "One thing that's incredibly important about mentors is that they have ethical standards," Barbara Haas, former Group Vice President at NiSource, told me. "My bosses invariably, if push came to shove, would do what was right. That's really important to me. It's not just important that I like them and that they like me, but that they're worthy of my looking up to them. All my boss has to do is say something at a board meeting, and the whole decision goes his way. It's amazing to watch. He's also incredibly bright. It's fun to talk to him. I learn things every time I do."

Sue Swenson concurred. "It's a mistake to work for the wrong people who aren't trying to support and develop you," she explained. And women are more apt to be exploited than men in this way. "Maybe they feel they have to take the really crummy job because this is their big opportunity," Sue continued. "Men may be a little more selective because they believe they're going to be offered a couple of opportunities. Women sometimes jump at the first opportunity that's presented because they're afraid it's not going to come by again."

You may fear that if you say "no" you won't be offered a promotion again, and in some companies that may be true. And sometimes you may have to take one of those crummy jobs just to show that you have what it takes—"Hey, put me anywhere; I can do anything." That's a different mind-set, however, than, "I'm just so grateful to get even this job."

That said, many senior women had tremendous success using their bosses as advisers and teachers. "My bosses for the last fifteen years are all either VPs or CEOs of the largest banks in America," Terri Dial at Wells Fargo Bank told me. "And I've gained different benefits from different bosses. One boss taught me credit in its more theoretical applications. And another taught me street-smart credit. And a third taught me street-smart anything—whether it was management, politics of an organization, or hiring people. He would be frank about that—he said it like it was—so I didn't have to try to read between the lines. And yet another boss taught me how to think. These folks were a really good source of information and learning. This professional network of bosses has probably been the most valuable group for me over the years. There's no question that they're giving me more than I'm giving back. These were people who were giving more than just what a boss would do to develop me. They were developing me beyond my job."

Sometimes your boss can help you gain entrée into an elite circle. One executive woman explained how her boss had tried to do that for her. "I remember when I had just been hired as a mid-manager in a new industry. My boss had been in the business a lot longer than I had. He had gone to all the right schools and worked at well-respected companies. He knew all of those people on a personal basis. He was trying to figure out how to get me to know those people a little bit better. He said, 'Well, it's a lot easier for me because I can go in and ask them how their wife is or how their kid is. I've known them all these years, and it's a good beginning for conversation. You haven't known them all this time, so it's a lot harder for you to break the ice.'" He gave this high-potential woman pointers and helped ease her connections.

When you're asking your boss for advice and support, make sure that you don't drain his or her valuable time. It can be helpful to schedule regular one-on-one meetings to air issues that perplex you.

## Look for Mentors Outside Your Company

Professional relationships besides the one you form with your boss are vital. As you move ahead, it's people who give you promotions. You have to know people, and to get the big jobs, you're weighed against other people. As one executive woman told me, "You know, it's a bit of a beauty contest out there—both for men and for women—and you have to have your own faction voting for you."

Although your boss may be a great adviser and supporter, it can be an ineffective career management strategy to limit yourself to just this one individual. To get ahead, you also need to have champions who will stand behind you when you're up for a promotion or when the going gets tough. These are people whom you can use as sounding boards without fear of consequences—especially if they are not your immediate bosses. Besides, when you have just one mentor, you can sell yourself short. You may constantly turn to this individual for advice in a reenactment of the parent-child relationship. As women, we have a tendency to second-guess ourselves anyway because we're different. We can ignore our own intuition. Having only one or a small number of mentors can hurt us because it teaches us not to follow our intuition, not to solve problems for ourselves.

In fact, in addition to the sidekick effect, sometimes having your boss as your only mentor can be a real liability. If, for example, you're unhappy in your current position and you're wondering if your company or department is right for you, that would be an issue better discussed with someone outside your organization. If you turn to your boss with these concerns, he or she can question your loyalty. You may even miss out on important assignments because your boss may be unsure if you're going to stay on the job long enough to finish your work responsibly.

> **DEVELOP A COALITION:** *To get ahead, you need to have a "faction" that will stand behind you when you're up for a promotion or when the going gets tough. Develop a broad base of relationships with different kinds of people inside and outside your company.*

So rather than trying to find that one person who is going to do it all for you, it's useful to follow in the footsteps of many senior executive women. They developed a broad base of relationships with different kinds of people (many of whom were outside their companies) who helped them in their careers. Such "foreigners" to your corporate culture have a fresh and different viewpoint—an outsider perspective that you may find illuminating.

For example, in reflecting on her supporters, an executive at a large pharmaceuticals company relied on two people external to her organization. "They are both outside consultants," she told me. "One is in San Francisco, and the other is in New York City. One is male and the other is female. They're both more than ten years older than I am. They provide a reality check and mentor me as I've gotten more involved in investor relations. They have really turned into good resources for me."

Julie England at Texas Instruments had bounced back after "peace broke out" with the help of a former division vice president from her past. "After more than five years, I went back to him, and I said, 'Please tell me about the high-growth areas in semiconductors, and who are the leaders.' I hoped these leaders would be willing to take a risk on a person who has been out of that business for five years. He coached me on it. He told me where to go, and I made a cold call on a manager who was soon to be in my future. I turned up on a short list of potential quality managers, and my old division VP was there to validate that I was the right choice. And the man for whom I was quality manager is the CEO today.

"But I also had two women outside the company who are about ten years older than I am," Julie continued. "They have a passion for helping women reach their full potential. They are key relationships for me. They encouraged and supported me for over fifteen years, and that has made a big difference."

If you are only one of a handful of women at your level in your company, you may also feel it imperative to search outside your organization for advisers. You may lack for female role models, and there may be no one inside the company with whom you can unburden yourself when it comes to your career and the unique issues you face as a woman. As one senior woman told me, "When you're one-of-a-kind, it's hard to know who you can talk to about issues around difficulties you have being a women, difficulties you have being one-of-a-kind in anything." These outside relationships can help you keep a sense of perspective, and they can also be very safe.

In addition to her bosses, Carlene Burgess at Entergy also used a colleague as an adviser. "I had one professional relationship that I felt was important to me when I was Manager of Methods and Procedures. He was Manager of Security there. He and I worked for the same VP and the same department, and we spent a lot of time together. We'd go to lunch and talk about what was going well. He had a degree in psychology, and I always joked that he was my personal counselor. But he was a good mentor. We really talked. He has moved on, but I still call him every three or four months."

The overall message of having advisers of different genders, ethnicities, age groups, and levels—whether they work in your company or outside—is *don't have just one.* That limits your perspective. Even though you might think you're getting your needs met with that one person, probably you're not. A variety of supporters represents a cross-section of people you'll be managing and working with. They offer many different points of view. They interpret the world and deal with problems differently than you or your boss might.

I had a Japanese-American male adviser who taught me how to better roll with the punches. He taught me groundedness. There was a word he would always use, *bachi,* which means, essentially, "what goes around comes around." If you say something bad to someone, and then you stub your toe—that's a bachi. He taught me the importance of treating people with respect. He taught me that if you give and give and give, it will become yours. He conveyed a gentleness that I hadn't internalized before.

Besides, it can be very time-consuming for a single chosen mentor when you depend on him or her for all of your career advice. That individual may feel obligated to be available to you, and it can be too great a burden. It's not healthy for either of you.

Think of an aircraft carrier. You can build an enormous seaworthy boat from many tons of steel if you distribute the weight evenly over a sufficiently wide surface. But if you consolidate that same weight into one giant lump of steel, the great mass will sink and sink fast. Your search for supporters follows the same law of physics. If you spread out the weight of your needs and questions, everyone does well—you all float. But if you are too dependent on any one person, both you and your chosen mentor may be pulled under by the weight of responsibility.

It's important, therefore, to increase the surface area of your contacts. If you distribute your problems evenly, you'll get enough suggestions and data to be able to solve them without dwelling on them too much or getting bogged down and isolated in trying to figure them out all by yourself. In business, you will always find issues that require you to consult with others. If you only have one person to ask, you may feel reluctant, because you've just approached him or her for something else, and you don't want to be a bother. On the other hand, if you have a dozen people that you bounce ideas off of, you can always find one of them to help you when you need it.

## How Do You Find the Right People?

Often supportive relationships develop based on a personal connection with someone you've grown to trust (and who has grown to trust you) as a result of working on a corporate board or a project in another department, someone who has noticed your career development, or someone who takes a special interest in you because you've performed under extraordinary circumstances.

That's what happened to Evie Byrnes, Vice President at American Management Systems, who worked for more than twenty years in engineering and data systems at AT&T. "At AT&T," she explained, "the first sponsor I had was a by-product of my results orientation. He was the head of engineering, and we were working on a long-range engineering project, a system that had an annual cycle.

If the system wasn't ready by January, they would have to wait a whole year to put it into operation. In December, they found a major flaw in a critical part of the system. They had IBM and everyone else in to assess what could be done about it, and they all advised AT&T to give up on it.

"My boss called a meeting and told us that we'd worked very hard and we'd built this system, but there was a critical flaw, and no one believed it could be remedied in time for the January cycle. I listened. Here I am a 'greenie.' But my nature was not to give up. I said to myself, 'Gee, we're giving up in December? This isn't due till January!'

"When everyone left the meeting, I spoke to my boss. 'Would you mind if I try to rescue the system?' I asked.

"'Well, what have we got to lose?' he replied. So he let me proceed to do that. I started working on it day and night, seven days a week. I gave my friends and family IOUs for Christmas. I wanted to make it happen and, as a matter of fact, I did make it happen. So that established me both with the Management Information Systems community and with the engineering department.

"Eventually that boss became very powerful at AT&T. He used to say, 'I won't believe it cannot be done by such and such a date until Evie Byrnes tells me it can't be done.' He became my champion. You can make allies along the way if you just stick to your own set of principles."

Evie won over this important supporter because of her hard work, her competence, her commitment, her ingenuity, and the extraordinary outcome she produced. But sometimes finding influencers goes back to simple chemistry. Perhaps the best way to ferret out coaches in your career is to identify people with whom you have such rapport. You trust their integrity; you know they will maintain confidentiality; you believe you can truly respect them and that they are respected and valued within their company. And they trust and value you.

Carlene Ellis of Intel had that kind of chemistry with one of her early supporters. "We stay in touch, no matter what," she told me. "I've worked for him; I've worked beside him; I've worked against him, as a competitor. He has been married two or three times, and I know his kids and all of his wives. He's kind of a soul mate. No matter what he does or where he is, I'll know about it. He sends every headhunter call he gets to me, and I still like him!"

Should you ask someone to be your advocate and supporter? That depends. If the relationship works with your boss, certainly you can ask if he or she will mentor you. Patricia Martin, a mid-level manager at Clorox, found other ways to get help and create an alliance without posing the "Will you be my mentor?" question directly. That's usually just too intimidating. To ask someone to be your mentor means that you're hitching your wagon to their star, and, as we've seen, it can be too great a responsibility for any one person.

"Generally I find people who I think are really good at something that I'm still working on developing," she told me. "I'm pretty honest about the fact that I have a lot to learn. I'll say, 'This is something I admire you for. Can you give me some advice?' I have never been turned down by anybody whom I've approached. I suppose it's flattering to be asked." This seems a good way to test the waters. There are folks in your company and industry who have an excellent grasp of issues and concepts that are new to you. It takes just a bit of vulnerability and honesty on your part to approach them and say, "You know what? I need help with this." You're asking for direction with a specific problem, not your whole career. And a more wide-ranging supportive relationship can grow from such an overture if, after the initial interactions, you find that you "click" with each other.

Indeed, recently I held a workshop for clinical psychologists who wanted to integrate their skills into the business community. At the end of the session, a dozen or so psychologists came up to me and either asked me to be their mentor or whether I thought any of the other panelists would be a good mentor for them. I advised them to reframe their question. A better approach would be: "Are you willing to be a sounding board for me?" "Can I call you if I have a question or need help with a specific issue?"

People are always asking Linda LoRe, the CEO of Frederick's of Hollywood, if she would be their mentor. And her response is always the same: "Be yourself. Get out there, and when you have an issue to talk through with someone you respect, I'm available. I've always been the champion of the underdog," Linda continued. I like to help people succeed who have struggled, but have worked hard. I like to help people who are bright and enthusiastic and have had some kind of situation that held them back, and I like to see them push through it."

Linda is a huge proponent of building relationships with people you admire and respect, and who take an interest in you and your career. Like many of the other executives I interviewed, however, she's not a big fan of the formalized and structured mentoring programs some corporations offer their employees.

## Reciprocity

In this chapter I have discussed the importance of finding a variety of people who are sounding boards and can help you in your career. It's also critical that the mentor believes he or she is benefiting from the relationship and interaction. It must be a reciprocal relationship.

Often mentors want to feel that they are helping someone else—giving back for all the times others had helped them to advance their careers. Sometimes they want to better understand the challenges and needs of the younger generation so they can become more attuned to the realities of the current workforce and business environment. And at other times, they look to their mentoring relationships for something more specific. For instance, I have a reciprocal relationship with a retired vice chairman at a large bank. The former president of the university at which I received my Ph.D. recommended that I call this man. He felt that Steve could introduce me to the CEOs of large companies.

When I went in to talk with Steve, we bonded on a professional and personal level. He has always been available to help me in any way he can. Although he cares about my progress, I believe that this relationship works because Steve, in part, perceives me as a means to one of his cherished goals. By taking me under his wing, he can help me make a difference in an area in which he has a great interest—the advancement of talented women into the executive ranks. He is passionate about the subject and worked hard to promote women while he was at the bank. However, as a retiree, he knows that he cannot have the same level of influence now as he once had. And he understands that I can help him. It's through me that he is able to advance more women, and that's important to him. That's the reciprocity of the relationship.

Another form of reciprocity can be achieved when you become an adviser to others. We all want to help other people and to feel that we're making a difference in their lives. When you become an adviser for someone beneath you in the corporate hierarchy, it provides an avenue for you, as a more experienced businessperson, to give back and help others, which is all part of human nature anyway. It can make you feel good about yourself when you serve others in this way. And such positive self-esteem can help you do a better job too.

Besides, being an adviser to someone else can enhance your own career in several ways:

- It can reinforce your confidence when you realize that you really do know what you're talking about and that other people find your advice valuable.

- Teaching someone else imposes on you the necessity to reach a certain level of clarity about how to deal with a particular problem.

- It helps you understand the issues that others are facing, which may be quite similar to yours. Consequently, you may feel less alone in your own struggles.

- Your protégé can also bring a different perspective. You may learn new ways to solve problems. By hearing what's important to others, you may learn how to better motivate and inspire others.

In fact, an effective way to counterbalance having mentors is to become one yourself. Taking on this role allows you to walk in the shoes of your mentors—to see how much is too much, in terms of your own needs and demands.

> **BECOME AN ADVISER FOR SOMEONE ELSE:** *It provides an avenue for you to give back and to help others. It also helps you better understand the issues others are facing.*

## Driving Your Own Career

Think of taking responsibility for your career as being similar to driving your car. When you're behind the wheel, you have a destination in mind, and you generally know how to get there. But should an animal run into the road or should you encounter construction, you swerve or take a detour rather than staying on the same trajectory that you might have used the last time. When you adjust and adapt to the changes that arise, you actually stay in greater control of your destiny than if you ignore them or depend on others to tell you what to do. This means that you're really taking responsibility for your own safety and your journey.

You may stop along the way for directions and repairs (input from an adviser or mentor), but you are still in control of the destiny and timing of your career, slowing down or speeding up as necessary. On the other hand, when you rely too heavily on a single person, you can become the passenger rather than the driver. It's possible to begin believing that the other individual knows better than you do and even to feel like a victim when situations go badly.

I can't emphasize enough the importance of taking responsibility for your own career destiny, whether you have one mentor, a dozen mentors, or decide to go it alone. In Part III, I offer you many ways in which to do so.

# LIFE AT
# THE TOP:
# CREATING
# A ROAD MAP
# FOR SUCCESS

# 9 Having It All and Having a Life:

## *Making Choices About Marriage, Family, and Career*

"**I**'m so confused," Judy told me. "I want to get married and have kids, but I worry that a family will interfere with my promotion potential."

At thirty-six, Judy has made good progress in her career; she heads a department within a large financial institution and sees that the way is clear for her to move up. "I know I'm on the fast track, but if I'm ever going to have children, I probably have only five years left to do that," she complained. "I don't know if I've advanced far enough that I can afford the time and energy it takes to have a child. On top of that, I've been dating a man for five years, and I'm still not sure if he's the right guy. I know I want to have children before it's too late. Maybe I should bite the bullet and get married to have kids. I don't know. Is it possible to have a successful career and a husband and children too?"

Judy faces a dilemma many mid-level women grapple with—can you have it all and still have a life? And the fact of the matter is, she really doesn't know what she wants. She has been so focused on her career and getting the job done for her company and clients that she has put her personal needs second.

Can you have it all and still have a life? It's a pivotal question. Judy's concerns are a central issue for many women already in the management pipeline who are at decision points both in their careers and in their personal lives. While there are no simple answers to work and family issues, in this chapter I will offer you the experience and advice of dozens of successful executive women who have already made their choices and are living with the results. It is my hope that their experiences and solutions will help you answer this question for yourself.

## To Be a Mother or Not to Be

The seventy senior executives whom I interviewed for my initial research resolved the marriage and motherhood issues in a variety of ways:

- Ninety percent of them were or had been married, but many had either chosen not to have children or had limited the size of their families.

- Forty-five percent had no children.

- Forty percent were married with no children.

- Forty-four percent had one or two children.

- Only 11 percent had three or more kids.

- More than half of the women who did have kids were over thirty when they gave birth to their first child.

- Six percent were unmarried and child-free while fewer than 5 percent were single, never-married moms.

- Approximately 20 percent of the executive women were divorced moms with primary responsibility for raising their children.

- Sixteen percent chose to adopt children.

Whether or not they decided to raise a family, most successful executive women viewed their work and family choices as *positive personal decisions, not as sacrifices.* That is, they were doing what they wanted to do, and didn't feel victimized by their circumstances or options. For instance, Liz Fetter, while she was President of Industry Markets at Pacific Telesis, had made a deliberate choice not to have children. "Basically I decided to run a large chunk of the company," she told me. "And I made a lot of choices that helped support that decision. It's really a matter of individual choices along the way."

In comparison, Gale Duff-Bloom, J. C. Penney's President of Company Communications and Corporate Image, had three children by her late twenties. She did not seriously focus on her career until *after* the children were born and her mother moved in with her to take care of the kids while Gale was at work.

## When the Decision Is "No"

Many of the child-free senior women expressed the sentiment that you just can't do it all and do it well. For instance, Karen Wegmann, Executive Vice President of Corporate Communications at Wells Fargo Bank, gave me her reasoning: "You can either have a great job and a great marriage and okay kids, or you can have an okay job and an okay marriage and great kids. It's very hard to have all three."

As you move up the career ladder, it can be difficult enough just to maintain your relationship with a spouse, let alone give birth to kids, raise them, and keep them out of harm's way. In fact, from the point of view of those executive women who chose to remain child-free, if you don't want children, it's perfectly acceptable not to have them. There's no need to feel guilty about it or unfulfilled.

One woman, for instance, spoke of her limitations in terms of time, energy, and biology. "Life is a series of making choices," she told me. "Doing anything well requires a high degree of commitment. You can translate that into time and energy. The fact is there are only so many hours in a day. During the boom years in my industry, there was a lot of work to be found, and I did it. That's not to say I didn't have a social life, but what I'm finding out more and more now that I'm married is that marriage takes time and energy too. I got married when I was a little older—forty—and I'm set in my ways! I'm used to doing what I want to do, how I want to do it, when I want to do it. And living with someone—that level of commitment—requires time and compromises. It can be done, but anybody who does it feels the tension between work and wanting to excel at a profession and having a family and wanting to excel at that as well. And there's biology—you have to sleep. We tried to have kids, but I had an early, spontaneous miscarriage—the pregnancy just didn't take. So if it works out, it works out, and if it doesn't, it doesn't."

There's also the issue of desire. Some women have very strong desires to become mothers, and others don't. If your maternal instincts are not speaking loudly to you, then it may be more important for you to listen to those internal voices.

Some women spoke of expectations they had based on their own families of origin, and how they believed they couldn't be the kind of mothers their stay-at-home moms had been. They really appreciated the parenting they had received and didn't want to relegate child-rearing to nannies or other surrogates. Consequently, they felt that to have children, they would have had to relinquish their careers. It was an either/or proposition.

For others, these issues were complicated by difficult family arrangements. As one executive told me, "For the first seven years that we were married, I'd wonder if I should have children. But because my husband is a pediatric social worker, he's with kids all the time. We're both very independent. He didn't want to be the primary caregiver, and he would have been forced into that role. Or I would have had to change careers. I get a lot of satisfaction from my work. Being a mother was not something I used to dream about. Besides, I can't imagine how I could have worked as much as I have and had children and focused on them too."

---

LISTEN TO YOUR INTERNAL VOICE: *Some women have a strong desire to become mothers, while others don't.*

---

Although some of these women may have decided that having children was not important to them, they didn't totally turn off their maternal instincts. Many derived great satisfaction from nurturing their careers. And some have nurtured other people and continue to do so without having kids of their own. For instance, Joanne, Director of Human Resources at a large accounting firm, brought a nineteen-year-old unmarried mother and her newborn into her home to provide the young woman and her baby a vehicle to transition into life. "They stayed with me for about eighteen months, and now the mother is working at a hospital," Joanne told me.

Not only did this young woman and her infant benefit from Joanne's caring and concern, but this arrangement also enhanced Joanne's life and career. "It taught me a lot," she explained. "I learned what women go through who have to put their kids into daycare so they can go to work. It gave me a lot more understanding of the issues and a lot more empathy. It kept me from becoming more set in my ways."

Other executives didn't want to have kids, but they still needed a sense of family, and so they created a close circle of friends. Many also found satisfaction in mentoring young women. The fact that these senior executive women decided against raising a family does not mean that they lead unfulfilled lives. They made the choice of not having children, and they didn't feel they were missing anything. This is what they wanted; it was a personal choice.

## When the Decision Is "Yes"

When I interviewed Ellen Gordon, President of Tootsie Roll Industries, she had been married for forty-five years and had four daughters ranging in age from twenty-six to forty-three. Similarly, Ruth Handler, the former CEO of Mattel, raised two children, Barbara and Kenneth (after whom the famous dolls were named), while she and her husband ran their successful company. These veteran businesswomen seemed to have been able to "have it all." Indeed, as noted above, 55 percent of the senior executives whom I interviewed for my research were mothers.

As my statistics suggest, it is possible to balance children with a highly successful business career. Sometimes the choice to have kids is based on timing and self-confidence. For instance, Shirley Buccieri of Transamerica Corporation needed to feel secure in her position prior to having a family. She was married for more than eighteen years before her daughter (who was three at the time of our interview) was born. "My husband and I just finally said, 'Let's try now,'" she explained.

Shirley gave birth to her daughter the year after she made partner at the firm. "It was good timing for my husband and me," she told me. "We really made a conscious decision to have her. We said, 'Things look like they're in good order, so why don't we try?' The timing has to work out right."

Other women understood that having children might limit their career options or slow their trajectory—but they still chose to have families. One executive had been married for thirty years and had two teenage boys at the time of my interview. "That's one reason I think I moved a little more slowly in my career," she said, referring to her sons. "I didn't start out knowing, at all, that I would move into the executive ranks. I began as a professional and then slowly was able to move up in a business career."

And one executive who had been married for twenty years told me, "It is incredibly difficult to be a CEO and have children, unless your husband is going to be the wife, and most men don't want to do that. I think it's a choice. If somebody asked me, 'Do you want the CEO job of your division right now?' I would say, 'no' because I can't give seventy hours a week. I can't fly all over the country. Physically I could. I have childcare and a husband who would put up with it, but I don't want to. I would not leave my child that much."

This woman made it clear that she had chosen this route. People make it sound as if these career choices are imposed on them, and that's a fallacy. Such an attitude takes the power away from a woman's ability to choose, and it also enhances the stereotype that women can't and don't want to handle the top jobs.

Perhaps a woman can climb higher on the corporate ladder if she doesn't have to balance the additional responsibilities that offspring can bring. Alternatively, many executive mothers told me that the vicissitudes of parenthood have taught them volumes about how to manage their time and other people. In addition, like Joanne, many learned to become more "human," and they developed a greater sensitivity to others' needs. As one woman said, "I did notice a change in me when I had my children. It really gave me a different perspective about what's important in life. I don't think I had that prior to my children. Before, I tended to be a workaholic, but I don't want to do that anymore." Raising children also teaches one how to motivate people with different personalities and needs. It is an enriching life experience.

## What Do You Want to Do?

Often members of the up-and-coming generation of managers feel hampered because they are certain that senior women have set a precedent—not to have children, not to have a life. This next wave of businesswomen believes that they are expected to remain child-free. They sometimes feel frustration and even animosity toward the senior women and the "model" they've established because many of them want to become mothers even as they ascend in their careers. These younger women feel victimized by their perceptions of the "sacrifices" executive women have made in order to advance into the upper echelons. "It's just not fair," they complain.

I'd like to set the record straight here. First of all, clearly, you can be a mother and a successful businesswoman. Some of the executive women I interviewed chose to do so *at the same time.* Others had a family early and grew into their careers later as time allowed, or they went all out for the career first and had a family later. Below, I will describe how some of these mothers manage their busy lives.

Alternatively, the idea that you don't have to have children can be liberating. Following a Windows in the Glass Ceiling workshop, a mid-level manager approached me to tell me how refreshing it was to hear from women who didn't want to be mothers. "I always thought I was a little strange to not want to have children," she confessed. "It was so validating for me to know that other women have also made that choice and that there was no guilt attached to their decision."

So how do you choose the best route for yourself? First of all, I believe there is no such thing as a precedent when it comes to having a family. It's up to you to make the personal choices that you want—not to base your decisions on the erroneous notion that some sort of standard has been established. Secondly, the senior women did not make sacrifices—they made choices. They did or didn't have children because that's what they wanted to do. My interviewees encountered some tradeoffs, of course, on both sides of the issue—there's no question about that. But these women accepted the reality that they could have it all, *just not all at once,* and they proceeded from there.

What about Judy, the confused mid-level manager who was unsure whether to marry and become a mother? She had spent many years building her career, and after some constructive soul-searching she decided that now was the time for her to stop and focus on her personal life. That didn't mean she would drop her professional life, but she decided to work on what she wanted personally. In order to achieve her personal goals, she knew she couldn't continue on for another five years with the same man and then decide she was with the wrong person. To gain some clarity, she took time to review what she wanted in her life and bump up those unresolved issues on her list of priorities.

If she did want to marry, she needed to establish what was important to her in a spouse. Did her current partner have the attributes she was looking for? If so, she could build that relationship with the same care and deliberateness that she had built her career. If not, it would be time to change the dynamics and be open to seeking out another potential husband. She even considered what it would be like to have a child without a partner. Just as she often asked for advice and counsel in her career, she sought the advice of a confidant to help her think through her decision.

Finally, Judy decided to spend less time at work and more on her personal life. She reduced her hours from sixty to fifty a week and decided not to take work home over the weekends. This allowed her to spend more time with the man she was considering marrying. She hoped that this would give her the information she needed to make an informed decision.

There are many options and paths available to you. The bottom line is that you must clearly understand what you want and what your priorities are, and then line up the resources to make it all happen, or not, as the case may be. It may be time to step up to the plate and make a decision.

> **BE REALISTIC:** *Executive women accepted the reality that they could have it all, just not all at once.*

## Managing the Family

Almost every executive mom whom I interviewed has either had a house manager, a housekeeper, a nanny, a supportive spouse, and/or someone else who provided crucial logistical and emotional support. If you hope to move up in your career and raise a family simultaneously, it's imperative that you get those relationships and systems into place in advance. Otherwise, you will be miserable, and so will your kids and partner.

All of the senior executive women had to make some family adjustments in order to have kids. For instance, Dawn Lepore, CIO at Charles Schwab, decided at age forty-three that she wanted to have a child. She knew that she couldn't do everything. She liked her demanding career, but she also wanted the child to be born into a loving, stable family. She and her husband talked about the situation for months. They agreed that they wanted to have a baby. Finally, her husband, who was an executive at Visa, said, "Dawn, your career is very important to you. You're on a faster track than I am. I think you should continue to work, and I will stay home and take care of our child." They made a conscious and well-thought-out decision.

And that's exactly what happened. Dawn gave birth to a healthy baby boy, and her husband stayed home with him. Dawn has had to make some choices in her professional life as well. Since the birth of her son, she doesn't attend as many evening functions as she used to, and she tries to spend as much quality time at home as possible.

Like Dawn, many executive mothers look to their husbands for help and support. Even if they were unable or unwilling to resign from their own positions and take over at home, these men provide the needed safety net that allows their wives to soar in their careers. They become partners in childrearing. Carol Hochman, CEO of Danskin, has full-time help with the kids, but her husband is involved too. "He is able to deliver the emotional help and the consistency when I have to be overseas," she told me. Her situation is common among senior executive women.

Sometimes a husband's help requires a bit of negotiation. Maggie Wilderotter, the CEO of a start-up company, Wink Communications, told an Executive Women's Alliance audience that she and her husband made an agreement about their shifting family roles when she took her demanding new position. "This has been a very high-growth experience for me," she explained. "I've never run a start-up before. It's a tough challenge. I'm on the road eighty-five percent of the time. I have two wonderful kids, eleven and fourteen. The reason I'm able to do what I do is because of my husband, who is a terrific individual. He picks up the slack for me at home. But it's an ebb and flow. He and I made a deal that for the first two years I was at Wink, I was going to be pretty much under water. By the beginning of next year, my goal is to have the team assembled and the right pieces in place so that I don't have to continue at this pace."

Other women relied on their mothers to help out. For instance, Gale Duff-Bloom of J. C. Penney had three adult children at the time of our interview. She had given birth to them when she was in her mid- to late-twenties. When I asked her how she had managed all that, she told me that her career had come about inadvertently—as a result of her mother moving in with her family.

"I had not planned to go back for a career," she explained. "Not at that stage. But my dad passed away, and my mother came to live with me. My mom had worked her whole life as a nurse, and she decided she didn't want to work anymore, that she wanted to get to know her grandchildren, because we had lived apart. But after about three months of my mom and I in the house together all day long, I started volunteering for everything I could find. I was volunteering about twenty hours a week. Finally I asked my mom, 'Are you going to go back to work?' and she said, 'Absolutely not.' She needed us and we enjoyed having her, but we couldn't stay there together all day.

"That's why I started my career. And by the time it got going, I had that built-in support system, and it was fabulous. Whenever I was home, I took over and did all the work. She didn't have to do all of it. There were times when we had people come in to clean so she didn't have to do those things, but she was there for my children."

If you're divorced or single or otherwise don't have a househusband or someone near and dear to take care of your family, then you must arrange—just as you would for any project—a support system to cover for you at home:

- Consciously think through what your responsibilities are and prioritize your time so you use it most effectively.

- Prioritize what is essential and what is not (see Chapter 10).

- Delegate the activities you shouldn't or don't choose to spend time on—including many of the domestic chores—and don't feel guilty about it. Pay someone else to cook, landscape, or pick up the dry cleaning. Your time is too valuable to waste on distracting tasks you don't enjoy. (If you love gardening or cooking and find them a welcome diversion, go ahead and indulge yourself. If not, find someone to relieve your burden.)

- Learn to let go. If the beds aren't made every day, so what?

One executive mother has a house manager who takes care of everything—paying the bills, going to the market, calling the plumber, fixing the meals—so she can focus on what's important to her: spending quality time with her family and working. Of course, you don't need to hire someone like that if you have a partner who is willing to pitch in.

Another senior woman, the mother of four grown daughters, told me, "I was told eleven years ago, when I went charging off on this career, that I can't have it all, and I had to make choices and live with those choices. Well, I don't do things as perfectly as I would like to do them sometimes, but I still find that it works."

Again, it's a matter of personal choice, accommodation, and negotiation.

## Children Can Limit Your Free Time

Despite the joy they bring, children can have a chilling effect on your own personal time and your ability to socialize with others or create large groups of alliances. After all, there are only so many hours in the day, and being a good parent may be your top priority. "Free time" can become a scarce commodity in your life.

One woman told me she plays with her grandchildren when she has time off. "I have these two six-year-old grandsons. That's my community volunteer work. They grow so fast; I just spend a lot of my free time with them." When I interviewed Cindy Hawkins, she was Vice President and Controller at 3Com and had two children (aged four and six), and the issue of free time was important to her. "My husband and I don't have much free time, and when we do, we choose to spend time as a family, rather than with friends. Our kids are very hungry for us and our attention."

When I asked one executive woman how she managed to have time to take care of kids, age five and twelve, and maintain a relationship and work full-time, she replied, "That's my life. There's not much else." She could see that her women colleagues who were either single or without kids had many more social interactions. "I just don't have the time," she admitted. "I have minimal social interactions with colleagues. There are a couple of colleagues whom my husband and I will get together with for no other reason than to socialize, but it's not strategic. They're friends."

> GET GOOD HELP: *If you hope to move up in your career and raise a family simultaneously, it's imperative that you put support systems into place in advance. Otherwise, you will be miserable and so will your kids and partner.*

You need to make your own decisions about what relationships and friendships are important to you and your family. It may seem overly calculated, but many executive women consciously choose which relationships are vital and commit to spending a certain amount of time each quarter with these people over the course of a year. They openly communicate to these "chosen people" the importance they place on the friendship and their level of commitment. Given the extreme demands on your time and energy, it is critical that you make similar choices and communicate your commitment and expectations to others. Conflict and hard feelings occur when expectations are not clearly expressed and/or are unmet.

## Involving Your Children in the Decisions

Carlene Ellis of Intel, a divorced mother of two, talked about engaging her grade-school-age children in decision-making when it came to hiring babysitters. If she had to decide who would be taking care of them when she needed to travel to off-site meetings, she made these decisions with her children's input at family meetings. These sessions not only created mutual commitment with her kids, but the meetings also taught her children how to communicate effectively, manage priorities, deal with conflict, and make decisions. They learned valuable lessons about responsibility.

Family meetings are a great way to manage family decisions and crises. In their book *Disciplining Your Preschooler and Feeling Good About It,* Dr. Mitch and Susan Golant give guidelines for establishing these meetings on a timely basis. If you think you want to try this approach, you might find it helpful to set up an appointment or a regular meeting time with your children and partner every Saturday morning to talk. When you treat this time seriously, your children will learn to respect its value. Also, be cognizant of your children's attention span. Preschoolers can only handle perhaps ten minutes, while older children can be engaged for a half-hour or more. Also be sure to shut off your pager and let the voice-mail take your calls. This time together is important.

Discuss only one topic—too many may confuse the issues. The clearer your goals are, the more effective you will be in coming to some consensus. Suspend all traditional family roles. Everyone gets equal time because everyone's input is important. This helps your children to feel valued and respected. And use good communication skills. That means making eye contact, really listening, using "I" statements such as "I don't like it when you're not careful" (rather than accusatory "What's wrong with you!" allegations). If necessary, leave the solution open. You might all get a better sense of how to proceed after you've had a chance to sleep on everyone's input. And plan ahead for the next meeting. You can be thinking about solutions in the intervening days.

> ESTABLISH FAMILY MEETINGS: *They create mutual commitment and teach your children how to be responsible, communicate effectively, manage priorities, deal with conflict, and make decisions.*

Perhaps the most important part of any meeting with your kids is the expression of love. It's essential for them to understand that although you may be busy and overwhelmed, they still come first in your book.

As mentioned above, you can have it all, but maybe not all at once. Most successful women seem to accomplish their goals in series. My best advice to you is not to try to do it all simultaneously, but rather in stages. Otherwise you, your family, your friends, and your work may suffer.

## Husbands, Wives, and Significant Others

Relationships can wither when you devote almost all of your time and energy to your career. In fact, a former boss of mine once told me how disgruntled his wife had become when she felt excluded and unappreciated in his life. The only way she could get through to him was to reach him in his own world. In frustration, she requested him to "treat me like I'm one of your projects going bad!" Her request fit into his work paradigm, and he could then clearly relate to her concern! Sometimes we need someone to remind us of the importance of our primary relationships, or we wake up at fifty, unhappily divorced, and wondering now what?

When two hard-charging people focus exclusively on their careers, neither has much time to build the partnership. (By the way, that partnership-building time can also include time alone for recharging your batteries so you can be more refreshed when you are with each other. As one executive said to her partner, "I'll be a better person if I can get away for an hour and exercise.") In fact, I have found only a handful of senior executive women are married to men who are also in the senior executive ranks. Instead, many of their spouses are teachers, consultants, entrepreneurs, or general contractors. These positions give them more options. For instance, Carol Hochman of Danskin told me that her husband works on Wall Street and makes substantially more money than she does. But he does have more flexibility in his day, so it works for them.

Although dual working couples are often in different fields, usually the partner of a businesswoman needs enough business savvy so the couple can relate to one another. There has to be a feeling that each person understands the other's world. Partners also need to make time for the relationship and themselves. When a couple's positions and lines of business are quite similar and the demands on their time are equivalent, it adds a level of complexity. Often both people have evening and early-morning commitments and have to juggle their travel schedules to meet the family's needs. It's workable—there are couples who make it happen—but it can be difficult.

I have also found that managerial women have procedures in place at work that enable them to accomplish their goals efficiently, and they have people to whom they can delegate certain tasks. But often these expectations are transferred to their home and personal lives. We do have to remember that delegating and consistently asking family members to do things for us may be an ineffective way to develop intimacy. Personal relationships require a lot more give and take than the superior/subordinate relationships that develop in the workplace. Ordering family members around conveys a lack of respect. Besides, we must realize that we can't and shouldn't strive for the same level of efficiency at home as we do at work. It's difficult enough when you don't have children—when you do, efficiency is truly an absurd concept!

A common discussion item during the Executive Women's Alliance is the inverse relationship between success in one's career and success in one's sex life. Typically, the higher your career attainments, the greater the pressures and responsibilities. Work begins to consume all of your time and concentration. In fact, highly successful people think about their work even when they're not on the job. As you can imagine, this sort of distraction can dampen your sex drive. When your stress levels increase, sex can be less pleasurable, and you may not even think about it as much. This situation is worsened when both spouses are in demanding careers.

It's important to realize that this reaction is common; other individuals in prominent corporate positions experience this loss too. Just having that knowledge can remove some of the apprehension you may be experiencing—this change in your behavior is not aberrant. Of course, any action you may take to relieve stress—such as exercising, having a massage, or going on a vacation—can reignite the spark. See Chapter 10 for some helpful suggestions in that regard.

## For Love or Money

Corporate marriages can also be undermined by conflicts surrounding money and status. Carole Hyatt, an author and career specialist, has investigated the earning power of executive women. Some of the statistics Carole found include:

- Approximately 29 percent of working wives earn more than their husbands, up from 21 percent in 1988.

- Among married female executives at Fortune 1000 companies, 75 percent earn more than their husbands.

- Forty-eight percent of working wives now provide 50 percent or more of their family's income.

Since money is often equated with control and power in our society, we can surmise that the higher earnings among executive women are a possible source of conflict with their spouses. These conflicts over who's in charge may also negatively impact the quality and frequency of a couple's lovemaking. In that instance, I highly recommend marital counseling. Many divorces occur because of money and status issues.

Karen Elliott House, President of International at Dow Jones, expressed irritation with the status quo when she discussed this subject with me. "It's hard for people to deal with 'great women with inferior husbands.' It's hard for the husband to deal with it; it's hard for the company to deal with it. People get all tensed up about promoting a smart woman. They wonder, 'What's her husband going to do? How will he handle her big promotion?'" It is not a company's duty to protect someone's marriage, but it is the responsibility of the couple to work the situation through. Although this problem can be pervasive, it can also be handled lightheartedly. For instance, Dennis Thatcher, husband of former British Prime Minister Margaret Thatcher, created the Dennis Thatcher Society to give the spouses of prominent women some prestige and an ego boost.

What if you find yourself surpassing your spouse? This can be an asset. Lori Mirek, in her position as Senior Vice President and General Manager at America Online, told a Windows in the Glass Ceiling audience, "I have a wonderful husband. He's a COO and CFO at a start-up company. We have two little angels under five years old. Interestingly, my husband wants me to make more money than he does. We're in a neck-and-neck race right now, depending on the value of our stocks."

While some men may bask in their wives' success and gladly partake in the financial rewards, it's important to be aware that for some husbands this could become a huge issue. The best protection is an ounce of prevention. If you're a high-potential woman, you're probably going to be moving up in your career, and may even be making more money than your spouse one day. Conversations with your husband about resentments that might arise need to take place before the fact. Raise issues such as, "What if I get a promotion and start earning more than you do? What if I have a bigger title? How would you feel about that?" Usually it's easier to talk about such eventualities before they occur. If your husband is alerted that the traditional balance may be tipped, it could diminish future conflicts.

However, from my experience, men don't have as much trouble with their wives' success as we might expect. Typically, they just want to feel respected, appreciated, and valued. They may, however, tie their identity to their careers and their earning power. If your husband's sense of self is so closely bound to those markers, and you find that you have surpassed him in the career arena, he may need to reframe where he derives his feelings of self-worth and recognition in society and at home. One executive woman helped her husband with that. Before the fact, she reassured him that money and career status were not the only ways for him to contribute to the marriage. "I value you for what you bring in more personal, less tangible ways," she told him, "like taking care of the kids emotionally and physically, managing the household, and handling our finances."

According to Carole Hyatt, a minimum of 2 million men acknowledge that it is their choice to become househusbands. In fact, if your husband has taken over the care of the children and the home, it might help for him to perceive this role as his new "job." After all, if you were to hire others to provide childcare, transportation, home repair services, cleaning and so on, it would place a greater financial burden on the family. As one woman with a househusband told me, "We sought professional counseling at the time we made the decision, to make sure it was going to work for us. My husband has been one of those unusual men who has taken the role of staying at home with the children as a job. I get up at 5:30 A.M. and so does he. I tell him he is so much more organized at home than I would ever be." Even if your spouse is not the primary breadwinner, he is still contributing financially to the family. But if you try such an arrangement and sense that it's not working, seek counseling. Deal with the issues up front, honestly and early.

Lora Colflesh had a disparity in her household, but she and her partner adjusted to it well. Lora's husband is a schoolteacher, whereas she is Vice President of Human Resource Operations at Sun Microsystems. "It can be difficult when you make more money than your spouse, and when you have more professional activities to attend. I have tended to work with more men than women, so it helps if you're married to a very secure man. We have worked it out so we both enjoy each other's career choices and our life together."

There were times when Lora's husband was the only male spouse at company events, and it was very uncomfortable, although he has come to have a good time. "Earlier in my career I was the only woman on the management team," she explained, "and I used to travel to France with my peers and my boss. All of our spouses came along. While we were working, they went to the beach; they went on tours; they just had a grand old time. Because he was the only man, my husband felt awkward at first, but he got into it, and he had fun. He had to learn how to get comfortable with the situation; he actually likes it when I travel and take him. Now, particularly being at Sun, there are more women who bring their husbands. He's not the only one, so it's more fun."

Often marriages work well when communication is open and boundaries are clearly established. Nancy Hobbs, General Manager of AirTouch Cellular, seems to have an excellent rapport with her husband. "We're both really strong personalities," she explained. "He's not somebody I'm going to be able to run over and always get my way. We communicate well. He's very quick to say, 'You're stepping over the line,' or 'I don't like this.' So there's no resentment. And if I get out of balance, if he really feels as if I'm working too many hours or too intensely, or there's not enough time for our relationship, he's not one of those guys who's going to suffer in silence. He comes right out and says, 'We need to talk. This isn't working for me.'"

Nancy and her husband have a great relationship. They have a lot of fun together, and, most importantly, they're friends. Although they have many interests in common, they also maintain a sense of integrity. "I like to sail," she told me, "but I won't scrub down the boat with him. I don't like to clean it. I draw the line somewhere."

## Commuter Marriages

Several senior executive women whom I interviewed were involved in commuter marriages—they and their husbands lived and/or worked in different cities. Such marriages can be healthy if both parties agree to it and the arrangement fits their lifestyle. Some of these couples have, as one woman put it, "atrocious phone bills." They talk to each other every day, "because that's part of the deal." These couples also spend a great deal of time on airplanes.

When Sue Swenson was CEO of Cellular One, she lived in the San Francisco Bay area while her husband lived in San Diego. Her husband thoroughly enjoys surfing, and the waves are better in San Diego than in northern California. Every weekend, Sue would fly to San Diego to be with her husband. Their pets stayed with him since he had more time to take care of them. She would fly back to San Francisco early Monday morning. (Her flight to work from San Diego was often shorter than her commute to San Francisco from Marin County across the Golden Gate Bridge.)

Sue loved this arrangement because it was a getaway for her. When she was in San Diego, she was truly away. She felt as if she were on vacation every weekend. Being on her own during the week also freed her to do whatever she needed to for the sake of work: business dinners, late meetings. She didn't feel guilty or need to be home; she could work as late as she wanted.

## The Superwoman Syndrome

From my vantage point, Superwoman is dead. The mere notion of this mythical beast causes everyone great waves of stress. She makes businesswomen under her influence quake with fear because they believe they must be perfect at everything they do—and she doesn't do men much good either. She threatens them by pushing them to keep up with women who work at unrealistic and sometimes inhuman levels.

Banishing Superwoman is tied to letting go of your perfectionistic tendencies and delegating—that is, loosening your control over certain situations. Linda Lewis, Senior Vice President of Learning and Training at Charles Schwab, explained how perfectionism could destroy relationships. "My doctoral research focused on married female doctoral students, among whom there is a very, very high rate of divorce. I was analyzing role reversals in the allocation of domestic responsibilities, among other variables. What made a difference was the ability of the woman to not be Superwoman, to give up this 'perfection syndrome.'"

As the women in Linda's research were going about their doctoral studies, they tried to divvy up the work to be done at home. For example, they would say to their spouses or significant others, "Here's the shopping list; go to the store and get X, Y, and Z." The spouses would return, having bought Jell-O at 89 cents a package, and the women would have fits because it was on sale for two for 89 cents at a different market. Some women would refold the laundry because it wasn't folded just right or rewash the dishes. "It's important for you to let go and understand that your role as a woman in leadership requires you to delegate," Linda explained. "Then step back and let go. That can be the hardest thing for some of us to do."

It's important to let down once in a while. We are all human, after all, prone to mistakes and messes from time to time. Linda LoRe, CEO of Frederick's of Hollywood, once said, "You have to give yourself permission to have a bad hair day once in a while. I read a report that stated that eighty-six percent of the female population believes that when their hair looks bad, they have a bad day. So plan-

ning to have a bad hair day when you need one is really important."
Indeed, by not getting everything quite finished or by taking your
children to work occasionally, you create a more relaxed environment for everyone. You don't need to work at a hundred and ten
percent. Eighty percent of your capacity is often sufficient. In fact,
as a high-achiever, your 80 percent is probably the equivalent of
most other employees' 150 percent.

> **BANISH SUPERWOMAN:** *Let go of your perfectionistic ten-
> dencies and loosen your need for control. Give yourself per-
> mission to "have a bad hair day."*

Relax, enjoy, and be gentle on yourself. In the next chapter, we'll
look at ways to help you find balance in your life as you progress in
your career.

# 10 | The Juggling Act:

## Making Choices About Work Time and Personal Time

How many hours a week do you typically work? Forty? Probably not. From my experience, high-potential women often put in fifty, sixty, even eighty hours a week—and sometimes more—as they forge their way to the top. That's tough! There's no room for a home or personal life. We are working at least as hard, if not harder, than our male colleagues, but men often have a support system to take care of the household and other responsibilities. Frequently, unless we create it ourselves, we don't.

You may feel emotionally and physically drained from spending so much time at the office. The C.O.R.E. attribute of Endurance is paramount in getting ahead. You must be strong in body, mind, and spirit in order to move up. When I asked Carol Bartz, the CEO of Autodesk, how she coped with it all, she told me, "It's really like a big juggling act. You've got a lot of balls in the air. You can't keep all of them at the same height at the same time." The trick is not to let any one of them hit the floor; you've got to catch them before they fall.

If you can't manage or feel overly burdened by all of the pressures you must shoulder, you run the risk of burnout—and a possible end to your corporate aspirations. Finding a balance is essential to your career and your future.

## Burnout: When It's Time to Get Out

Some of my interviewees made it to senior level, but then didn't want to go any further. They were exhausted, burned out. One woman executive told me her dream was to quit her job and sail around the world. "Work is not my raison d'etre," she explained.

When I asked another senior woman what her next step would be, she startled me when she blurted out, "My career path is out of here! That's the plan, though I haven't figured out where I want to go. I know I want to do something totally different, something that's more real, something that people can relate to. My metaphor is, I want to sell running shoes on the beach. Earlier in my career, I thought that's what I would want to do—have a small business. You know, it still sounds appealing to me."

Indeed, a few of the women with whom I spoke had felt exhausted from their climb and were ready to pack it in. One woman complained of working seventy to eighty hours a week, including through her lunch breaks. "It's pretty dumb," she admitted. "It doesn't give me any time to rejuvenate. And I'm really getting bored." It seemed her whole life revolved around eating, sleeping, and working. "And the trouble is," she continued, "most of my friends are people I know from the office." Even weekends were no refuge for her. "On Saturdays, I've become a vegetable," she complained. "I used to do all sorts of fun things. But last week, I even missed the kids' soccer game. I had to complete a performance appraisal for one of my employees. When I finished, I cooked dinner, and we rented a movie. I fell asleep on the sofa!"

Some women leave for personal reasons. In a high-profile move, Brenda Barnes, President of Pepsi-Cola, North America, left the company because, as she explained to me, "I needed to spend more time with my children." In our conversation she made it clear that she did it for herself, her own needs, not necessarily for her kids. But Brenda has not abandoned the fray completely. She keeps her foot in the corporate world by serving on corporate boards. She doesn't want to take on another high-powered position right now, but she stays connected.

Interestingly, however, most of the women who were ready for a change in their lives did not have any regrets about where they were.

They'd made choices, not sacrifices. Still, they were saying, "I'm tired. I don't want to do this anymore." It was not a matter of them wishing they never had taken on the corporate climb in the first place, but they were ready for a dramatic change. They had learned many lessons along the way—lessons that they cherish and would not give up for anything; lessons that have been woven throughout this book.

I have found that women who remain in the corporate world do so because they know it is what they really want to do. And they take enough time out—vacations and time off—to create balance in their lives. They don't just burn themselves out. It's common sense that you last longer if you enjoy your job and take care of yourself. This is not a sprint; it's a marathon. In order to be successful for the long term, you have to pace yourself. That also enables others to do the same, so your team doesn't burn out as well.

## Put Your Life in Order

Jack Parks, CEO of Basic American Foods, believes that at his company, the priorities should be family, God, and self, first; Basic American Foods, second. He tries to emulate those values. He doesn't work endless hours without regard for his family or his personal health. He takes some alone time three or four hours a week to get in touch with what's important to him by riding his horse and playing the piano. He loves rainy weekend weather so he can stop and "veg out." Jack tries to keep a balance in his life in order to endure the challenges he faces in his job.

> FIND A BALANCE: *You must be strong in body, mind, and spirit in order to move up. If you can't manage or feel overly burdened by all of the pressures you must shoulder, you run the risk of burnout. Pace yourself and take care of yourself.*

Other CEOs spoke to me about the importance of having a supportive partner who understands you and your career. It's helpful to have someone who grasps the business world—its demands and what it takes to be successful. If you're unhappy at home, it's awfully hard to be productive at work. As Alan Buckwalter, CEO of Chase Bank of Texas, explained, "I would recommend that people take time to smell the flowers from time to time. Spend time with your family. Build relationships. When you're on your deathbed, the people who are going to come visit you are your family and close friends. But, admittedly, this is difficult advice to follow, given the demands of your position."

Ruth Handler, the cofounder and former CEO of Mattel, was a business executive long before droves of women entered the corporate world. She and her husband, Elliot, had founded Mattel with a partner in the 1940s. And in a voice that bespoke the wear and tear of eighty-some years, she shared some realities for women in business from her perspective.

"You've got to find some way to deal with your personal life so that it doesn't interfere with your job," she explained. "I think that is a female's biggest problem. A man can keep his personal life separate from his business activities. A woman has a harder time doing that. But she has to find the way to separate the two. Too often the home environment interferes with the job, and I don't think they can run together."

Ruth was talking about compartmentalizing. "Leave home issues at home," Ruth continued. "Don't let them intrude. In general, men don't bring them to the office. Women, because they're homemakers by nature or societal standards, have still got to manage at home and figure out what to do with their kids and the cooking and the shopping. Oh, sure, if they get a husband who is like mine and comes close to sharing fifty percent of the burden, that helps. But some men are still not geared to that." Ruth believed that a businesswoman must be willing to exert superhuman energy and strength. It can be difficult, but it is important to put your life in order. In fact, it's imperative.

## First, Take Care of Yourself Personally

Lisa, a mid-level manager at a large insurance company, recently told me that she arose at 3:45 A.M. every morning, left the house at 4:30 and was at her desk by 5 A.M. She jammed from 5 A.M. until 7 P.M., when she finally went home, ate, slept, and repeated the same routine the next morning. She even went into the office on many weekends. Lisa allowed people on her staff to take lunch breaks at noon and to work out, but she didn't feel she could permit herself the same indulgences.

After becoming quite ill with bronchial pneumonia, however, Lisa finally heeded her boss's advice. When she came back to work after three and a half weeks of sick leave, which included a brief hospital stay, her boss insisted, "I want you to take an hour lunch break every day, even if that means going for a walk. And get some sleep!" She reluctantly complied, yet found that she actually accomplished just as much while treating herself and her employees with more sensitivity. There is a valuable lesson to be derived from Lisa's difficult experience. No job, no matter how wonderful or how much you want to excel in it, is worth risking your health. Lack of sleep and exercise or not eating healthfully can take a terrible toll.

We give and do for other people, but often don't take care of ourselves. We forget that, in the long run, we're no good to others or to our company if we've run ourselves into the ground. Think of it this way: When you're preparing for take-off, the airplane safety video instructs you on how to put on your own oxygen mask before assisting your children with theirs. The same is true in relation to your work. You can't take care of others—including your job, company, family, and community—unless you focus on your own well-being first.

Sometimes that requires making major adjustments in your life. When Gloria Everett of Globalstar was around fifty years old, she started wondering if she had the stamina to advance in her career. "Someone asked me whether I had the energy for a specific job I was looking at within the company," she explained. "I said, 'Yes, of course I do.' But then I thought about it. I was going through a divorce, so I was going to need all of the energy I could muster. I decided that I was a little too heavy, so I lost weight. I needed some exercise, and I started doing that." Gloria recognized that she needed to rejuvenate, and all of these actions seemed to free up her energy.

"Today, thank goodness, I have good health, and I really do have a high degree of stamina. The hours in this new job are as long as anybody else's, and I'm doing well at it. But the truth is, as hard and as long as you are working, you must re-evaluate every once in a while whether you're doing the right things for yourself."

Taking care of yourself can be as monumental as leaving an unhappy marriage, but it can also be as simple as getting enough sleep. Although some of us need more than others do, sleep is essential. It's a time for your body to renew itself, recharge, and revitalize.

> BE KIND TO YOURSELF: *You can't take care of others—including your job, company, family, and community—unless you focus on your own well-being first.*

One executive woman confided that the big signal that she's in trouble is when she finds herself up late at night (long after she has forsaken the three-mile run and is down to sleeping only five hours a night), going for the Bakers Unsweetened Chocolate in the pantry. "My husband hides it, but when I find it, I throw on a little confectioner's sugar, nuke it in the microwave, and just sit there and eat it," she admitted. "I know it's disgusting, but that's my signal to get back on track. The first thing I take care of is the sleep. I get rid of the late-night and early-morning meetings so I can sleep in. The next night is an eight-hour night. Once I've slept, I'm much better at jogging and resisting that chocolate. And once I've taken care of the physical, the rest starts to track. It's much easier to deal with the emotional and intellectual parts of life when the physical is in order."

It is important to take the time once in a while to step outside your body, look at yourself, and say, "Am I living a healthy day or am I reaching for the proverbial unsweetened chocolate?"

Unfortunately, in addition to dispensing with sleep, we often also overlook the benefits of exercise. Science has proven that regular physical activity can add years to your life and life to your years. The energy you cultivate through physical activity will make you physically stronger, while reducing stress and uplifting your mental attitude. During a good workout, your brain releases endorphins, the body's natural pain relievers. These chemicals promote a sense of calm and well-being.

Perhaps you believe that you can't find the time to exercise. Thirty to sixty minutes a day, three times a week, may feel like an extravagance. But if you think about it creatively, you are sure to come up with ways to work physical activity into your day. For instance, Pat Meredith, in her position as Executive Vice President at Canadian Imperial Bank of Commerce, fit exercise into her busy schedule by walking to work. Her home was a three-minute drive (or a ten-minute walk) from the office. She made the commitment to walk to work every day, rain or shine. If she didn't walk, she didn't get the exercise she needed. It was as simple as that.

If you travel a lot, you can use the exercise facilities that many hotels offer rather than spending evenings working or watching television in your room. And if your job keeps you at home, enjoyable weekend activities like gardening, bike riding, long walks, and tennis can help maintain good levels of fitness. Think about the number of times you jump into the car to run to the store or get your hair cut five minutes away. How about walking or riding your bike instead? It could be a fun activity to do with one of your children, your partner, or a friend. At the very least once a day, use the stairs in your office building rather than the elevator. Stay alert to exercise opportunities all around you; you'll find them if you're looking for them.

You may derive additional energy and endurance not only from physical activities but also from a spiritual practice. For some people that means meditating, going to church, walking on the beach, backpacking in the mountains—whatever gives you a sense of peace, perspective, and purpose.

One senior executive woman said, "I am religious. I go to church every Sunday. Believing in a Higher Power helps me a lot." Linda LoRe also spoke of the importance of spirituality—the part of you that taps into whatever motivates you at a deeper level. "It doesn't matter what it is that you believe in, as long as you honor it," she explained. "For me, it happens to be a very real, true spiritual practice that helps motivate me." Everyone has a different way of going about it, but don't deny yourself the opportunity to gain your endurance from different areas of your life.

And don't underestimate the need for your business accomplishments, because they are fortifying, and they reinforce positive aspects of your personality. But if you only get your endurance by relishing your work achievements, pretty soon you're going to run out of steam. You must integrate career successes with the rest of your life. And remember to take time for your family and friends. Being with loved ones nourishes and nurtures you.

## Take Those Vacations!

Taking your allotted vacations is another wonderful way to take care of yourself while improving your job performance. Many mid-level women say, "I don't have time to take two weeks off. I can't do that." In fact, one manager's biggest fear as she was moving up into executive ranks was that she could never be gone for more than three or four days at a time because people would realize they didn't really need her. Questioning the value we add to our company and those around us is common among high achievers. Being cognizant of the contribution you make is healthy. But being overly demanding of yourself can be a result of a deeper questioning of your own self-worth. A lack of self-esteem—believing you are never doing enough—can cause you to become exhausted and emotionally "empty." With all of the demands on your time, it is easy to miss when you have become exhausted.

Vacations can even help you progress in your career. If you've taken a new job recently, you will have noticed that for the first several months you are aware of all kinds of things that nobody else in the department sees. That's because you come in with a fresh, new perspective. Once you've been in a job for a while, however, you may become habituated to it—you lose your sense of perspective. The best way to continually renew your vision is to stand back and cultivate activities that are unrelated to work. That means taking a vacation and completely walking away from the day-to-day difficulties that bog you down in your job. After resting your mind and body, you may come back with reinvigorated energy and insight.

Maggie Wilderotter, CEO of Wink Communications, explained that she takes six weeks off a year and encourages her employees to take their vacations too. "I need those breaks when I'm working very long hours day in and day out, to step away from what we do and then be able to hit it again fresh. That's probably the one sacred cow that I have maintained and will continue to maintain. It recharges me and also gives me time with my family, which I think is really important."

> **TAKE YOUR VACATIONS:** *The best way for you to renew your vision is to walk away from the day-to-day details of your job. Your people need the break from you as much as you need the break from them.*

Vacations are also vital for your staff—and not just their vacations, but yours too! Linda LoRe, CEO of Frederick's of Hollywood, told me, "We can set the bar so high for ourselves that we forget that others are human and need to get away too—not to mention that they need to get away from us. Your people need the break from you as much as you need the break from them. Vacations rejuvenate everyone."

If you believe that you can't completely walk away from the company and be incommunicado for weeks on end, think again. Have you not communicated with your coworkers (boss, staff, colleagues) enough that they can handle most things while you're gone? Who are you training to replace you? Let one key person at work know how to reach you, if absolutely necessary. Empower them to make seasoned judgments and decisions. Everything might not get done "perfectly" or as you would have done it. However, you might be surprised at just how much they learn and how well they manage without you.

There are also ways to take mini-vacations. For instance, you might consider a weekend or a day at a spa with colleagues or clients as a way to mix pleasure with work. Spas have become quite popular among businesswomen. In fact, female employees are beginning to submit receipts for reimbursement for spa outings and treatments as client entertainment in the same way that men charge in rounds of golf. And companies are starting to see the value of increased self-care activities. Your female clients may really enjoy spending the day at a spa with you rather than attending a sporting event. But this form of activity may be unfamiliar to your company. In that case, you may have to present a business case as to why the activity is important to relationships and/or business development. Sometimes taking a client to a spa and charging it in (and apologizing later if you have to) is better than first asking permission—especially if the activity helps you close a deal!

Between your vacations and your client excursions, you might follow Clorox Chief Financial Officer Karen Rose's advice for creating mini-breaks. "I consistently read a lot of fiction to maintain my own emotional and intellectual balance," she explained. "I think fiction is so valuable. It teaches you lessons in life. It provides an opportunity for self-reflection and helps you examine your values and confirm them. Everything is so fast-paced in our lives, but fiction is slow-paced entertainment. It gives you a mini-vacation." Karen reads what she considers to be good literature, as well as what she calls "mind candy." If you enjoy reading, fiction is valuable in that it takes you away and gives you perspective.

## Take Care of Yourself Professionally

In Chapter 7, I advised you to just be yourself. But in order for you to do that, you have to know yourself. That takes introspection, which usually requires some down time. It can be phenomenally helpful to take an entire day to examine the direction of your life. But how often do you do that? Most high-achieving women are running a thousand miles an hour. They're either taking care of the kids, working, or trying to squeeze in some exercise. Even when they're home with family, they're answering e-mails, returning calls, or finishing a domestic or work-related project.

It is so important to get away from the house or office and just be with yourself. Even if you are an extreme extrovert, you need some alone time to center yourself and gain perspective on your life and long-term goals. It is important to run your thoughts and insights past people who are important to you for feedback, validation, and support. To help you identify your career goals, I suggest that you refer to Your Career Road Map in Chapter 13. This will help you gain clarity on who you are, your strengths and weaknesses, how others perceive you, and what is important to your company. From this analysis, you can better determine what would be an enjoyable and productive career path for you.

In today's business environment, many executive women and up-and-coming executives have an executive coach. The coach is usually someone from outside the company who is hired on a retainer for a specified amount of time or is paid hourly on an as-needed basis. These coaches help the women make sound judgments and often provide them with the support they need to take calculated risks. In the coaching I do with senior executives and mid-managers, often my clients need a sounding board in someone who understands their business challenges and can identify the behavioral and psychological patterns that assist and impede their ability to be successful.

Businesswomen often need to deal with the intersection of their careers with their personal lives. A clinical psychologist without a business background may not understand the business pressures you feel, while a boss or mentor may render only business guidance. Through assessments and other methodologies, an executive coach can assist you both professionally as well as personally. It may help you to know that you're not alone in some of the issues you're dealing with.

If you have agreed to take on a big new job and if you have a good sponsor or manager who really wants you to succeed, you might negotiate for a coach. You could say, for instance, "I would really like to do a great job at this assignment. Could I have an executive coach for the next six weeks to two months to help me get off on the right foot?" If you feel you need an executive coach and one is not forthcoming from your boss, you may want to hire one yourself. Although you may find a list of names of executive coaches in various directories and handbooks, from my experience the best way to find a quality coach is to ask for referrals from someone who is using a coach.

It's also vital to create a great support system for yourself at your job. Professionally, that means building a high-performance team of people whom you trust and who are capable, so if something goes

> HIRE AN EXECUTIVE COACH: *A coach can help you make sound judgments and can provide you with the support you need to take calculated risks.*

wrong for any member of the team, the other people can step in and fill the gap. I recently heard the story of a phenomenal executive at a high-tech firm—one of the best leaders in the field. She was running the network division of her company, which is one of its most essential parts, when her child was diagnosed with a fatal disease and was given only a year to live. At the same time, her husband decided he wanted a divorce; he just couldn't handle it. For four months, she stayed at home, and the team closed the gap around her and ran the business unit. Nobody knew.

This woman was one level from CEO of a 16-billion-dollar corporation. Her high-performance team got her through the most difficult period of her life. And today she's one of the top-ranking executives in that industry.

Several senior women spoke to me about relying on their friends for advice and support, but these were not merely tender, positive interactions. As Lori Mirek of America Online explains, "I choose folks for these relationships who are objective. I have very dear friends who are always positive, and that's nice. But those aren't the friends I actually learn the most from. I look toward people who can objectively say, 'Lori, that doesn't make any sense at all. Why would you want to do that?' or 'Lori, I just listened to you outline all these different alternatives from a career perspective, and the only one you spoke passionately about was this one. Did you realize that?'"

Sometimes you need a friend who will really listen to you and honestly challenge what you're saying, even if you don't want to hear it—a friend who can tell you, "You know what? This isn't working for you. Walk away from it." Or, "I know you're scared, but I think you should go for it!" And, of course, you have to be able to listen to the advice and accept it.

For, in truth, the only way you get value out of these relationships is if you heed the advice your friend gives. He or she is giving up personal time to listen to and help you. If you always ask for advice and then do whatever you please anyway, your friend may not invest that sort of energy in the future. Even more importantly, some of the best feedback you get may anger you when you hear it the first time. As Lori Mirek explained, "It's the best friends I've had who have been able to say, 'You really didn't do that right.' Or, 'Did you realize the impact of what you did there?' It's hard to hear that sometimes, but I challenge you to listen to the part of the feedback that you dislike the most. All feedback is valuable, whether it's saying, 'Wow, you did a great job on that presentation yesterday.' Or, 'You didn't, and here's what you missed.'"

The quality of your relationships is important. You will never have enough time in your life to develop friendships with everyone you meet, so it's important to gravitate toward solid, extraordinary relationships. Lori Mirek, for instance, feels comfortable with fewer, but really high-quality friendships. "It takes a lot of work to build these up over time. We have this common code. When I call and say, 'Corette, I really need your help,' she knows. She calls right back and is there to help. I do the same thing for these friends when they call with a code red. That's a critical part of being able to get through some of the tougher issues and inflection points in my life."

Some of the best advice can come from people with whom you would never want to develop a close friendship. They are very different from you; they see the world through their own eyes, and engage in dissimilar behaviors and interests from you. But they also see what you don't—your blind spots. When you encounter people who "totally rub you the wrong way," be grateful! One of these days, they could offer you the best insights and advice you will ever receive—if you're willing to be vulnerable and ask for their opinions. Then be quiet and truly listen to their perspective! Thank them for their candor and honestly think about what they said. You may even want to offer to be a sounding board for them, when they want a different perspective.

## Prioritizing Your Life

Many people believe their lives will become easier once they move into more senior ranks—they'll finally be able to call the shots and have more control over their fate. But often that's not the case. For one thing, with a move up, you may work even longer hours than you do now. One woman told me she puts in at least sixty to eighty hours a week. In her previous job, she had thought working fifty or sixty hours a week was quite a bit, and she believed that once she was promoted to vice president, things were going to calm down a little bit. Clearly they didn't.

Whether we're inherently deeply nurturing or because we're perfectionist–workaholics, women tend to be of the mind-set that we have to do it all. However, one of the single biggest career-limiting mistakes you can make is to forget to prioritize. You run yourself ragged doing the urgent but unimportant tasks and never getting to the more complex ones. It is important to remember that the smaller tasks usually take more time to complete than you expect, and the larger ones typically take less time than you expect.

It is important to prioritize and set aside blocks of time to work on the most important (and usually more complex) tasks first. The smaller tasks can fit into the small spaces of time around the edges— between phone calls, on your way back from the water fountain or the bathroom. A nemesis to accomplishing your priorities is perfectionism. Once the objectives of a task have been satisfied, stop fiddling with it. Call it done and move on to the next priority. There are always going to be little adjustments you could make, but you begin to reach the point of diminishing returns. Other people and the universe will give you feedback if there are bigger changes that need to be made.

Another challenge to accomplishing priorities is delegating, but then wanting to micro-manage. It is important to remember that when you delegate a task to another person and reach an agreement as to the priority and time line to accomplish the task, you let the person do it as he or she deems appropriate. Check in on them to see how they are coming along, but let go of the mechanics.

> **ESTABLISH PRIORITIES:** *One of the single biggest career-limiting mistakes you can make is to forget to prioritize.*

Lori Mirek, in her recent executive positions at high-technology companies, often encountered the challenges of perfectionism and delegating. She has had some big jobs that literally cried out for prioritizing, and she seemed to have mastered the art. "I often have five hundred things that I need to do," she explained. "Prioritization, to me, means picking the right five responsibilities that really have an impact and that can be accomplished, and focusing on them; delegating the next forty-five to the outstanding team I have working for me—and then letting them do them; and then forgetting about numbers fifty-one to five hundred.

"Where I often see folks get off track is either they don't prioritize, or they prioritize with poor judgment. But mostly, at the middle-management level—because you've pretty much weeded out the first two by the time you get to middle management—they just can't drop responsibilities fifty-one to five hundred. That's what trips them up. But, candidly, by the time you get to number fifty-one, you probably should have already re-evaluated if the top fifty are still the top fifty, because things change so rapidly in business these days."

Diane Harris, in her position as Vice President of Corporate Development at Bausch & Lomb, had a different but equally valuable perspective in terms of prioritizing relationships. The further along she had progressed in her career, the more she wanted to spend her time in business with people about whom she could have good feelings. "Qualities like trust have become more important, as well as respect, learning, sharing information, and mentoring," she told me. "Before, I was just focused on getting the job done, but today I find myself spending more quality time with individuals. Life is too short for me to spend energy on people who don't have the same values that I would want to have in my personal friendships." That doesn't mean that Diane has no instrumental relationships to get the job done, but she puts more energy into the deserving relationships that bring her the most pleasure.

"When somebody burns me on something, I'm much less likely to go back and try to reconstruct a relationship," she explained. "I'm not going to put my energy into it. That person showed who he or she is. I can write off the relationship more easily now than I might have before."

This sense of independence tends to increase as you mature and progress in your career. You may not have to bend over backward for as many people as you used to. You get to know yourself better and to understand your values and how you want to spend your time. You start to prioritize more. "I delegate more than I used to," Diane continued. "That's good because it's more developmental for people. I'm also probably more discerning in some ways."

It's important to remember that you're the one making the choices in your life. So when you start hearing yourself whine, "This is really awful. I'm working too hard. I don't have time to exercise or be with my family. I'm really overwhelmed," you must realize that you've arranged your life this way. If you want balance in your life, ask yourself, "What are my personal priorities? What things really count for me?" Of course, it's up to you to decide what comes first and what comes last, and then stick to it.

As one senior executive woman put it, "The things that are important to me are my family and the ability to be able to use the talents that God gave me. When someone asks me to do something that isn't within that realm, I can very happily smile and say 'No, but thanks for asking.'" If you haven't learned to say 'no' to what is unimportant to you, you will never be able to find balance. And, frankly, I don't think you'll ever be able to find a great deal of happiness in your life. There are so many things to do with so many people and not enough time. You have to be able to make choices to truly be happy."

## Personal Crises Can Shift Your Priorities

Just because the many women I have spoken with have become quite successful in their work lives does not mean that they are immune from the vicissitudes of life. Like all of us, they have had to cope with life-threatening illnesses, family tragedies and deaths, divorce, or other personal traumas. But, rather than embittering them, these difficult experiences have, in one way or another, enriched these women's lives and humanized them. And these events have often served as catalysts for their changed perspectives. Perhaps this is a symbol of executive women's deep reserves of resiliency.

Several senior women have found that bouts with cancer (either

their own or in a loved one) had altered their lives immeasurably. Linda LoRe's story is particularly moving. The oldest of eight
children, Linda started her career as a department store salesperson
when she was seventeen. In 1986, at age thirty-two, she was diagnosed with malignant melanoma and was told that if the doctors
didn't get it all, if it had advanced too far, she would die. Understandably, the prognosis was terrifying to her.

By then, Linda had risen to a senior management position at a
major southern California department store that had just gone
through an acquisition. She was in a troubled marriage and was
commuting to work sixty miles each way. "Probably four or five days
into the cancer, right after the operation, I literally spent one day
and night just thinking about what this life is all about," she told
me. "I said to myself, 'I'm not sure if I'm going to live, so how do I
want to spend the rest of my days?' It was a wake-up call."

Linda realized that life is precious. "Suddenly it became much
more important to know who I am and to be on my path than it was
to have a title, bring home a big paycheck, and so on. Being a Type-
A personality and a responsibility-oriented person—my character
has always been the same; I didn't give up any of that—that was a
drastic change for me. But at that moment 'Linda' really emerged.
And it has taken me the better part of the last twelve years to shed
some of those tapes of 'You have to do this; you have to do that,' and
really go into 'What is this life all about and who am I really? Am I
happy? Am I doing the things I need to do in order to be who I want
to be? Am I really on my life's path?'"

Linda changed her life the year after she had cancer. She quit her
job at the department store and started working for Giorgio. She
moved closer to the office and no longer spent four hours a day commuting. And she got a divorce.

"I realized that I'm in charge of my own life, and unless I take responsibility for it, no one else is going to," she continued. "I had
been holding everything inside, trying to be perfect at everything.
That was my nemesis. When any kind of anger came at me from
someone else, I would ask 'What's wrong with me?' and try to fix
everything around me. Instead of expressing my fear and anger in an
active way, I would hold my emotions inside, and they manifested

themselves in the destruction of my body. I realized that I was a participant in my own recovery, and that how I feel and think have everything to do with my health, my well-being, and the quality of my life. The illness started me on a completely new path." Fortunately, Linda survived it, and it made her stronger.

Lora Colflesh, the Vice President of Human Resource Operations at Sun Microsystems, was diagnosed with breast cancer a year before I met her. Her illness awakened her to the kindness of others. "Even people whom I had worked with years before took the time to call and write and express their concern and empathy. It was not something that I expected." The outpouring of concern and good wishes from people whom Lora worked with at Sun, past colleagues, family, and friends was stunning to her. It made her rethink everything.

"Friendships are important, and doing good work is important, but getting stressed out or fighting battles or playing office politics just don't matter anymore. It's not worth it. My priorities have changed. I've become less focused on being in the ultimate job. I'm less willing to put all of my energy into my career. And the good news is that I feel more balanced. It's curious to me because while I don't feel I'm performing at the same level as I did before, people I've interviewed think I'm working even more productively than before. It was sort of a funny feeling at first, and it made me a little bit nervous. I know I am still effective, and my work, personal life, and health are much stronger because of my new lifestyle. It just took a little getting used to the change of pace. It's wonderful."

Another woman attributed part of her success to her nursing her husband through cancer. "You ask why I'm successful? I think the first ten years, it was due to my focus and hard work, but in the last ten years, it's been because I've had a change in perspective—I'm able to balance work and not let it overwhelm me.

"I think that change was largely due to my husband's cancer. He almost died. He had a bone marrow transplant, and I had to take three months off from work to take care of him. He had to take a year off. It was one of those things where nothing else really mattered. Fortunately, we both had good jobs and a lot of support from our businesses, and we could afford to go through that and not come out destitute. I don't want to make it sound as if our jobs don't matter. The income, the prestige to some extent, and the mental satisfaction are really important, but they are not the only thing."

A sense of balance and perspective about work have become really important to this woman. "When it comes right down to it," she told me, "my job really matters, and my career does too, but not if they're out of balance with my personal life, my health, and my spiritual well-being."

When I interviewed one senior executive woman, she talked about the double whammy of her father's death and her divorce in one year, which nearly stopped her in her tracks. But these twin disasters also taught her about the value of those around her. "It was overwhelming to me how people in my broad network just reached out and gave and gave and gave without me even asking," she confided. "And I know I was worthless. I mean, I was literally worthless for six to eight months. It was all I could do to just get to work. Their concern was wonderful."

Lori Hricik, Executive Vice President at Chase Manhattan Bank, also endured a terrible year when her father and father-in-law passed away within weeks of each other. She received more than a thousand cards from people. Until that point, she hadn't realized how many lives she had touched. Lori had always been thinking ahead, telling herself, "I've got to do more." She felt she needed to leave a legacy before she retired. But in this time of difficulty, she was given the opportunity to appreciate how much impact she had already made.

Of course, none of us would wish for these misfortunes in order to help us put our professional and personal houses in order. However, we can learn powerful lessons from these women's difficulties. When lives hang in the balance, our true natures and values emerge. You can, for a moment, put yourself in the shoes of one of these women, and ask yourself the questions Linda LoRe posed when she faced her own mortality at the age of thirty-two:

- What is my life all about?

- Who am I, really?

- Am I happy?

- Am I doing the things I need to do in order to be who I really am and to be happy?

- How do I need to change?

- Am I really on my life's path?

If nothing else, these questions will help you focus on your real priorities and perhaps find some balance.

## Finding a Balance

Despite all the difficulties these women may encounter, it is a mistake to assume that there is no room for a full life at the executive level. The fact is that many successful women say that they do have fulfilling, rounded lives—but only because they demand it and deliberately make room for it with some occasional complex maneuvering.

I asked Carol Bartz of Autodesk how she handled her jobs as CEO and mom. She told me, "Whatever it is that I'm doing, I'm really focused on that. So when I'm working I'm very focused on work, and when I'm with my daughter I'm very focused on her."

Some women need to compartmentalize their lives that way because otherwise they may feel too scattered to be any good at anything. One executive mother I interviewed told me that in her household they have a master calendar on their refrigerator. Her husband is also a high-powered businessperson, and they have two young children, ages three and five. Whatever goes on that master calendar is what they do. And if it doesn't get on the calendar, it doesn't get done.

Others think in terms of performing daily triage with the competing demands and priorities in their lives. They deal with the most urgent matters first—whether those priorities are professional, physical, emotional, or spiritual—and never attempt to grapple with them all at once. For these women, the balance in their lives can change daily. By setting ground rules and expectations and keeping communication open, they find a way to live meaningful lives while meeting the demanding needs of their careers.

Intel's Carlene Ellis is a divorced mother of two children. She has taken her preadolescent son to work, so she could spend time with him and he could feel a part of what she does. Rather than compartmentalizing, however, she seems to merge family with work. "My life on the planet is twenty-four hours a day, seven days a week," she explained. "I tend to work at 10 P.M. if I want to and pick up my son and go to lunch at 11:30 A.M. if I want to. I probably don't do the separation of work and home and the separation of relationships into professional and nonprofessional really well. But I never divided my life up this way because I don't think this way. My children understand my work."

This approach may not work for everyone, however. In some industries, stereotypes still abound. Karen Elliott House, President of International at Dow Jones, told me, "Men get all kinds of credit taking their kids around, but women don't. We actually did a story on this recently. If a woman walks into a meeting with her kids, people will say, 'Why can't she manage?' But if a man walks in with his kids, people will say, 'What a great father!' It's absolutely instinctive." And, of course, it's unfair.

Still, even some male executives insist on balance. IBM's former CEO John Akers set aside half an hour at his office every day to take a nap or just have time alone. We all need a feeling of equilibrium in order to work at our best.

## Living a Well-Rounded Life

We might also think of balance as living a well-rounded life, but that notion can mean different things to different people. I asked one woman what a well-rounded life was and whether she had one, and she told me, "Yes, my life is extremely well rounded. I get my exercise when I play golf with my coworkers and clients. I like to entertain, so I give dinner parties for clients and colleagues. I get to travel all over the world for my job." This woman was unmarried and child-free. Her sole focus was her career. She loved what she did and didn't want to do anything else. And I guess within the parameters she had established, her life was indeed well rounded.

Other women, of course, have a different understanding of the concept. It is important to be aware of the wider world around you. Be careful not to become so isolated and insulated by your business concerns that you don't read newspapers or go to the movies. As I've emphasized, talking about current events is a perfect icebreaker in business situations, but, beyond that, knowledge of society at large contributes to your becoming a more whole person and your understanding of the big picture. Of course, children help in that regard too.

> **DEVELOP YOURSELF OUTSIDE YOUR WORK ENVIRONMENT:** *You will not only gain new skills and sensitivities to your job, but you will also become a role model for others.*

For Christiane Michaels, President of Waverly Lifestyle, a well-rounded life means incorporating relaxation and even play. "I watch men all the time," she told me. "We'll all get on a plane, and all I think about is business, business, business—getting it done, the next problem, the next solution. These guys, they go and read a spy novel or the newspaper. Once we get to our destination, they play golf. It doesn't make them less effective. They're just able to put work aside and play. In fact, their whole motivation is 'Let's play!'" I suspect this attitude allows men to get their job done, develop relationships with some key people, and enjoy their careers. They also tend not to burn out as quickly as some women do.

When I interviewed Linda Holsonback, she was Vice President of Managed Care Operations at Blue Shield. She told me, "It's important to have some joy and meaning in what you do every day." For Linda LoRe, that means exercising. "I work out. I think it's very important to keep healthy. I also enjoy taking hikes and getting out into nature."

Karen Rose, Chief Financial Officer at Clorox, is the president of the board of directors at a nonprofit theater group in San Francisco. "It's like running a small business with profit-and-loss responsibility—with lots of emphasis on the 'loss,' believe me. I tear my hair out. But I have made the most wonderful relationships in my life. I have learned skills that I didn't learn in corporate America. And I've gotten things done. I feel as though I've made a contribution. Those are things that help me in keeping a little sanity in the total scheme of things."

Susan Weir, in her role as Vice President at McKesson, had a sixteen-year-old daughter and three stepsons in their late twenties when I interviewed her. When I asked how she thought she got where she was, she said, "I'm a well-rounded person, and that has something to do with it. I'm involved in community activities; I'm on boards. I bring that to my job and company, and I think the organization values it. I try to lead somewhat of a balanced life. It was difficult in the beginning. I had separated my professional and personal life, and then I recognized that I'm a real person too. I became a much more successful person when I learned to integrate both of those aspects."

When you take the time to develop yourself outside your own work environment, you not only gain these new skills and sensitivities to your job, but you also become an example for others to do the same.

## Creating a Well-Rounded Life for Yourself

At the beginning of each year, I work with my staff on creating well-rounded lives. We each get a marker and a flip-chart page. We take turns enumerating the various areas of our lives that are important to us: health, leisure, spirit, travel, work, family, friends. Then we talk about how much time we can realistically devote to each of those areas. We have even gone so far as to list the days of the week and the hours that we might focus on these activities. Of course, any such plan requires flexibility, but it shows every member of the group what the competing demands are for each person's time.

> CREATE A WELL-ROUNDED LIFE FOR YOURSELF: *Assess what a well-rounded life means to you, and communicate your needs and wants to others.*

This little exercise makes us more human and gives us a different level of understanding and commitment to each other as people. It helps us establish expectations. For instance, some people explained that they did not want to work evenings because they had competing demands that took a higher priority. That gave me the opportunity, as the manager, to say, "I may need you to work on an evening from time to time." I began to understand their desires, and they heard my needs. We agreed that I would keep evening work to a bare minimum, but that when I truly needed them, they would be flexible to accommodate the business demands. I wouldn't have known their expectations, nor would they have known mine, if not for this beneficial exercise. As a result, we grew to appreciate each other more. You too might consider meeting with your team to establish expectations and open dialogue.

The overall message here is to identify what is important to you and your loved ones, and then do your best to communicate your needs and desires to your boss and co-workers as well as to your family. These insights will help you prioritize your commitments and have passion around what you do at work and at home.

Linda LoRe once explained to me, "The thing that has helped me maintain balance more than anything is that I have always loved what I do. If you have a passion for that, it creates all kinds of positive opportunities for you in business as well as in your personal life."

People sometimes tell me that I work too much. "Why don't you stop and smell the roses?" people ask me. My firm belief is that you don't have to stop and smell the roses, if you carry them with you. If you love what you're doing and you surround yourself with positive people, you won't have to stop to smell the roses because you'll be carrying them with you too.

## The Value of Staying the Course

It is important for women's collective advancement that they do not burn out, but rather stay the course—remain within the corporate world, even when the going gets tough. In order to make lasting change—to get more women into the executive ranks, to impact corporate culture, to influence the decision-making process, which includes who gets hired and who gets fired—movement must come from within the corporation itself. That means more women must be on board. If you burn out or flee to entrepreneurial enterprises, you will lose what collective clout you do have within your company.

Besides, the balance is shifting. In 1999 and with great fanfare, Carleton Fiorina was plucked from her position as Lucent Technologies group president (at a $20 billion division) to become CEO of Hewlett-Packard, the world's second-largest computer company. Her closest competitor for the job was another woman—Ann M. Livermore, an H-P insider, remarkable in this traditionally male-dominated industry. Although in newspaper interviews Carly made optimistic statements, such as, "I hope that everyone has figured out there is not a glass ceiling," I believe her rise to power signals that change is afoot, but we haven't quite reached the promised land yet.

It's important to bear in mind that for most people who make it into the senior ranks, it can take twenty-five to thirty years of business experience to reach the level of CEO. If we bail out too soon or burn out when the going gets tough, we are never going to make a change in the status quo.

Although more entrepreneurial options may be open to you, I would urge you not to give up. Be patient. Find a balance. Keep working. Times are changing.

# 11 Career Strategies of High-Level Minority Women

"One of the things that has helped me is that I really don't care what people think about me—either positively or negatively," Anita told me, with some vehemence. "I care what I think, and I have to walk with my own integrity because there is no one for me to follow. That's why I don't look for mentors. I would like to create them, and I use my boss in that way when I can, but I don't expect anything from people. I expect to have to do it by myself, even though I know I don't and can't do it by myself.

"But I have to do what I think is best because I don't have a lot of support, guidance, or mentoring. Part of that for me is feeling comfortable just being who I am. That is my strength, and that means letting people know what I think."

This senior executive African-American woman voices the feelings and concerns of many women of color as they make their arduous climb up the corporate ladder. Independent, wary, motivated, hard-working, Anita epitomizes the difficulties that many women of color face as they seek to move ahead in corporate America.

In this chapter, we will look at some of the different choices and career advancement strategies of aspiring minority women. Today women of color comprise only 0.1 percent of all top executives. Minority women, however, made up 17 percent of the executives in my study. And I have found that while on some levels, the career experiences of senior executive women of color are no different from those of their white counterparts, in many ways these women face an additional set of challenges. I will be sharing with you many of the issues that these women raised. But I can't pretend that I fully grasp all of them, since I'm white and subject to my own interpretations and life experiences. And, since 75 percent of the women of color I interviewed were African-American, many of the concepts presented in this chapter will reflect their views.

Remember, today the biggest challenge for companies is to find qualified and diverse talent. By the year 2002, ethnic minorities are projected to comprise more than 50 percent of the workforce, with 25 percent of working minorities being women. Companies will be competing against each other for the best talent, especially among women of color. Despite the obvious obstacles, you are sitting in a good place if you're smart about what company and career you choose.

> TODAY'S BIGGEST CORPORATE CHALLENGE: *Finding qualified and diverse talent. Companies will be competing against each other for the best talent, especially women of color.*

## How They Got There

Many women of color spoke to me about what it took for them to reach the executive levels, and from our discussions it is clear that the four critical success factors—Competence, Outcomes, Relationships, Endurance (C.O.R.E.)—apply to white and minority alike. Moreover, like their white peers, these women did not buy into the six myths that can slow a woman's progress.

All of the women of color, for instance, attributed their success to achieving results through tenacity, relationships, and very hard work. I was often told that if women have to work twice as hard to be seen as half as good, then minority women have to work five times as hard. One woman, the General Counsel at a large company, told me that she made it into the senior executive ranks because she works very hard to make her boss look good, and she overcompensates in areas where she believes she has deficits. "You have to be a quick study in order to make it in the business world," she added.

Michele Hooper, in her position as President of the International Business Group at Caremark International, was known for taking on difficult assignments that gave her a high profile. "People invited me into the executive suite because of my analytical ability, my bottom-line orientation, and my listening skills," she explained. "I'm actionable and reasonable. I have an attitude for getting things done, and I get things done." Michele felt empowered, and she also described herself as a risk-taker. Reputation was of the utmost importance to her. "It's extremely important to take responsibility for a business," she told me, "to have bottom-line profit-and-loss responsibility, to lead, and to play in a complex market—that is, to enjoy and be able to manage the complexity of business."

Michele also had keen interests in developing professional relationships outside her office that afforded her the opportunity to be a player in community-based activities at the board level. There she displayed her leadership in numerous other organizations. These involvements helped her hone her skills inside her company and also gave her the chance to give back to the community.

Another woman also believed that she made it into the executive ranks because she accomplished her goals through her good relationships with others. "I don't lie. I'm very trustworthy," she told me. "It's important to be true to your word and to establish yourself by returning phone calls and staying on top of things." This woman also believed it was important to pay attention to reciprocal alliances. "I always have something to give," she told me. "If I do, I can always return later if I need help. You can't constantly ask someone, 'Can you help me?' You've got to be able to give back too."

Bobbi Gutman, Corporate Vice President and Director of Global Diversity at Motorola, felt she has been so successful because of her trust in God. She too is committed to honesty. "People say that I'm a breath of fresh air because I'm willing to tell the truth," she explained. "I refuse to get into the 'norm box.'" Bobbi says what she believes and doesn't do much artificial chitchat. "Although I'm friendly and approachable, I have little faith in networking. That's extremely artificial," she told me. Bobbi genuinely likes the corporate environment. She fits there.

Since many of these high-achieving minority women followed the same path as their white cohorts, it would stand to reason that they would also fall prey to some of the same myths along the way.

For instance, Leonade Jones, in her position as Treasurer of The Washington Post Company, told me, "I was pretty naive at first. I worked hard, I kept my head down, and I believed that I would get noticed. Now I know—you have to position yourself to get recognized." Leonade encourages female coworkers to make sure that others are aware of their achievements. "You need to be intentional and proactive in the visibility you get," she told me.

## Who Are They?

Although there are similarities among all senior executive women, there are also some significant demographic differences between whites and minorities. For instance, the women of color whom I interviewed had fewer children than their white counterparts. None of the minority women had more than two children, as compared to up to four for the whites in my study. They also gave birth to their babies later in life. The average age for a minority executive woman to have her first child was thirty-three. The whites, on average, produced their first offspring by the age of thirty. (In fact, the youngest minority mother was twenty-eight when she had her first child, whereas for the whites, the youngest mom was twenty.)

Linda Keene, an African-American woman with an MBA from Harvard, who is Vice President of Market Development at American Express Financial Advisors, had made manager level before she had a son. "I feel it's extremely important, especially for people of color, to have a track record before they go off and have children," she explained. "You need to have sufficient time to demonstrate your abilities and prove yourself before taking on the demands of motherhood."

Although marriage rates were the same, divorce rates in my study differed between these two populations. Fifty percent of the white executives were divorced—about the same as the national average. But the divorce rate was only 40 percent for the minority women whom I researched. Although there is no clear-cut reason as to why this discrepancy exists, I often heard that a stable and supportive home life was essential for the women of color to endure the physical and psychological demands of their careers. Because the women of color feel judged and not fully understood in the work environment, they need to have strong, supportive marriages at home.

Educational differences were quite significant as well. Thirty-eight percent of the minority women whom I interviewed had a Ph.D. or a J.D. (Doctor of Jurisprudence), whereas only 19 percent of white women were educated at the doctoral level. Sixty-two percent of the women of color had master's degrees versus 57 percent of the white women. Indeed, all of the executive women of color I interviewed had graduate degrees, as compared to three quarters of white women, and almost all of them received their degrees from Ivy League schools.

These differences are notable. Many minority women believed they had to overachieve. For instance, a mid-level manager from a large pharmaceuticals company told me why she felt she *had* to get an MBA. "I don't want the lack of a piece of paper to stand in the way of my next promotion," she explained. "If they're looking for some reason to not promote me, they're not going to blame it on that. They'd have to blame it on my performance, which is good." This woman went back to school not because she wanted to, but because she felt it a necessity. She didn't want that strike against her too. "I'm even contemplating getting my Ph.D. for the same reasons," she continued, "although I don't want to. I don't want to give them any reason to question my credibility. I don't want my intelligence or credentials to be unfairly challenged."

Perhaps it is for the same reasons that the other minority women felt that they needed to delay childbearing until after they had reached a significant milestone in their careers, or that they had to have the best education or keep their marriages intact. Like many minority women, this mid-level manager felt unjustly judged. In fact, to counteract prejudice, many women of color were far more conscientious about the companies they chose to work for than their white female colleagues.

## Due Diligence

Given the scarcity of talent, minority women executives have become proactive about the companies they choose to work for. Unlike their white counterparts, they engaged in much more due diligence when it came to career choices. They researched which companies had minorities in the upper echelons and also which ones had women. If they saw executives of the same ethnicity and/or gender, these women believed they had a better chance of making it. For instance, Linda Keene told me she went to companies that were more open to diversity. She was very intentional in her career and tried to maximize her opportunities for success.

A mid-level manager at an insurance conglomerate told me that up-and-coming women of color should look at the overall company, and ask questions such as, "Does it really match who I am?" She is learning that lesson the hard way. Her company has a culture that, she believes, conflicts with her values. "I feel strongly about honesty. I want to feel that what I'm doing is credible. I have recently joined this company and am beginning to see things that are borderline dishonest. I know I don't want to be a part of that, but do I speak up or keep my mouth shut? Voicing my concerns is going to create a lot of conflict."

She also advised aspiring minority women seeking a job to interview their potential manager, not just allow the manager to interview them. "You have to see if you have something in common and can build a good rapport. Often minorities are so interested in landing a job, they don't think about what a manager can do to help or hurt their career. It's important to find out as much as you can, especially if the manager doesn't understand us or has some deep-seated feelings about people of color." If you can't get along with that manager, your best bet is to look elsewhere.

## Having a Plan

Seventy-five percent of the women of color in my study had well-defined, carefully mapped-out career paths, as compared to only 27 percent of the white women. One woman, for example, decided that she wanted to be the first minority woman chief patent counsel in the United States, and she carefully navigated her career to achieve her goal.

"I read the right magazines and books in order to 'break the code' of moving into the senior levels," she told me. Carla was determined to get exactly what she wanted, and she was analytical and calculated in her efforts. "I knew I had to win by continuing to move up within the system," she explained. "So I learned the rules and then played by them. I used them to my advantage."

She also told me that she never thought of herself as different, although at times she was treated as "less than." "I had to learn to cope with that," she said. In order to do so, she blocked out many of those negative feelings. Carla was hell-bent on making it through the system.

Mary Evans, a mid-level manager in the banking field, found a different way to achieve her goals. "The last few years I have not encountered a lot of problems because of the business I'm in," she explained. "To a large extent, my production is based on me. My superiors are looking for output. We're all on separate tracks here. If you don't produce, you don't stay. I was the first African-American in the office. I don't think they had a lot of expectations for me, but in three years, here I am, assistant branch manager. I feel comfortable, and I do my business the way I want to." Racial differences haven't mattered—Mary competes against herself. She is thriving in a what-have-you-done-for-me-lately corporate culture.

## Trust

I believe that the differences that have emerged from my study between executive women of color and whites in family dynamics, educational striving, due diligence, and intentionality in career choices revolve around issues of mistrust. Many senior executive minority women spoke to me about the difficulties they had in trusting their situations and their coworkers. They often felt unfairly judged. It was also more difficult for minority women to develop relationships with top executives, who might feel uncomfortable with racial differences. And many complained of being stymied in their quest for promotions. As one African-American middle manager told me, "We're going after the same things as the Caucasian women, but they have the competitive edge. Every one of us has a story about how we worked on the same project, we had a better education, and did a better job, but because they wanted a woman for the job, the white woman got the promotion."

These trust issues emerge from current slights as well as lifelong encounters with prejudice. One African-American executive vice president believed, as she grew up, that she really couldn't trust people. She felt she was being judged based on the color of her skin rather than her capability and likability, and so she didn't believe that others saw her for who she actually was. Another explained that she was more guarded with others because she too lacked a level of trust. She occasionally discussed minor personal issues with professional colleagues, but not often. She believed that race is still an issue, and a lot of people do not deal with it. Who could blame these women for being distrustful?

I personally experienced this wariness and skepticism about my motives when I called executive women of color to request interviews for my research. In my original study, I had interviewed sixty-five senior executive women, only two of whom were minorities. I wanted to better understand the challenges and concerns of women of color, but the next three I called turned me down flat. It wasn't until I reached one female executive of color who was willing to introduce me to other minority executives that suddenly doors opened that I never could have budged by myself. I proceeded to interview ten more women of color.

When I explored these issues with my interviewees, they explained how they had been hurt by racial prejudices. One told me, "It's a double-edged sword. I don't feel understood, and I don't trust the motives of others either." This woman had earned a J.D. at an Ivy League university, and she had "worked like a dog." She delayed childbearing until she was in her forties. Even then, she had to beg for every promotion. "They would not have given them to me if I had not asked for them."

Another woman told me people did not give her opportunities before they truly believed she was ready; they wouldn't take a risk on her as they would on a white woman. "And then, if I am promoted," she continued, "I don't know whether people view me as an individual or as a token. So it's hard for me to trust people because I don't know where they're coming from."

Anita, the strong-minded woman who lacked mentors or supporters, believed that her subordinates, peers, and, on one occasion, even her boss expected her to behave differently as a manager than they would a white man. "They expect me to be a caretaker," she complained. "I won't go so far as to say that they see me as 'Mammy.' I don't think anyone could see me that way very easily! But there is an expectation that I'll be a kinder, gentler manager, that I'll tolerate some things a white manager wouldn't be expected to tolerate. They think I should cuddle and care for people more. But that's not my nature, so it creates difficulty for me."

A mid-level manager told me she felt unprepared for the political games that are played in corporations. "Sometimes I see a war between white women and African-American women," she explained. "If there was a problem between another employee and me, and I went to the manager, I was always devalued. It couldn't be that the other person had done these things to me. My manager said, 'You must be misunderstanding her; perhaps you're overreacting.' He made it seem as if I was the one creating the problem, although this other employee had a history of not getting along with others." I could nearly hear this woman's silent scream: "It's just not fair!" And I agree with her—it's not!

One of the biggest differences in the experience of minority women executives occurs in the way they manage their professional relationships. Because of the distrust they feel, they tend to maintain an even greater separation between their personal and professional lives. Many are extremely prudent in what they share with others—and they don't reveal much. As one mid-level manager told me, "I work with these people, but during my time after hours, I don't want to socialize with them. I don't want to go to the company picnic; I want to be with people who I enjoy. Other people feel, 'You don't want to be with us.' Actually, that's not true. I've been with them for hours all day. I just want to go home, relax, and be with my family and friends."

Part of her reluctance came from her skepticism of others' motives. She was already one or two out of a hundred in her work area, but in the larger group she felt even more isolated. In their misguided attempts to connect with her, she felt that others bombard her with questions about her personal life in these social situations. "We tend to be private," she told me. "I'm afraid someone is going to start drinking and then feel he can ask me anything. I don't want to pull back; that can hurt my career. But if I do divulge too much, I'll come back to work on Monday and find that everyone knows it. People let their hair down, and it comes back to haunt you."

Another woman told me that sometimes she feels as if she's two people. "One is open to the bigger world, and yet I slide into the other track when I'm with other African-Americans. I feel very relaxed. I can say or do anything. No one is going to judge me. In the broader world, I'm always concerned about how I look and what I say. There's always tension. Am I doing everything to make everyone know I can do the job? Do they just need a black face on this committee, or do they want me because of my expertise?"

It's basic human nature to want to be appreciated for our talents, to feel that we're adding value, to be understood. Denied these positive strokes, we become hopeless. Or we feel victimized and walk around with a chip on our shoulder. A great deal of systemic and organizational change needs to occur in order for corporations to create a culture and an environment that appreciate and reward a diversity of thoughts and behaviors. (Corporate recommendations will be highlighted later in this chapter.) Unfortunately, not all companies have an inclusive culture. However, the women of color who have been successful seem to be able to move beyond the mistrust and feelings of hopelessness.

> **THE SYSTEM NEEDS TO CHANGE:** *A great deal of systemic and organizational change needs to occur in order for corporations to create a culture and an environment that appreciate and reward a diversity of thoughts and behaviors.*

"Those of us who have made it have learned to get past that," one woman told me. "But there are a number of minorities who are still apprehensive and still feel there are whites who are out to get them. That keeps a lot of good people of color out of high-paying jobs. It doesn't make any difference how much education you have. With that attitude you won't get ahead. If you let other people define your life for you, that will stop you.

"In order for me to live the American dream," she continued, "I can look to people and see the good in them. Realize that people cannot put you down unless you allow them to. Look at yourself, who you are, what you want to do, and move on. When I feel there's something I want to do, no one can stop me from doing it. It may take me a little longer to get there, but no one will stop me."

What should you do if you feel mistrusted and mistrustful? Perhaps it's wise to give others the benefit of the doubt and not be as suspect of their intentions. If you feel that someone is "grilling" you at a corporate picnic by asking you unwelcomed questions, realize that they are probably just trying to get acquainted in the only way they know how. If you are uncomfortable with their questioning, start asking them questions about themselves—like where did they grow up, how many children were there in their family, and so on.

Often interactions become a product of self-fulfilling prophecies. People tend to show up as you perceive them and expect them to. If you change your perception and expectation of how they will behave, perhaps they will begin to behave differently. For instance, for a month try to see your boss as someone who likes you, who wants you to be successful, who understands and supports you. If you act as if he or she has good intentions for you and your career, see how your relationship changes. It will take time and a true commitment on your part to honestly believe that your boss's motives are good, but it's worth a shot.

> TRY TO ESTABLISH TRUST: *It's wise to give others the benefit of the doubt and not always be as suspect of their intentions.*

## Feeling Different, Fitting In, or *Not* . . .

Unfortunately, in business today, people still tend to hire others who are most like themselves, people with whom they feel "comfortable." Historically, that means white males hiring white males. Professional women are still an unknown to many men. That kind of unfamiliarity creates obstacles for all aspiring women, but it is particularly troublesome for the advancement of high-potential minority women. "I think white men are on the inside," one senior executive woman of color told me, "and they have created a huge network among themselves. It's natural for them to operate that way—it's like the water they swim in—and the rest of us are trying to get into the pool, but we don't swim the same way and need fresher water."

As the minority women see it, at least the white women can create relationships based on the fact that they're similar to someone's daughter or wife or sister. "I don't have that advantage," one woman told me. "I am completely strange to these folks. They don't have a clue about me; they don't know what to expect. If they would just treat me like the other managers, that would be fine. But that's not how things get done."

She went on to explain that there were a few Caucasian women in her company who have been able to make a relationship with the CEO because he perceives them as his "kid sisters." "I've actually heard senior vice presidents say about women around here, 'She's like my kid sister.' The woman would resent it, but it has gotten her access, which she otherwise wouldn't have. And it doesn't even occur to him that he's not saying that to *me*—it's not possible for him to see me as his kid sister. So there have been some hurdles. But I just keep going. You just have to find a different way around."

Although many people are still uncomfortable with diversity, some of the minority women saw their distinctiveness as a way to create more visibility for themselves. They didn't fit in, and they stopped trying. People notice them, and they took that as a positive. Their independence provided them with a different level of freedom.

For instance, Anita didn't always dress "corporate," yet she made it into the executive levels of a conservative company. "A lot of times I would come to work in silk pants with a casual top and earrings swinging down to here," she said, pointing to the middle of her neck. "One of the unwritten rules when I joined this company four years ago was that executive women didn't come to work wearing pants or earrings that moved. And I said, 'We'll see about this!' The same rules don't necessarily apply. So I've gotten away with more stuff. My head has been shaved, and nobody said anything but 'it must be a cultural thing.'"

Because she feels it's futile for her to try to "fit in" with the dominant culture, Anita has become a maverick. She's willing to push the envelope. "All I need is for people to let me in and be willing to hear me, separate from my style," she said. "I want them to accept that we can create a team and work together. I was brought into this organization to accomplish something, and I want to do that job. Outside, I've got other things I do. I'm active in church. I have friends. I have a husband at home. So I don't need to belong here. I've got a family."

No one challenged Anita about her huge earrings, shaved head, and colorful casual clothes. Her coworkers couldn't put her into a category they understood—sister, wife, daughter, mother, or even friend, since many didn't have friends of another race. In order to feel connected with other professionals, Anita and many other women of color have created "affinity groups" at work.

## Affinity Groups

Since many high-level women of color felt isolated in their jobs, they voiced the need to have relationships with others who were like them. I found that about half of their relationships were with other minorities, both men and women. This is extremely high when compared to white women, who had, on average, less than 5 percent of their professional relationships with people of color. For women of color, these minority alliances occurred within the context of affinity groups: an informal collection of same-race individuals who share a personal connection and common concerns. The participants in these groups are typically of both genders and at various levels within one or several companies. They act as a support for one another, allowing each other to share feelings and experiences more openly.

Many minority women spoke of their involvement with their affinity groups—some seeing it as a lifesaver. One woman, for instance, believed that she was closest to other professional women of color—especially those who had "walked through the same fire" that she had. For some, the group represented common ground upon which to build friendships and further their careers. No one else could really understand them, these women believed. And although the support is more often personal than professional, members of the group mentor each other and open doors for one another, recommending associates for promotion, where appropriate.

"I have more trust for people who are already more like me by culture and color," an African-American woman told me. "I tend to doubt people. They don't see their own biases. I feel closer to people who are black because they understand what I'm dealing with and what role race plays in my life." This executive made a point to constantly mentor younger African-Americans.

Another explained that differences in income, education, and status within the company among affinity group members made little difference to her. "Believe it or not, I get a lot more information from people below me than above me. And that group is a reality check for me in terms of, 'Remember who you are. Remember the whole context that you operate in. And don't forget us.'"

> **VARY YOUR CONNECTIONS:** *It's important to find personal and professional support among your peers and people with whom you feel comfortable. To further your career advancement and personal growth, however, it is also important to involve yourself in informal groups that include both minority and white businesspeople.*

Other executive women of color suggest that one be careful about spending too much time in affinity groups, thereby excluding whites and other races from one's life. Bobbi Gutman, Corporate Vice President at Motorola, said, "When we accept people of different races and genders into our lives, we are more likely to be welcomed into their world." And when I asked Leonade Jones of The Washington Post Company about the activities or functions she thought were the most beneficial in helping her get to know people and soliciting their help for her career, she talked about nonprofit work. She urged minority women to go outside their affinity groups and get involved in mainstream communities if they wished to get ahead.

Mary Evans, who works in the banking industry, saw affinity groups as "one of our downfalls." "You stick with people that you feel comfortable with," she explained. "We as African-Americans see ourselves as our race. I'm in A.K.A., a black women's sorority. I always know that if I'm in need, I can go to one of those people anyplace in the world, and we will pull together. So it's not a bad thing; we just need to keep it in perspective. I think these groups started during slavery in the South. People couldn't talk freely on the plantations during the day, but at night they could. It was a matter of feeling comfortable and protected. We're protecting our feelings from what we perceive as people who would come along and hurt us. But in most cases it's paranoia. It's a perception, not reality."

It's important to find personal and professional support among your peers and people with whom you feel comfortable. To further your career advancement and personal growth, however, it is also important to involve yourself in informal groups that include both minority and white businesspeople.

## Cultural Issues

Many conflicts in the workplace arise from subtle cultural clashes— the elusive but real disparities between an individual's ethnic culture and the corporate culture in which she finds herself. For instance, today American companies value people who are assertive, goal-oriented, and direct. But those traits aren't necessarily appreciated in other cultures.

Asian-Americans, for instance, might have been raised to be more focused on the group rather than their individual needs. In Asian cultures, group accomplishments are rewarded over personal ones. An Asian-American might believe that she would please her boss by showing up on time, working hard, and being a competent part of the team. But in the United States, you also need to promote your personal accomplishments in order to get ahead. Your visibility and individual relationships with your superiors can make or break your promotions.

These same sorts of culture clashes exist between the African-American and white cultures. One woman of color told me that her mother had raised her with the words, "Don't think too highly of yourself." "It was her way to protect me from disappointments," she explained. "A lot of people grow up without good self-esteem. As minority women, we tend not to pat ourselves on the back. We may be the ones doing all the work, and other people may get all the credit for it, but we may not speak up at meetings and say, 'Oh, that was my work!' I am passive in most cases, and I don't push. I was raised that way." With that kind of upbringing, it's harder to be assertive.

Unfortunately, when people are raised with cultural values and expectations that are not exhibited in American companies, they can be penalized for it. They feel they don't fit, and what they have to offer is unappreciated, since their values clash with those established by people making the judgments. There may be a perception of them as not having "leadership qualities," when, in reality, they are a different type of leader, and the wonderful qualities they do possess aren't valued.

For instance, one African-American woman told me she was raised with the value that you help another person in need. "If I see you're struggling, I'm willing to stop and help you," she explained. "It goes back to slavery. If someone in the community didn't have food, we helped out, we gave what we could. But in a big company, it's every man for himself. You have your job to do. So when I reach out to someone, my superiors will ask me, 'Why are you distracting yourself with someone else's problems?' Sometimes it's hard to work through the culture if it conflicts with your values."

I have also heard African-American non-executive employees voice their frustration with people of their own ethnicity who make it to the senior levels and then act as if they're no longer black. Forgetting about or not acknowledging same-race individuals is a huge "faux pas" as minorities advance in their career. In the executive coaching I do with people of color, I have found that there is an implicit (and oftentimes explicit) understanding that, if you are a person of color, you take the time to communicate and take care of one another.

One African-American manager tried to explain, "You know, all African-Americans are supposed to connect with each other—like a huge family. We come from a sharing community. It goes against the grain of who you are and what you were taught; it's a big slap in the face if you don't want to associate with other black people. But there's envy from some members of the community. They'll say, 'Just because you went to college, and you have this big job, you think you're better than the rest of us.' It's complicated. As a group, we're more critical of our own than other groups. Yet we're also very supportive. I know even though they may be jealous, they're out there, pulling for me." They expect that they will often be ignored by whites, but feel slighted and insulted when ignored by same-race individuals.

All of this boils down to the many difficulties women of color face as they move into the senior levels. Not only do they have to perform on the job (and often they are very high achievers), but they also must work to preserve their connection with their communities and families of origin whom they don't want to leave behind. It's a tall order.

One woman of color admitted, "I've been faking it." She has tried to become more like the dominant culture, but it has taken an emotional toll on her to fit in and be perceived as being competent. And some women struggle with the feeling that they shouldn't be too successful or they'll be ostracized from their community. Then they won't fit anywhere.

A person from a minority background may always be conscious of racial stereotypes and may constantly wonder how she's being perceived. Such a heritage may make you conscientious about being competent, or worried about others' assumptions about your competence. You may second-guess yourself: Do I have two strikes against me already? Is discrimination still prevalent? How will that impact me? Will I get the same opportunities as a white person, given that I'm just as competent and as knowledgeable? These insecurities can take more of a psychological toll on you than you may realize. If your thought processes are straying from the work at hand because you're concerned about how others judge you, you may not work to your capacity. You may even miss what others are saying to you.

Some individuals can't handle the strain or the frustration and opt out. "Why should I continue to do this?" they ask themselves. They leave their organizations, not because they lack ambition or knowledge, but because they perceive the institutional barriers as insurmountable. Some move to other companies in the hope of finding better opportunities, while others become entrepreneurs.

## What Companies Can Do

Questions of racial inequality and prejudice have dogged our society since before its inception. They are not easily solved, but I don't believe they're intractable. After all, some women of color have broken through and made it to the senior executive ranks. How can we make it easier for more high-potential women to follow in their footsteps with, perhaps, less pain? Changing individual perceptions, attitudes, and behaviors is an important first step in creating an inclusive work environment. However, sustainable change will occur only when individual efforts are coupled with organizational and systemic change.

At a minimum, it is important for corporations to have a mission statement that institutionalizes a commitment to diversity. The CEO must truly believe in the importance of a company policy promoting a diverse workforce and require compliance with such a stated policy. From executive vice presidents and division heads enforcing it within their business units to mid-level managers and below with their employees, everyone must participate.

Progressive companies like Marriott International and Pitney Bowes (which *Fortune* magazine has ranked among the top fifty companies for blacks, Asians, and Hispanics to work for) have taken the initiative in tying executive salaries and bonuses to demonstrated increases in a diversified workforce. In 1998, the bonuses of 300 Marriott executives were linked to their having reached their diversity goals.

Pitney Bowes has instituted numerous programs that reflect its commitment to diversity. The company consistently links its diversity objectives to its business planning process, called "Elements of Success." Its business unit presidents also chair the Diversity Leadership Council. This sends a strong signal of senior leadership involvement.

> *Changing individual perceptions, attitudes, and behaviors is an important first step in creating an inclusive work environment. However, sustainable change will occur only when individual efforts are coupled with organizational and systemic change.*

In speaking with CEOs, I asked what their companies were doing to help women of color advance in their careers. Several had effective programs in place and some worthy suggestions. Rick Belluzzo, former CEO of Silicon Graphics and currently Group Vice President at Microsoft, for instance, told me, "I really believe in diversity. It goes back to the talent issue. If you exclude large groups of people from being successful in your company, you're creating a problem in being able to get enough strength and talent to be successful. One of the biggest issues I have worked very hard to deal with I called 'hiring for discomfort.' You know, if someone feels that he is not really comfortable hiring this minority person, I say, 'Who cares whether you're comfortable or not. If the person is qualified, and you need someone, hire her.'"

Rick felt that hiring a diverse group was a good business move. "If everyone talked the same and acted the same and had the same style, you'd really limit yourself," he explained. "Having completely different orientations in a company is a key factor to success. So I have to say to my people, 'It may be a little bit harder to communicate, it may be a little bit uncomfortable at times, but we've got to understand that this is a good thing to do.' I want to make this a more inclusive environment. You know, those decisions made in the men's room are not necessarily the best ones."

Rick also encouraged semi-formal mentorship within his company. "You have to go out of your way to make sure you provide a bridge for developmental opportunities," he said. "You need to have some structure to it, but ultimately a good mentoring situation has to come naturally."

Jim Preston, retired CEO of Avon, noted that times were changing. "One of my predecessors was seen as the quintessential CEO," he explained. "Some of his buddies were on the board; there were few women. It was truly a good ol' boy network. They went hunting and fishing together, played cards, and drank and smoked cigars." But today's CEO recognizes the realities of globalization and diversity. More than 80 percent of new entrants into the Avon workforce are women and minorities, Jim explained. "We need to understand what it takes to attract the best and the brightest people. We need to *want* the diversity of thought, ideas, and decisions, and not be threatened by them."

Jim explained that when he works with women of color, he deals with the individual, not the gender or race. "Besides," he said, "those differences seem to blur as they move up in their careers."

In a July 1999 interview for *Fortune* magazine, Rich McGinn, CEO of Lucent Technologies, said, "Diversity is a competitive advantage. Different people approach similar problems in different ways." Alan Buckwalter, CEO of Chase Bank of Texas, shares that view. He firmly believes that achieving diversity makes good business sense. "If we, as a bank, don't mirror the community that we're in, ultimately our customers are going to go somewhere that does."

The other issue is the necessity of change. "This part is a little harder to sell," Alan admitted, "particularly to folks who have been doing the same thing for a long time and have been successful at it. They're apt to say, 'It's gotten me to where I am, so why should I change?' The only person who likes change is a baby. But if we keep doing things in the same way, we're not going to get different results. With a diverse employee base, we'll get a lot of fresh ideas. Some may be quite radical, perhaps, but that's what you need in a world that's changing as rapidly as the one we live in."

Alan made it clear that you don't get different ideas by hiring people who look like you and come from the same background. "You're just going to have the same old, same old. And people who've had to scramble to get where they are oftentimes are going to have a better work ethic and will feel more driven to succeed, as opposed to the person who's had it all handed to him on a silver platter."

Historically, the companies that pursue diversity outperform the S&P 500. In order to be effective in creating an inclusive corporate culture, I have found a few additional strategies that I suggest companies focus on—and then measure their outcomes. For instance, hiring practices are critical; companies need to devote attention to employing a diverse group of people. In addition to typical recruitment efforts at well-known universities, companies should develop strong recruiting ties to colleges and universities that have traditionally attracted ethnic minorities. They must also ensure that they have a diverse group of recruiters who are knowledgeable and sensitive to the cultural and racial differences of potential employees.

Companies should also pay attention to the number and compensation levels of minorities in executive positions and on their boards of directors. Not only are meeting such criteria imperative to being named on well-known lists, such as *Fortune*'s "The 50 Best Companies for Asians, Blacks, and Hispanics," but it also sends a clear message that the company values diversity at the highest levels. As mentioned earlier, people of color closely scrutinize the minority representation and compensation at the executive levels at companies before accepting a position.

The company's performance evaluation and succession planning processes also should be linked to diversity objectives. These quantifiable and measurable promotion criteria should be standardized, enforced, and tied to compensation. We must also ensure that minorities receive leadership development training and coaching as part of their development plans.

There are many other small but significant ways that a company can enhance diversity in its workforce.

- Companies should regularly conduct "cultural audits," engaging employee focus groups to determine diversity objectives and strategies.

- Companies need to ensure that they are working with minority vendors, contractors, suppliers, and alliances.

- Charitable contributions should target programs that benefit minorities.

- Companies should consistently encourage the sharing of diverse ideas and perceptions.

- They need to encourage employees to think of new and innovative ways to market their products and/or services to their own cultural group.

## What Ethnic Minorities Believe Will Help

How do you get more women of color into upper corporate levels? Promote them! Easy enough, but "it is not *that* easy," some of the women of color cautioned. "It's one thing to promote me," one woman told me, "but if you don't give me some support, I may fall flat on my face. Companies have to understand how hard it is to be the only person of color within a work group. There have been times when I wished there was someone who looked like me to whom I could say, 'I'm having a real bad day today.' "

Self-knowledge and motivation are important first steps. Mary Evans told me, "Minorities need to understand that no one is going to give you everything. You have to help yourself. You need to get a good education—you need the tools to work with. And that includes understanding corporate politics, so people don't think you have a chip on your shoulder or an attitude."

Communication is also key. It's important that we learn how to talk to each other and feel comfortable. Companies need to open dialogues to help us understand one another. Such discussions will help corporate minority women see that those in the dominant culture really do care, and white women can begin to understand who their minority coworkers are and the issues they struggle with. We need to listen to each other and to start looking at ways we can enhance each other's lives. The worst thing is for women to undermine or come into conflict with one another. After all, we're *both* minorities in the corporate world, and we need to pull together.

As one woman of color told me, "We all need to start talking to each other. Try to understand my culture, where I came from, and what my feelings are. And when we talk about cultures, I need to understand your culture too. It's not a one-way street. Until we can say

COMPANIES NEED TO OPEN DIALOGUES TO HELP US UNDERSTAND ONE ANOTHER. *Such discussions will help corporate minority women see that those in the dominant culture really do care, and white women can begin to understand who their minority coworkers are, and the issues they struggle with.*

what we really want and expect, I don't think we'll cross the divide. We need to better understand each other, no matter what your race, gender or nationality. Companies need to help people feel included."

It's only by truly getting to know another person that one understands his or her motives, behavior, and language. Bobbi Gutman, for instance, told me she preferred to work with people—whether male or female, black or white—who are able to look beyond the surface, people who are introspective and willing to probe beneath the issue at hand. "I like to work with people who don't just see me as black or see others as who they expect them to be, but who they really are."

Although in this chapter we have focused on the advancement of women of color, true diversity is creating an environment of openness to differences in attitudes, perceptions, and behaviors. According to Herschel Herndon, Director of Global Diversity at The Stanley Works, "To become truly effective at addressing diversity, a company must focus on the full utilization of the skills and capabilities of every single employee." This needs to include ethnic minorities, people with different sexual orientations, women, and white males. "In other words," he said, "at the very minimum, every employee must recognize a personal and/or business benefit—preferably both—when true diversity is implemented. If we only focus on small parts of diversity, we miss the breadth and depth associated with the full spectrum of power under the diversity umbrella."

# 12 | Going to the Top:
## Fifteen Proven Strategies That Will Advance Your Career

I have already emphasized that you must take calculated risks and move beyond activities that are comfortable, taking on profit-and-loss responsibilities where possible. Above all else, you must also understand what makes you happy, what you want out of life, and what you are capable of enduring to achieve the goals you have set for yourself. If you believe you have that kind of clarity and commitment about your work, it's important to come to grips with the challenges and reality of executive life: which opportunities are possible within your company, as well as the benefits, rewards, and costs of every career move. You must talk to people who have followed the path to which you aspire in order to discover what you should do, step by step, to reach your ultimate goal.

The following fifteen points will help you clarify what you must do and how you may need to adapt your behavior in order to move ahead. They come straight from the triumphs, failures, and experiences of senior executive women and their CEOs. If you follow them, you too will increase your chances of finding windows in the glass ceiling and climbing through.

## 1. Display Leadership

People love being led by a great leader. And they want to like and respect their leaders too. What does it take to make a good leader? Tom Engibous of Texas Instruments told me, you must develop "incredible followership." People who work for great leaders want to run up the hill with their rifles and charge the enemy. The CEOs with whom I spoke had many opinions on how you can become a great leader. These included:

- Creating a successful track record

- Assembling a team that grows, achieves its bottom line and a set of targets, continues to expand, and does so relatively consistently every year

- Driving execution: getting the job done

- Making sure that the train leaves the station on time

Ask yourself the following leadership questions:

*1. Can I develop a good strategic plan?* Do you know where the market is going and where your place can be in it? When you develop a strategic plan, rather than just asking, "What are the big market opportunities?" you must also ask, "Where can I play in the market, bring value, and establish customer loyalty?" You have to understand the global and domestic market trends—and that can vary greatly depending on which industry you're in.

Remember, the tactical skills and behaviors important for accomplishing your goals as an individual contributor or a manager are not sufficient to propel you to the senior ranks. You need to develop your ability to think strategically.

*2. Do I have a strong desire to win?* Do you like to compete? Sue Swenson, President of Leap Wireless International and former CEO of Cellular One, admitted to being highly competitive. "In adversarial or negative situations or ones where it looks like there's no chance in hell we could ever do well, there's a spirit inside me that says, 'You know what? We can really do this.'" Sue believes that competitive force allows her and her team to push through some of the firewalls they encounter.

*3. Can I build productive teamwork within my organization?* Do you know how to turn your people on? It's not just delegating and having your people do things for you, but knowing what inherently motivates them so that they produce for the team in the most efficient and enthusiastic way possible. You also need to reward risk-taking and failure. Encouraging your team to take big, yet informed, risks can be critical to your organization's longevity.

Do you know how to develop people? It's important to hire the right employees and then get out of their way, to let them have their own mistakes and successes. And sometimes, even as a leader, you're not the boss, but a member of a team. Jim Preston of Avon recalled that some of the most productive meetings he ever held occurred when members of his team challenged one another's ideas instead of his decreeing, "This is the way it's going to be." They bounced ideas off each other before finally making a decision.

This sort of team-building applies domestically and internationally. David Pottruck, CEO of Charles Schwab, recalled that the best management decisions are made when there is a diversity of ideas presented to reflect the global marketplace your company serves. "We have a large operation in the United Kingdom," he explained. "One of the executives there called the executive to whom he reported in the States and said, 'I think we have an issue of major concern.' The U.S. person talked with him a little, and that was it. We have lots of issues of major concern. But our person in England was saying, in the typically understated British way, 'The roof is falling in. We need big-time help.'"

Unless you make a concerted effort to be sensitive to cultural differences, you can run into trouble. You have to go out of your way to understand how cultural differences operate. As David Pottruck stressed, it is important to have diversity on your team, be highly attuned to cultural differences, and listen to everyone's ideas to make good global decisions.

*4. Do I have strong interpersonal skills?* Jan Peters, CEO of MediaOne, stressed the importance of emotional intelligence. The bigger the business group you'll be managing, the more you'll be dealing with employees and clients. "You have to be able to communicate and be evenhanded. It's important to limit emotional ups and downs and justly deal with others based on merit," she stated. And many CEOs spoke of the need to be tough yet compassionate and to understand the softer side of business. Are you reasonably open? Are you fair-minded? You need to balance your head and your heart to be an effective leader.

**5. Do I know how to engage people?** Sue Swenson said, "I have been told, and after all these years I tend to believe, that I have the ability to engage anyone and everyone. People feel comfortable with me. I can get total strangers to tell me their life story, and it's not because I'm nosy. I'm truly interested in people." People skills are key.

Rick Belluzzo, Group Vice President at Microsoft and former CEO of SGI, summed up leadership qualities when he said, "I think it ultimately comes down to, first, a combination of having the ability to take complex or challenging situations and bring clarity to them in terms of what to do and what path to pursue. Second, it's the ability to mobilize an organization toward achieving the result you choose. That involves setting plans, motivating people, sharing a vision, dealing with poor performers, building a model, and making it stick. Third, there's communication and dealing with people—the softer side of business—which includes getting and developing the right people, building a team, and being able to communicate." Perhaps good leadership comes down to being aware—knowing yourself and being attuned to the needs and desires of others and to the marketplace, so that you can develop well-thought-out and creative solutions that can be scaled to the entire organization.

## 2. Don't Take Everything So Personally

I have written much about the perils of perfectionism. Besides its other drawbacks, it can also lead to taking everything around us and ourselves extremely seriously. We personalize the feedback that others give us, rather than seeing it as their perception and comments on our behavior. We become upset. Our reaction makes those around us feel uncomfortable. They can't be themselves and be honest. They walk on eggshells, afraid of how we'll react.

When men are criticized or reprimanded or when they discover they didn't get a much-coveted job, they tend to become visibly and externally angry. Women, on the other hand, seem to express that same emotion of anger inwardly; for us, it translates into hurt feelings. In fact, we become upset with ourselves, not with the messenger or the situation. If someone says, "You know, you probably could have done that differently," we often reply, "Oh, I knew that.

I shouldn't have done that. What was I thinking?" I, I, I . . . and we ruminate on the issue for the next several days rather than saying, "Okay, I hear you. I'll change my behavior next time. Thanks for pointing it out."

How can you depersonalize criticism? Think of the advice Dr. Spock gave new parents. If a child did something improper, parents were advised to criticize the behavior ("I don't like that you wrote with markers on the wall!")—not the person ("You're a bad, bad girl!"). We learned to do that as parents, but we often don't interpret the criticism we receive from others in the same way, especially in work-related situations.

When you perceive feedback as terribly personal (taking it to mean "You're bad," instead of "I don't like your behavior"), it becomes very difficult to change. In fact, you may believe that you must alter who you are rather than just your actions. So the next time you receive criticism, interpret the comments as someone's personal feedback about your behavior. Just think about changing what you *do,* not who you *are.* You can change behavior; it doesn't get at your core. When you think of criticism in this way, it isn't as devastating. It is just the world giving you some feedback about how you might adjust your course so you can arrive at your destination more quickly and gracefully.

---

DON'T TAKE IT SO PERSONALLY: *The next time you receive criticism, interpret the comments as someone's feedback about your behavior. Think about changing what you do, not who you are.*

---

And, interestingly, by changing the paradigm of how you view criticism directed at you, you will also begin to deliver it differently. When you're upset with someone, your lesson is not to malign the person. Rather, comment on his or her behavior. If you truly believe that it's the behavior you're censuring, it will be easier for you to criticize others and allow your frustration to vent. Otherwise, you may be tempted to withhold feedback because you believe you're assailing the person, and don't want to cause hurt.

If you tend to take criticism extremely personally and get defensive or believe that failures are an attack against you as an individual, the negative feedback may be touching an old childhood wound that hasn't been resolved. Intense reactions may indicate that you need to go deeper in your understanding of yourself and your responses. Psychotherapy can be helpful in this regard.

## 3. Find Your Passion

We all need to have a true passion—something that motivates us to get up in the morning and make an impact. Sometimes we find our passion in our work; we believe what we're doing will change the world for the better. Sometimes we find it in something more personal.

Mike Murphy, a Vice President at American Management Systems, explained how his passion helped him overcome a devastating loss. Before working at AMS, Mike thought that he would try his hand at an entrepreneurial venture and make big dollars along the way, but instead his efforts ended in near total bankruptcy.

"Decisions are made by your heart, your brain, and your stomach," Mike explained. Unfortunately, he didn't listen to his brain, and his brain knew the odds were against him. Other companies were already in this line of business, and all the recent start-ups had failed. Mike's brain knew not to go down that path; statistically, success was improbable. But his heart and gut motivated him to do it anyway. Sadly, with the exception of his house and his wife and kids, he lost everything, including his children's college fund and his retirement money. He struggled with depression after such a huge failure.

"You have to ask yourself why you want to get up in the morning," he admitted. But Mike found a way. He moved a picture of his two children to the night table where it was the first thing he saw when he awoke each morning. In the photograph, his four-year-old son was sitting on a split-rail fence. His daughter, age two at the time, was holding a lavender flower and was leaning her head on her brother's shoulder. It was perfect.

This photo reminded Mike of what was really important in his life. He knew that he had to pick himself up, dust himself off, and start all over again because of his kids.

I cannot overstate the importance of having passion, self-direction, and purpose in what you do. That's what keeps people having fun and not burning out. Love what you do—have passion about it. It's what sustains and nourishes you.

## 4. Expect Crises

Crises are inevitable. From my experience, you must anticipate that you will have to manage major disruptions three or four times a year (or maybe more or less for some people)—it's just part of life. If you have that expectation going into each year, then you'll see each difficult episode as one of the inescapable crises you knew would hit sooner or later.

We try to manage our careers and lives so closely that we're jolted when a major snafu occurs. We find ourselves taking it personally; after all, we've tried so hard to make everything run smoothly, how could this be happening? Working moms, especially, have so much going on in their lives, they don't have time for emergencies. They have allotted spaces in their lives for work, family, friends, and, hopefully, themselves, but there's not a place for crises.

It's healthier and more realistic, however, to expect these emergencies. There are always setbacks. When they come to pass, you can say to yourself, "Aha, that's one of them!" and then deal with it. It has nothing to do with you. In fact, often the crisis takes place outside what you've done—don't take it personally! You can never take one moment in time as the final decision on your life.

But you need to find a place in your life for crises—set your expectations in advance. When you're allocating time for various activities in your career, be sure to establish contingency plans for exigencies that may arise. Think of it this way: Subconsciously you may anticipate that your kids or your aging parents may become ill; you know these events will occur, and you have plans in place in case of emergency. You might look at work crises in the same way. Just as you can't control your children's or parents' health, you should expect and plan for the unexpected work crisis.

## 5. Be Aware of Your Attitude

Sue Swenson, President of Leap Wireless International, is one of the most upbeat executives I've met. "The only thing you can't recover from is death," she told me. "People will come in and say, 'Oh, my God. Things are just so terrible!' And I'll ask, 'Did someone die?' If the answer is no, then we can fix it. Nothing is beyond repair. I have a fundamental belief that you move toward what you think about. So if you hold a positive attitude, you generally are going to end up in a positive place. But if you focus on the negative, you will end up there."

Like Sue Swenson, you need a positive spirit to advance in your career. The skill-sets you've developed, and the personal attributes, experiences, and strategic alliances you've amassed are all vital for your success. But you also need the conviction and the confidence in yourself to say, "I can do that!" and believe it. In fact, you need to believe it to such a degree that others believe it too.

It's amazing how much influence you have as a manager. Sometimes you can forget that people look up to you when you enter a room. One of the first qualities they notice is your nonverbal communication: Are you slump-shouldered or enthusiastic? What sort of verbal remarks do you make? Once you make it to a managerial level, you need a positive attitude that empowers the people who work for you. Without followers, it's awfully difficult to be a leader.

You can apply that kind of positive attitude to your personal career goals too. If you want to progress in your career, you must act like someone who has already made it. Senior management promotes people who fit their leadership profile and whom they can visualize in advanced positions. If you're already acting like a member of the team, it can be a natural fit. When you have confidence that promotions will come, you become more relaxed about them—and, more often than not, they do come.

> ACT LIKE YOU HAVE ALREADY MADE IT: *Senior management promotes people whom they can visualize in executive positions.*

Besides, negativity will only work against you. Jim Preston, re- tired CEO of Avon, advised, "Stop complaining about why you haven't made it yet. Rather, act like you've already made it, and that will help your career in the long run."

Lori Mirek, in her role as Senior Vice President at America On- line, used to believe that the best thing she could do was to be direct with her boss, even if it meant consistently raising negative issues. After all, she thought she was being "professional." She didn't un- derstand the impact of her negativity until she took a job at Oracle. "One of my senior directors was such a consistent pleasure to work with," she explained. "I finally sat back and asked myself, 'Why is that? Why is this one guy so fabulous?'

"It was because he approached every problem with, 'Hmm. Let's figure out this problem together,' Or, 'Let's utilize this relationship and see how we can get them to help us.' He was always positive. Now, no matter how brilliant or hard-working the folks are on my teams, I find myself gravitating toward the people who have that can-do attitude. It's contagious."

How do you develop such a positive attitude? You might emu- late a role model the way Lori did. Also, look for how you can fix problems and improve situations, but never start off with a com- plaint or an excuse. In fact, refrain from volunteering an excuse for anything. There's always logic and a reason for why things are the way they are. Think in terms of: *"This is where we are, how can we change or fix the problem?"*

And by all means, adhere to the eleventh commandment, "Thou Shall Not Whine!" If you feel victimized in a situation, oth- ers will perceive you as a victim too. And no one will want to be around you if you express bitterness. For instance, if your company has just gone through a merger, and you're unhappy with your new position or boss, your natural response may be, "It's not fair. This wasn't what I was promised!" However, if you go into your new role with that attitude, you'll be, according to one senior executive who lived through such an experience, "dead meat." It's better to take charge of your own fate. Change jobs, if you must. That's more ap- propriate than staying in a position that makes you unhappy and causes you to whine and complain. Remember, once you fall into the trap of being perceived as a victim, it is quite difficult to get yourself out of it. In fact, senior management will avoid you if that's how you're feeling or behaving.

> **ADHERE TO THE ELEVENTH COMMANDMENT: THOU SHALT NOT WHINE!** *If you feel victimized in a situation, others will perceive you as a victim too. No one will want to be around you if you express bitterness.*

Another attitudinal issue has to do with your perceived commitment to the corporation. Think about the casual conversations you have in the hallways and bathroom. If all that the leaders of the organization hear about is your commitment to your family or your leisure time (and I don't mean to imply that you shouldn't have strong commitments to family and fun), you may impede your career progress. Higher-ups need to hear about your commitment to and your great new ideas for improving the company. If you only talk about your children or vacations, they may never learn about your innovative insights for the company.

Gloria Everett at Globalstar explained, "I have a daughter. At the right time and moment, I brag a great deal about her. And when she was ill, people in the office knew. She had a life-threatening horseback riding accident, and they knew that. They're aware of my concerns. But she is not always the major topic of discussion when I'm at lunch or when I'm in the hallways." Gloria is strategic about what she shares with whom.

Also pay attention to your attitude toward work and travel schedules. Be careful about how you portray your availability. You don't have to work weekends or a hundred hours a week, but how flexible are you? How mobile? Some organizations make provisions for workers to telecommute; flex-time schedules and job sharing are workable options. And at some corporations, mobility is a big issue, whereas at others it isn't.

Gloria Everett explained, "We've asked a number of employees to spend three to six months in foreign countries. Some have said 'no.' I don't think it has been the 'kiss of death.' In fact, I know it hasn't been. But some have said 'yes.' And in an international environment, that could help them in the future."

If you don't want to travel because you need to spend time with your family, certainly you shouldn't take a job that requires constant globetrotting. You may want to stay open to some travel, however. To say, "I won't travel," when your job may include an incidental trip twice a year, can work against you in the long run. Rather than making such a blanket statement and closing all your options, you can always say, "Sorry, I can't make it to *this* meeting because . . ." Remember, if you claim that you won't travel, you may also be denying yourself the one trip a year to London or Paris.

Another attitudinal error is to voice your concerns about another person too loudly. Why make it known that you would never work for Phil or Karen? Perhaps your next advancement will mean working for Karen, who has just been promoted. Maybe you can live with it for a year, you might even learn something. Sometimes our greatest learning opportunities come from working with people who see the world differently than we do. Why state up front that you'll never take a certain position or work under a specific person or in a particular department, or never agree to a relocation? Maybe you can't relocate this month or this year, for instance, but things change. Perhaps you can relocate for a big promotion three years from now. Unfortunately, the same management team may remember that you once swore you would never move, so they skip over you when an opportunity arises.

All of these issues have to do with your portraying yourself in the best light possible. Your attitude makes all the difference when bosses are looking to give the next great opportunity to someone.

## 6. Never Be Afraid to Communicate, but Communicate Clearly

Many of the CEOs with whom I spoke explained that to advance in your career, you need to provide information in a manner that is actionable. It's inadvisable to go into a meeting and try to impress everyone with *all* that you know. Tailor your message to your audience. Nobody will give you points for showing them how technically competent you are by demonstrating all of the complexities and all the details that you've thought of. But they will give you points on making a complex issue clear to them. People are extremely busy. You want to make sure they take away the fundamental message you're trying to deliver. Provide your superiors with information they can make a decision with. Of course, you shouldn't talk down to your audience, but just recognize that many people won't have the technical background you may have. They're looking for guidance from you, which means they have to understand what you're saying.

And get to the point! Linda LoRe, CEO of Frederick's of Hollywood, explained, "One of the things that drives me crazy is when I ask someone what time it is, and they tell me how to make a watch. Top management people don't have time for the periphery." That doesn't mean you should be robot-like or leave important details out, but organize your thoughts and deliver them concisely, always focusing on the "so what"—what you recommend management do with the information you are presenting.

Linda believed that a fear of speaking up lies behind the disproportionately small number of women in leadership roles. "I've met some really dynamite women, and I'm pleased about that," she explained. "But considering that women now make up approximately fifty percent of the workforce, we don't have fifty percent of women in leadership. And many times—I think some of it's cultural or sociological—women are afraid to voice their opinion. I sit in meetings and watch this. Two or three women might speak, and you can always see that those are the ones who are going to make it somewhere because they're not afraid." From Linda's experience, if you turn in good reports or proposals but keep your mouth shut in meetings, you won't gain the visibility or credibility you need to get ahead.

Many women find themselves in this difficult position. They know they should contribute, but they don't because they fear being judged harshly. Unfortunately, as a consequence, they develop a reputation for being quiet and are perceived as having little value to add in meetings. There's no progress. Worse than being deemed imperfect, reticence can render one invisible!

Moreover, since these quiet women actually do have ideas to

contribute, often tension builds and churns within them. They become self-critical. "I should have said that," they silently berate themselves, "He said it first, but I *knew* that! Why didn't I just open my mouth?" Or, when they do finally speak up, their words emerge explosively; the resentment has been festering for a month or more. So now they're also labeled "rude" or "defensive" or "abrupt," and word gets out that they have a chip on their shoulder.

It is important to speak up when you believe you have something valuable to add. You need to make a positive impression if possible, so that higher-ups will remember you. Even if your contribution is imperfect the first time around, it will continue to improve. The fact is that the only way you get better at anything is to practice. So seize any opportunity you can to participate in discussions and offer your thoughtful ideas. The last thing you want to do is to present before the board when you have not run your ideas past any groups of people or when you have little experience speaking in front of groups.

But don't just talk idly. Outspoken high-potential women pick their topics carefully. You don't want to speak just to be heard. If you do, you'll get a reputation as somebody who always has something to say—or nothing to say—but talks a lot. Speak up, but do it in a "laser-like" manner.

You also have to know how to deliver your message. Linda LoRe suggested media or other public-speaking training as a way for women to advance their careers. Take a class or join an extracurricular group on speaking or debating. "It is one of the single skills to which I can attribute a good portion of my success," Linda explained. "Debating and public speaking teach you to organize your thoughts, listen thoroughly and quickly, and think on your feet. You can listen to a lot of material and still come back to make your point."

Also, don't hide from difficult interactions, and don't beat around the bush, especially if you have to deliver bad news. That's part of being forthright, which means more than just being honest. It's being straightforward and proactive in your honesty, and that takes a lot of courage. When you're leading a team or giving feedback to others, you might fall into the trap of telling them all the good news first. Sometimes time runs out before the negative feedback is ever delivered. Or there isn't enough time to focus on the constructive feedback and brainstorm solutions. While this may spare your employees' feelings, the real issues are not confronted, and therefore behaviors and difficult situations do not change. You must be clear and precise in your communication. If you choose to brainstorm possible solutions, do so after you have delivered all of your feedback.

Alan Buckwalter of Chase Bank of Texas commented on the importance of delivering tough messages early. He explained that the higher up you go in the hierarchy, the more time you spend on people issues. "So being honest and open and delivering tough messages are all important," he said. If someone is unable to perform at the level that's required, Alan recommended that he or she be redirected or allowed to find something else to do. All too often, because we feel compassionate, we try to soften the blow, and we let people who are struggling flail about too long. "They are suffering more than you are," Alan explained. "The best thing is to let that person move on. If you don't, he may be kicking the dog or mistreating his spouse or the kids or drinking to relieve his stress. Anyone who is performing poorly has ten times more stress than the person who is performing well but is overworked."

There is one caveat here, however. Sometimes if you're too forthright or assertive, you can be seen as a threat. Many senior men don't know what to do with us. Many have moms and daughters and wives at home, especially if they're in their fifties and sixties, but they don't have a professional "bucket" in which to put high-achieving women.

Executive women say it is important to calm that sense of threat. That means communicating in such a way that you're seen as a team player. Take into consideration what's occurring on the other side of the table. What kind of behavior are others expecting of you? What is the goal of your communication? Remember that in order for *communication* to happen—not just talking—both people must hear and understand each other's meaning. This doesn't mean that you must be somebody you're not. The objective is to get your needs met without alienating others. Do your best to understand the other person's perspective and desires before stating your own. In other words, "Seek first to understand, before being understood."

Being a good communicator also means being a good teacher. I've seen people derail because they keep their own territory well guarded and don't share information broadly. There's something really powerful about being a teacher. In fact, the more you share information about your area of expertise, the more powerful you become.

Also keep supervisors, colleagues, and subordinates in the loop, formally or informally. You can't communicate if you aren't actually talking to people! Also, remember the marketing/advertising "rule of six": You may have to repeat your message six times before people actually hear it. This is particularly true if you're advocating a change initiative or an innovative project. In many companies, you have to pre-sell your ideas, and that means getting out there, talking about them, and repeating yourself if you have to.

> **BECOME A TEACHER:** *The more you share information about your area of expertise, the more powerful you become.*

One of the most important traits that advances people in their careers is understanding how to probe, and how to ask questions and truly listen. "People don't ask the why, how, what, and where questions very often," Linda LoRe explains. "They listen to a presentation and say, 'Well, that sounds pretty good. What do the numbers look like?' You need to get underneath the underlying reason for this project." Pose questions such as: Where do you think it can go from here? How do you plan to execute this? What do you think about it? How do you feel about it? What do you think the pitfalls are? Why do you think that? Then, of course, carefully listen to the answers.

Indeed, listening is a vital part of communication. How often are you three sentences ahead of someone you're talking to, thinking about what you're going to say next? But, according to Jim Preston, rather than racing ahead with your own thoughts and suggestions, you have to look at the individual and ask, "Exactly what do you mean by that strategy?" Or, "Why do you think that will work?" Or, "What are some of the biggest challenges you think we might face by trying to implement that?"

Listening doesn't come naturally to many of us. We want to get our opinion out there because we want people to know that we add value. An excellent listening exercise is to repeat back what the other person has said. This is a good way to insure that you have heard his or her message. You might mirror statements by saying, "What I hear you saying is . . ." Jim Preston told me he had to take classes to polish his listening skills. Obviously it has paid off.

It may go without saying that you must listen to the concerns of your higher-ups. There can be awful consequences if you fail to communicate with those above you. One senior executive woman explained what happened to her because she never attended meetings designed to communicate a strategy that she and her boss had developed and had been advocating. "If I'd been there, I would have seen there was no communication going on. Nobody in that meeting was listening to the concerns of the major stakeholder—the CEO. If I had been there to see it, I'd have done something entirely different. I'll never let myself be cut out of critical communication meetings again."

It is also crucial, however, for you to pay attention to your employees and trust them. That's an important lesson you may forget as you move up the corporate ladder and spend less and less time with them. In fact, Liz Fetter of NorthPoint Communications shared a story of one of her greatest mistakes, and it revolved around her not listening to critical data from the people in the field who were actually doing the work for the company. She was running a large line of business for Pacific Bell and had been in the job for only a few months. The company was revamping one of its key operating systems; the change would affect phone service for half of California. It was the biggest "systems cut-over" as Liz called it, that Pacific Bell had ever attempted, and it involved enormous customers like AT&T, MCI, and AirTouch Cellular.

"There was no backup plan," Liz explained, "which should have been a five-alarm for me. But I was fairly new to the systems realm. As we were getting down to the deadline, which was over the Fourth of July weekend, we polled the people who were actually doing the work and who would be affected by the systems. We had outside experts, consultants, and the senior people telling us we were ready. But the front-line workers, the people dealing with the customers and doing the work, were exhibiting a great deal of apprehension. I was torn between what all of my employees were telling me—and their fear of change—and what my peers, the experts, and the senior officers were telling me.

"One fateful day, we decided to take a vote. I had the deciding vote, since my business unit was affected. I decided to go with the 'experts.' Friday before the Fourth of July, we were hitting one hundred percent of our due dates, but after the three-day weekend, we were hitting zero. Nothing. The system failed, and we were without the ability to provide services. It was one of the most profound experiences of my life; I realized that I was fundamentally responsible for a major screw-up. It affected the business in a very big way. I learned never to disregard what the people who are doing the work are saying. I vowed I would never make that mistake again. So, no matter what the experts are saying, the people who do the work probably know better."

Attending to nonverbal cues and body language is also important—especially if you want to present a proposal to your superior. Often someone's verbal and nonverbal communications are in conflict, and typically the nonverbal cues are a more accurate indicator of a person's emotions. When you sense an incongruence, seek for understanding. It is important to listen to and follow your intuition. Often women discount their inner voice, when usually it is the first signal that an issue may need further clarification.

Sometimes even your appearance communicates volumes about you. Sue Swenson of Leap Wireless International explained, "I recognize that I can't always look the way I want to because it impacts how people judge me." Sue then told me about the time she interviewed for a job. After a period of time, her new superior came back and said, "You have been selected, but the person I work for didn't want you because you don't look the part." Sue's hair was long, and she wore it down.

Sue got the job, but this interaction impacted her. "I've actually taken my appearance into consideration," she told me. "Now I think about who my audience is, and if my long hair is going to get in the way, then I wear it up. Or I wear a particular type of clothing. Unfortunately, the truth is that appearance does influence first impressions, and it will either allow me to get done what I want to get done or not. You have to acknowledge that. It's an unfortunate fact because, clearly, the substance has not changed, but it gets in the way of how people perceive you."

The objective is to communicate in such a way that people understand you. If static interferes, then your intended message will not get through.

One last point on communication: Many senior executive women consider themselves to be introverts, yet they work very hard to be perceived as leaders, to be more extroverted, and to draw others out. "My personality is pretty forceful," an admitted introvert explained, "so that would imply extrovert. But I had to take classes when I got out of college to learn how to speak extemporaneously in front of a group. I force myself to be in competition."

Yes, you can be an introvert and advance in your career. But you also have to be able to communicate to large groups of people. In fact, many CEOs are introverts who have learned extroverted behaviors. As one highly successful woman put it, "You'll probably find a lot of folks like me who actually prefer to lock themselves in the office and get a lot of work done or think about the next strategy, but who force themselves to get out, interact with others, shake hands, and play golf. It's part of the tradeoffs you make."

And if you happen to be an extrovert, think about which introvert behaviors you might exhibit and learn, such as being thoughtful or reflective before speaking. And pay particular attention to introverted individuals during meetings. Ask for their opinions; they may be sitting on a gold mine of unexpressed insights. Help them find their comfort zones. In truth, it's acceptable to be an introvert or an extrovert—but you need to learn how to balance the two.

## 7. Pick Your Fights

It's important to align your personal goals with your corporation's goals. You may have an important objective: You want to move up in your career, or you believe that a particular project has to be finished by a certain date. You may push it through, but perhaps it was not what your organization wanted you to focus on in the first place. Understand the blunder of Pyrrhic victories—winning the battle but losing the war. You must evaluate the big picture to know which battles you need to fight, and which you should just let go in order to win in the long run.

It's also important to be strategic about when and where you choose to make a stand. Take a position that you can support. When you have something important to say, align your behavior with your words, but speak softly. You will communicate your point much more effectively than if you launch into a tirade.

As one senior executive told me, "I get mad twice a year. January is out and December is out. I try to pick whatever battle I'm going to fight. I want it to be a strategic battle for the company. I don't want to always be the one out on a crusade. I choose only two in any twelve-month period. You can always approach me in December or January. It's safe. I won't get mad then!"

And save your chits until you really need them. We all know that one of the reasons we work so hard to develop relationships is that we may need the support of those with whom we are allied at a critical moment. But don't call in your strongest troops until you know they'll provide the maximum benefit possible for a specific situation.

And when you're engaged in battle, remember that emotions have to come out somehow—through crying, laughter, anger, and so on. From a psychological point of view, it is better to let your emotions out in a healthy way rather than to keep them bottled up. Women often let their negative emotions show through crying, rather than anger. When this happens in a business situation it may be uncomfortable for all parties involved. Elaine Agather, Chairman and CEO of Chase Bank, Dallas Metroplex, believes that crying is not a healthy way to solve a business problem. "When you're done crying," she will tell an employee, "let's deal with the issue at hand."

When we're upset, we all need to let off steam. If you don't release the tension through crying, anger, or physical activity, it stays in your body, emerging as physical complaints—headaches and stomachaches—or more serious illnesses, so that's not good either. My best advice is to tell the offending party that you're angry without crying or yelling. There's nothing wrong with saying, "I'm really upset about this. I need some time." You must handle your emotions effectively; it's a sign of maturity.

Then allow your emotions to emerge outside the work environment. If you need to, go outdoors and take a brisk walk. Come back when you're ready to deal with the situation in a constructive way. After the initial discharge of emotion, you can rechannel your energy to solve the problem.

## 8. Use Humor

We can get so caught up in advancing in our careers, deciding whether to have children, getting the family taken care of, and all the other things we must do daily, that sometimes we forget we just have to laugh about it all. We're on this earth for a relatively short period of time, and I believe that we're meant to be happy. It is important to remember to laugh at yourself and to joke about the situations you and your team find yourselves in. It defuses tensions, and it also can create group cohesion because everybody is having fun.

A senior executive working in the high-tech industry explained, "Don't let your ego get bigger than your sense of humor. It sounds trite, but in Silicon Valley, where I work, it's so easy to get caught up in 'important' things and in yourself that you lose sight of who you are. And sometimes you lose sight of having a little fun and putting everything into perspective."

Elaine Agather at Chase Bank found humor to be an effective tool when dealing with her mostly male clients, as well as her employees—nine out of ten of whom were men. Humor deflected tension.

Also, as I mention in relation to authenticity, it's important to demonstrate your geniality. A senior executive woman, in explaining some advice her boss gave her, said, "He told me, 'You have a really great personality and sense of humor, but you don't let anybody see that. You're very serious at work, and it only creeps out every once in a while. You should really let that show.'" That's great advice for everyone interested in living a healthy and enjoyable life!

## 9. Ask for Help

Asking for help is related to the executive virtue of being realistic. You need to know your strengths and weaknesses—what you're willing to do to move ahead and when you need assistance from your employees, your colleagues, and your superiors.

Often the managers and mentors of mid-level women advise them that to advance toward the executive levels, they need to learn how to do more "visioning," more high-level strategic planning, and less of the detail work. Whereas mid-level contributors often do the actual labor, an executive's job requires her to create and develop the larger systems, processes, and structures through which decisions are made. As you move forward in your career, you will be required to think more in terms of strategic execution (*What do we want to accomplish?*) versus tactical implementation (*How are we going to do it?*). You will be removing barriers that might prevent your employees from getting their job done. And the truth is that often the skills that have helped you get into mid-level management are insufficient to advance you into the more senior ranks.

To move forward, it's important to let go of some of the hands-on, getting-it-done-yourself activities, and to delegate those tasks to your direct reports. That will allow you more time to lead larger groups of people and take on more substantial responsibilities—goals that will help you move up into the senior ranks.

But remember, the right to delegate is also the right to follow up. Whenever you assign a task, by all means check in with your employees to see how they're doing. As a manager, it's your job to make sure your team succeeds. If you give an assignment that's due in a month, call your employees after two weeks to see how they are progressing. If you don't see the results you want, you can always step in at this point. But step in with plenty of time so that your employees can still be successful and your team can meet its objectives.

> FOLLOW UP! *Whenever you assign a task, check in with your employees to see how they're doing. It's your job to make sure your team succeeds.*

You can also ask for help from those above you in the corporate hierarchy. Part of being credible is the ability to juggle all the balls that have been handed to you. Don't be afraid to seek assistance if you feel you might drop some of them. As one senior executive woman explained, "Most people want to help you be successful, but you do have to ask."

When you have a difficult problem in front of you, you may need to ask your superiors for advice on how to solve it. The longer the trouble lingers, the worse it can become, and the more debilitating it is, not only to you but also to your staff. In asking for assistance, you might approach your boss or mentor with statements such as, "I don't understand this. Could you please help me out," or, "Some of my preliminary ideas on how to solve this issue include . . . Could you give me your feedback on my initial thoughts?" One senior woman told me, "I believe in spreading my problems around. It always helps me because I learn from folks who are watching me. They know my blind spots. I don't know them that well. I have a feeling where some of them are, but in a given situation I don't necessarily know. And I break down barriers by saying, 'I really don't know how to do this.' Or, 'What am I not seeing here?' I involve others in my situation, and sooner or later the situation begins to be resolved."

## 10. Remember, the Company Is Not Your Family

Never forget that neither the company nor your colleagues are your family. Do not believe it. Do not act like it. You've got to keep perspective.

Lora Colflesh, Vice President of Human Resource Operations at Sun Microsystems, explained, "This is a piece of advice that I've learned, not only through personal experience, but also because, having spent quite a few years in human resources, I often see people on their way out, as well as those who are on their way in. Whenever we talk about layoffs or changes, it's never Bob or Jane's decision. It's always 'the company' has decided. And the company will make the best decisions, as they see it, for the company." So no matter how good you are, no matter how loyal you've been, no matter what kind of value you can add, if the company decides that they're going to make a change, they're going to make a change. You may feel bad about it, but the company is going to do it anyway.

"Early in my career, I made that big mistake," Lora continued. "I thought, 'I am so nice, and I am so good, how could they possibly ask me to leave?' And they did. I shut down a division for a major company after having been there for one year. And I did such a good job closing it down, they actually let me turn the lights out, and then asked me to leave. They just said, 'Thank you. Goodbye.' I couldn't believe it. Fortunately, later they asked me to come back to a great assignment, which was the good news about this story. But I've seen it happen time and again."

The moral of this cautionary tale: Do your best for the company, and keep your goals aligned with the corporate objectives. However, never lose sight of the fact that *you* have to build and nourish your career—the company is not obligated to "take care" of you.

## 11. Make Strategic Moves

At the beginning of my career at IBM, we used to create and work from ten-year plans. These are now virtually obsolete. Some companies don't even create five-year plans anymore—because of the fast pace of change in business, two to three years is the maximum amount of time you can project.

We know that an important attribute of an executive is to move from the purely tactical to more strategic thinking and behaviors. This is true not only from a corporate standpoint (in shaping strategy for your company), but also for shaping your career strategy. It is vital, therefore, for you to have an end goal in mind. Visualize where you want to be in two- to three-year increments by creating your own three-year plan.

Ellen Hancock, CEO of Exodus Communications and former Chief Technology Officer at Apple Computer, advises to look two steps ahead when planning your career and to aim for a position that will ultimately lead you where you want to go. Once you have developed a high-level career strategy, you then must turn your attention toward performance at your current position rather than focusing on your next promotion. Companies change, and your skill-sets and interests evolve over time too. It's important for you to allow some flexibility as you navigate your career—and to understand that promotions are possible only if you do an excellent job in your current position.

In thinking about where you want to go and how you might get there, you might consider making a lateral move—especially if you want to broaden your base and/or get profit-and-loss experience. It is not a straight line up to the top; successful executives acquire a great deal of experience in varied areas of responsibility.

Beth Bull, Vice President and Finance Director at Texas Instruments, made two such moves, and they worked to her advantage. She took the first lateral move after being with Texas Instruments for only eighteen months. "TI's finance people have two responsibilities—cost accounting and financial planning," she explained. "I had started in financial planning, was doing well, and had gotten promoted once already. But I could see that the ultimate job I wanted required me to be responsible for both areas, so I made a lateral move into cost accounting, which a lot of people don't make, especially early in their careers. I knew what I was ultimately aspiring to. For my own knowledge, confidence, and performance, I needed to master both of those areas of expertise."

Not only did the new job help Beth's level of skills and knowledge, but she had taken a calculated risk. "I moved to a new organization at a time when I probably was on a short list for the next promotion in my original department," she explained. "Rather than working to my disadvantage, however, it demonstrated to other people that I was interested in building my skills and in continuous learning. I was not just finding a comfortable spot and growing there until I couldn't grow anymore."

Beth made a second critical—and again lateral—move when she accepted an assignment to become Finance Director for Texas Instruments, Asia, when she was six months pregnant. She trained in that job in Taipei, Taiwan, during her sixth, seventh, and eighth months of pregnancy, and then returned to Taipei with an eight-week-old child. "This lateral move had the same qualities as the first one; it was just sort of on steroids," she explained. "It was a bigger job, a better opportunity, and it required a physical move to a foreign country."

Beth had a vision of where she was, and where she wanted to be. This second move showed once again that she was willing to take a calculated risk, and that she had a career road map. She knew it would ultimately get her to her desired goal. Once more, she was engaging in continuous learning, and that was further evidence to her superiors that she was building her skills.

---

CONSIDER MAKING LATERAL MOVES: *They can help you broaden your base and get profit-and-loss experience. It's not a straight line up to the top. Successful women acquire a great deal of experience in varied areas of responsibility.*

---

For Linda LoRe, being strategic meant refusing a promotion. "That was considered corporate suicide," she explained. "I was working for a major retailer, and I knew I wasn't ready for the job they were asking me to take. I hadn't built the proper foundation for it, and turning down the promotion meant that it took me a little longer to get to the position that ultimately launched my career in senior management. But it also allowed me to develop some of the skills I needed to take the kind of risks I knew I would have to take. And it gave me courage and tenacity, based on the confidence I acquired by building that foundation." For Linda, refusing the promotion was a good long-term strategy. I would just remind you, however, that as emphasized in earlier chapters, don't be afraid to take a promotion, even if you aren't confident of your ability to do the new job. Often the best learning is a result of actually doing the new job. Remember, don't let fear or perfectionism get in the way.

In some companies it is commonplace that a person either move laterally or take a demotion if they're changing departments, especially if it means going from a staff to a line position. As you have seen, lateral moves can work to your advantage, but if you find yourself contemplating a demotion in order to broaden your base of experience and learning, talk with your adviser and champions inside your company to ascertain if it is truly necessary. If it isn't, try to make a lateral move, even if it's not a promotion, when you change departments. Remember, you bring a lot of skill and competencies to your next job, even though you may not have the exact experience they are looking for.

Several other senior executive women spoke of assuming their first management responsibilities as major turning points in their careers. One had been an individual contributor at a bank for twelve years. "It's great if you're a superstar, and if you want that as your career." she explained. "But the power in management is that you can take those skill-sets that allow you to be an individual contributor and multiply them among a team of twenty, two hundred, two thousand, or twenty thousand. The opportunity for me to manage a team was my first chance to show that I could take a group, organize them against a plan and objective, meet a budget, meet P&L responsibilities, and contribute to the results of the company. And I was able to do this in a much broader sense than I had as an individual contributor."

Keep in mind that your superiors will not give you a large team to manage until you've proven yourself with a smaller one. The virtue of taking on management responsibility is that you grow from running a small team, to a bigger team, to an even bigger team, until you have the credibility to manage large groups of people. If you haven't yet gotten a management assignment, I encourage you to look for and ask for it. If you're currently running a small team, seek opportunities for greater responsibility in your company. Watch for a new manager who needs help, new ideas, or initiative, and make yourself available.

## 12. Sometimes You Have to Go with the Flow

Most of us try to control, organize, and balance our lives, and we can get irritated when things don't go the way we want at work. But if we're alert and go with the flow, we can also use those glitches to our advantage. Sharon, one of the executive women I interviewed, found this strategy especially helpful in her career.

She and her partner planned what they thought was the perfect time to have their first baby. Sharon was working for a fabulous woman. "She was one of those bosses who is a mentor to me today;

I was in heaven working for her," she explained. "I got pregnant, and was just about ready to tell her when she quit. I was put into the acting senior vice president slot. I had six more months to go on the pregnancy, and now I was reporting to an all-male chain that did not have a reputation for taking good care of women or promoting them.

" 'Oh, God,' I thought, 'I've got only a couple of months to prove myself, and then I'm going to be out on maternity leave for four months, and my career will be screwed while I'm gone. They're going to put somebody in this job, which is, of course, rightly mine.' " Sure enough, despite all her good planning, that's exactly what happened. But, on hindsight, Sharon is glad that it did. "When I came back from maternity leave, and after I calmed down, I realized that I was working for a nice guy. He was not at all that demanding, and for the first time in my life, I worked a forty-hour week. It was the best year I ever had with my daughter, and I couldn't have planned that. Sometimes you gotta go with the flow."

Another executive shared a similar experience. Donna had been working at a large financial institution when she determined that the company was going to be acquired. She went through a period of shock, denial, and anger. "I thought I would just stick it out through the close. I'm going to honor my commitment, and then I'll leave. I grumbled for a few months, though I don't think I showed it. After six months, I started saying, 'Hey, these new folks are great. I really like their business strategy.' By year-end, the stock price had increased dramatically, and I actually—it wasn't about the money at that point, although the money kept me there—loved these people. They were great. They came out with a fabulous offer for me and my team. Everything worked out. I could never have planned that."

The trick, when you find yourself really disliking some aspect at work, is to step out of yourself and say, "Can I focus on a different part of my life?" or, "Is there a different way I can look at this so I can take advantage of it?" If there is, great. If not, then it may be time to go. But don't always assume that the path you had planned is the right one. There might be something better coming down the pipeline, if you can just be patient and trust the process. Flexibility, another executive virtue, is key.

## 13. Be Smart About Getting Promoted

How should you respond when you ask your boss for some advice or thoughts on your career and he or she says, "You're doing just fine. Keep it up"? Most people would interpret that as good news—after all, it seems as if your superior is pleased with your performance. But when the senior executive women at one of my recent workshops heard this feedback, they reared back in displeasure. "What that means," one senior woman bristled, "is that they don't want to lose you to someone else, but they also don't want you to take their job." Another added, "That's a real barrier. If only your boss knows you, you're not going anywhere."

Instead of resting on your laurels when you get that dubious pat on the back, you need to think about who is really going to promote you to the next level, not just give you the next title. It's less likely to be your boss than your boss's superiors or peers or somebody totally outside your group. You need to make your accomplishments known to them.

There are other promotion pitfalls as well. As a perfectionist, you may believe that no one could possibly do your job better than you can. But, if you can't be replaced, you won't be—which means you will never get that promotion. You have to encourage and develop your replacement; you must make it easy for others to move you along. Gloria Everett shared a personal story about how this issue hit home for her. "Recently our president retired at Globalstar," she explained. "Somebody came to me at an employees' lunch and asked, 'Gee, Gloria, could you be getting that job?'

"I said, 'No. If I were on the board, I don't know who I would replace me with.' Even if I were viewed as a perfect candidate, this wouldn't be the right time for me because I haven't developed my replacement. This was a reminder to me that I'm going to have to start making sure that happens."

It's also a fallacy to believe that in order to get promoted, you have to know everything about the new job. I find that many women who derail in their careers say, "Let me go off and learn the job first; I'll get perfect at it. Once I understand how to do the job, I'll take it." But the window of opportunity closes almost as quickly as it opens. There's little time to dawdle. Besides, I have met few people who have been promoted into a job they've done before! If they had, it wouldn't be called a promotion. But I have seen people move ahead quickly by figuring that they will plow in and learn on their feet, usually with terrific results. If they make mistakes, they rectify them later. Indeed, some of the most valuable experiences executive women have described occur when they've learned on the job. It was enriching for them—it pushed them ahead a lot more quickly in their careers and allowed them a lot more opportunity—and for their organizations as well.

As one senior executive woman explained, "No, we don't always know what we want to do and even if we do, that may not be where we're ultimately going. But I do have to think about where I might want to go. Maybe I want to be a CFO. Maybe I want to be the president. Maybe I want to be in investor relations, just for the heck of it. Maybe I want to be all these things. In my career, I've been in marketing, finance, investor relations, R&D, engineering, and operations. I didn't know the jobs when I went into them. But all that experience made me very qualified to take on a vice president of operations job."

It's also important for you to stay with a mainstream, highly visible business unit so that you are perceived as a key player and can attract the attention of those who can influence your career. One senior executive at AT&T told me that when she inadvertently discovered that a project she was running was a low priority within her corporation, she was out of there and onto a more highly regarded project in a matter of two weeks.

And, whatever you do, make sure others are aware of your contributions. As we have seen, it is a myth that if you do good work and keep your head down, people will notice you. While there may be a few terrific bosses who are always looking for great people working quietly in a corner, generally others must be made aware of your good work for you to advance. You want to have your name on the tip of the tongue of the executive who decides who should have the job you want.

Take opportunities to be noticed. If you just keep doing what you're doing, no one will tap you on the shoulder and say, "You've done a good job. We'll give you a promotion." You've got to let people know that you want to move up. But you can't approach

> MAINTAIN VISIBILITY: *Stay within a mainstream, highly visible business unit. You will be perceived as a key player and may attract the attention of those who can influence your career.*

them with statements such as, "I've just had a big win. Now what are you going to do for me?" An attitude of entitlement alienates and irritates higher-ups. However, you do need to leverage your success. When you are recognized for a substantive contribution, go to the person who heads up an area you'd like to become more involved in and say, "Based on my recent accomplishments, I'm ready for expanded opportunities and responsibilities." Ask for more *opportunity*, not for a promotion.

You're not necessarily going to be advanced just because you've just done a good job. Good work is imperative, but being noticed and having a good reputation (and some sponsorship) are probably even more important, particularly if you want to shoulder greater responsibility. People need to see you as a logical choice for a new position.

Of course, when you ask for an opportunity for advancement you can be turned down. As a mainframe sales rep at IBM, I learned that "no" is a good excuse to seek more information. If you've been denied a promotion, ask for more feedback on why. The response will tell you exactly what areas you need to develop. This is the perfect opportunity to ask for your boss's support and his or her commitment that if you achieve certain milestones, you will be promoted to the next level.

Will going back to school for an MBA or another graduate degree help in getting you a promotion? It may, but it may not. Nothing makes up for good business judgment. You can develop such insight from relationships, observation, experience, school—indeed, from just about every aspect of your life. Those executive women who have advanced degrees explain that it has helped them get in the door in a competitive environment, and it has expanded their professional alliances.

If you're thinking about going back to school for an advanced degree, evaluate the tradeoffs toward your eventual goals. An MBA can be a great way to reposition and repackage yourself if you're interested in making a career shift. But if you already have ten or more years under your belt, you've probably got the experience you need, and most likely you're well on your way to developing the alliances that will help you. If an advanced degree is not required or expected of executives in your company or industry, you might want to just keep going.

What if you're contemplating resigning? I'm all for being aggressive and challenging your company and trying to move up, but if you're unhappy where you are with your existing manager, you might first try investigating another department within your company to see if there's a better opportunity on someone else's team before you move out. Your human resources director, if trustworthy and reputable, is a great person to help you in shopping for a new position within the company.

Having the right corporate culture, one that matches your needs, is really important. For instance, some companies are more progressive about flexible work hours than others. You may need that at one moment in your life more than at another. If you fit into it, that's great. You're going to be putting in a lot of hours. If this is the path you choose, you need to make sure that you love the work you do and that you're in a culture that can help you grow and to which you can add value. Linda LoRe advised, "If you have an entrepreneurial spirit and you want to work in a corporation, it's best to find one that can embrace someone like you. If you are working your way up and you love the kind of business you're in and the company, make sure you can express your own ability to grow. Burnout doesn't come from working too many hours; it comes from not feeling valued."

But if it's clear to you that you will never get what you want from your current company, it may be time to move on. At that point, your external relationships and casting a wide net become especially important as sources of information, guidance, and potential opportunities.

If you choose to make a move, it is important to understand that the skills and behaviors that made you successful at one place may not be the talents that are important and valued at the next. "Understand the transition," Rick Belluzzo, Group Vice President at Microsoft, advised. "A good athlete doesn't necessarily make a good coach. Some of the new skills required are quite soft, like being adept in a political environment. A lot of people derail because of that." Remember to start your new job by asking a lot of questions and observing what skills, personalities, and behaviors are most rewarded.

If you are considering a big career move, it's wise to look to your own intuition. Ask yourself: What is really motivating my decision? Is it fear? Or is it passion? And watch out for your ego. Some people (men and women alike) are afraid to leave their companies because their identities are so attached to holding a certain title, level of responsibility, and control that they're afraid to unhook. If you are going to leave your company because you feel that it is no longer a fit for you, it is important for you to stay attuned to the lessons you can learn from the transition.

Above all, remember to take calculated risks. You probably know more than you think you do. If you have reached the level of mid-management, you bring many skills to the table, including those involving personal interaction and communication. You may be amazed to realize how much you actually know about your functional area and about your company that you didn't think you knew. Have confidence and trust yourself as you go for it!

## 14. Take Ownership of Your Career

I have made the point several times that it's vital for you to take responsibility for developing yourself and for advancing your career. Why not view yourself as your own business? Your capabilities comprise what you have to sell to your company. You need to keep your own best interests at heart while you're doing a really great job for your organization, because circumstances do change.

Taking ownership of your career means initiating whatever it is that you want to have happen in your work and your environment. (This goes back to the question of having a strong positive attitude versus feeling victimized.) Whatever challenge you seek—a promotion, additional responsibilities, the compensation you believe you deserve—it's up to you to strategically spur that along. There may even be occasions when you have to leave the company to find what you're looking for. So move on if it's not working for you. Or make it work where you are.

At one of my Windows in the Glass Ceiling workshops, a surprising number of women, having interviewed their bosses prior to our meeting, decided that their opportunities for advancement were limited at their current companies. Many thought about seeking their fortunes elsewhere. Once they heard the specific suggestions offered by the senior executives, as panel members or as coaches, they began to realize that they could effect change where they were. If you're truly unhappy where you are, and you feel that you're not getting the support or opportunities you need for advancement, don't let your self-limiting beliefs or the limiting beliefs of others hold you back. In today's business world, opportunities abound. It's wise, however, to carefully consider what such a dramatic change might mean to you in the long run.

The vice president of human resources at a large high-tech company counseled the group, "A couple of times when I've said, 'That's it! I'm leaving. It's not going to happen here, and I'm really angry,' it turned out to hurt me financially. Think about the financial impact before you resign." Not only are you looking for new challenges and opportunities, but you really need to consider your long-term financial situation. Leaving a company can be expensive to you, especially in corporations where stock, stock options, or retirement plans are a portion, if even only a small portion, of your compensation. They make a difference over the long term.

"Several of my colleagues have changed companies so often that they have no financial security at all," this executive continued. "They gave up 401(k) matching funds, pension plans, and stock options. They gave up good health plans to go to companies where coverage was poor, and then they got sick, and it wiped them out." If you think of yourself as a business, you need to ponder, "What am I giving up? And what am I gaining for my own financial security if I leave this company?" Balance both sides carefully.

In taking ownership of your career, continue to develop alliances outside your company. Sustain yourself by writing articles, winning awards, becoming involved in family or community activities that give you accolades external to your organization. You don't want to feel isolated or hopeless when you walk out of a meeting or when you weren't fully victorious or your ideas were rejected. Gaining positive feelings about yourself outside the workplace is a useful compensatory strategy, and it can help you create important relationships too.

And bear in mind that you're ultimately responsible for yourself. You're your own free agent and accountable for building your own skills. That's good for you, and ultimately it's also good for the company.

## 15. Remember, Hope Is Not a Strategy

# 13 | Constructing Your Road Map

In the personal coaching and workshops I've given to hundreds of high-potential mid-level women, certain questions and concerns continually arise:

- I would like a clear action plan of what should be some of my next steps to move forward. How do I develop a blueprint for my advancement?

- I know I need to cultivate more effective and helpful relationships and personal contacts. Where should I begin?

- I need a better understanding of my ultimate career goals. Are my current aspirations still appropriate to my needs?

- How can I develop more insight into how I'm perceived as a leader?

- What are the most important attributes I need to advance into the executive level? I'd like to identify where I measure up to the criteria and then develop a plan to close the gap between where I am now and where I need to be.

- I'd like a better understanding of what top management is looking for in selecting and grooming an executive.

These are typical questions that mid-level women ask—perhaps the very ones you have asked yourself. All of these women are seeking guidance—a road map, if you will—that can help them plot their course as they move forward in their careers. In this interactive workbook chapter, you will start to consider some of your answers to these pressing questions as you apply the C.O.R.E. elements to your own life, and you too will be able to develop a career road map that suits your unique life situation.

## Know What's Expected of You

In Chapters 2 and 3, you evaluated what you know about yourself and where you believe you stand in relation to the four C.O.R.E. critical success factors. But you also need to know precisely what your company values and how your superiors view your potential, vis-à-vis these factors. Jim Preston of Avon emphasized the importance of this by noting that women are rarely brought into their company's value structure—they're typically not told exactly what the organization considers to be vital. "Because they don't know what those values are, they can't aspire to them, and so they lose out on promotions," he explained.

Some companies—especially the newer high-tech giants—emphasize innovation. It is expected that you will be a relatively aggressive individual contributor, proactively voicing your ideas and concerns. In more traditional manufacturing organizations, on the other hand, teamwork is often stressed over individual contribution. How do you determine which experiences and behaviors are rewarded in your organization? That can take a bit of time and some detective work, but it is possible. In every company, no matter how big or small, you will find some people who know what's going on and are willing to be straight with you. You can ask them, "What are the unwritten values of this company? What does it really take to be promoted into the management team?" That will help you determine where you need to focus to be successful. Talk to several people, at different levels, if you can. Different points of view will help you get a fix on what is really going on.

The following exercise will help you in your quest. These questions emerged from my interviews with the CEOs, and what they suggested you do. To effectively create your career road map, you will need to set up a one-hour meeting to interview your manager or an adviser. You will be asking specific questions about your career path, as well as your company, industry, and leaders.

Although some people may think it naive to pose these questions, especially if you've been at the same company for a long while, it has been my experience in working with mid-level managers at large companies that these specific concerns are rarely discussed directly. In fact, sometimes mid-level professionals are surprised by the answers they receive. One woman discovered that her boss was quite impressed with her work. However, he was concerned about her potential for burnout because of the long hours she spent at work. "Focus more of your time on your family and yourself," he told this startled manager.

As you're interviewing your boss or mentor about your C.O.R.E. characteristics and other issues, record the essential points. I urge you to go to your manager, unless he or she is unsupportive. Otherwise, approach an adviser or other advocate with the following questions. And, of course, you should feel free to adapt and personalize them according to your situation:

- What do you currently view as my strengths?

- What do you see as my areas for development?

- What additional skills do you feel are important for me to develop as I progress in my career?

- What additional assignments and experience do you suggest I obtain?

- *Take a moment to think of possible way(s) you might gain these suggested skills/experiences and run them by your manager/adviser to check for validity.* Or ask: What suggestions do you have as to how I might gain these additional skills and experiences?

- What results do I need to produce to advance in my career? What can facilitate my producing those results?

- What relationships do I need to develop and/or maintain to help me progress in my career? This includes relationships inside the company (across multiple levels and functional departments) and outside the company (competitors, customers, vendors, the community, boards, etc.).

- *Take a moment to think of possible way(s) you might develop these relationships and run your ideas by your manager/adviser to check for validity.* Or ask: How do you suggest that I cultivate these relationships? Whom should I approach?

- Given the fast pace of change, what types of information do I need to acquire to stay intellectually current in my industry and in my field of expertise (business books, trade publications, journals, additional academic training, conferences/seminars, professional organizations, board experience, and so on)?

- What is your personal regimen to keep up with the pace? What do you do to recharge yourself? How do you maintain your intellectual, emotional, physical, and spiritual health?

- What types of work and personality styles are executives in this company looking for in high-potential, up-and-coming employees?

- How are decisions made in this company? What are the lines of communication to the senior executive team? Do I need to pre-sell my ideas?

- Are there other factors that we haven't discussed that are necessary for me to know or do in order to be promoted? What are the unwritten rules and values of the company?

- What would be the next two logical career moves for me?

## Evaluate What's Right for You

After you've interviewed your manager or adviser and understand his or her perception of your C.O.R.E. capabilities and the playing field, your next step is to evaluate what is right for you. Take some time for self-reflection, and ask yourself the following questions. Again, write down your reflections.

- Are these desired competencies something I'm capable of and want to fulfill?

- Can I develop the skills required? If it means returning to school, am I willing to do that?

- Am I capable of producing the outcomes that are expected? What kinds of support would I need at the office or at home?

- Do I have the wherewithal to create the relationships that my superior believes would be helpful?

- Do my personality, character, and value system match what is required here?

- Am I willing to adhere to most of the unwritten rules?

- What do I really want to do in my life? What legacy do I want to leave?

## Creating Your Road Map

In this section, I will detail a process for you to follow that I have found to be effective in coaching mid-level managers and executives in their career development. You will be using the three illustrations that follow to help you evaluate where you are in your career path and what you need to do to reach your goals.

Because each of us is on our own journey, I cannot define the specific steps that you must take to move ahead in your career. However, this book has been all about the underlying assumptions and values that senior executive women hold and what they believe to be imperative to their career advancement. Those behaviors and values are consistent, regardless of the individual path one is on. The steps and details will differ depending on your competencies, strengths, weaknesses, industry, and company.

First study the graphic called Your Career Road Map (pages 294–95). On it, you will find numerous personal factors surrounding your career path, including leisure, travel, health, family and friends, spirituality, reflection, and enlightenment. These are essential to your advancement and to your life's success and happiness. If managed well, the creativity, fun, and happiness from your personal life can recharge and re-energize your professional career. If not, these personal factors can conflict with and ultimately hinder your personal and professional success and happiness. Keep these personal factors in mind as you proceed to the chart for Your Personal Achievement Inventory on pages 296–97.

The purpose of Your Personal Achievement Inventory is to help you, as an aspiring corporate woman, to concretely visualize what you have already achieved. List on Your Personal Achievement Inventory the specific Competency, Outcome, Relationship, and Endurance (C.O.R.E.) factors that you have *already achieved*. Which skills, experiences, and credentials have you obtained? What outcomes or results have you produced? What relationships have you developed? How have you learned to endure—to take care of yourself in the process? You might refer back to your answers to the questions in Chapter 3, on pages 64–65. These are the steppingstones that have brought you to your current success. Many upwardly mobile female managers whom I coach or who have attended my seminars are astonished to see how far along the road they have already come, and you may be pleasantly surprised too.

## Your Action Plan

Next, take a look at pages 298–99, the chart for Your Executive Development Plan. Here you will be listing the long- and short-term goals that you have yet to accomplish—the steppingstones yet to lay down. You may base these on the many suggestions you have found throughout this book and/or on the feedback you have received from your boss or adviser. This exercise is valuable because it clarifies and simplifies what you need to focus on within the C.O.R.E. factors. It also asks you to identify which resources you will need to leverage to accomplish your goals.

As you fill out this form, keep in mind the competencies and attributes the senior executive women have stressed in each of the chapters:

- The importance of developing strategic and substantive relationships with key individuals

- Adding value to your company by producing desired and valued results

- Being gracious, kind, and trustworthy

- Proactively helping others achieve their goals

- Taking calculated risks

- Gaining profit-and-loss responsibilities

- Maintaining your physical, emotional, intellectual, and spiritual health

With these attributes and your boss's or adviser's comments in mind, list each short- or long-term goal, possible action steps you could take to achieve the goal, the resources you can leverage to help you complete the action item and when you expect to complete the task. Once you have finished this action plan, you will know exactly

REFLECTION

FAMILY

SPIRITUALITY

PARENTS

**Your Career Road Map**

# Your Personal Achievement Inventory

| Competencies | Outcomes |
| --- | --- |
| | |

| Relationships | Endurance | ✓ |
| --- | --- | --- |
| | | |

# Your Executive Development Plan

| Developmental Goals | Action Steps |
|---|---|
|  |  |

| | Timeframe | Resources | ✓ |
|---|---|---|---|
| | | | |

what you must do to move forward. I urge you to discuss Your Executive Development Plan with your boss or adviser to garner his or her insights and commitment to helping you accomplish your goals. As you complete each task, you can check it off in the column provided and transfer it to Your Personal Achievement Inventory.

I have seen this exercise work with corporate women. For example, one executive woman I was coaching was constantly worried that whatever she was doing wasn't good enough. Tina was unclear about her objectives or how she could achieve them. I asked her to fill out an Executive Development Plan, and she identified as one of her developmental goals the attainment of more clarity about what she was expected to contribute to the success of her organization. To achieve that goal, one of Tina's action steps was to set up regular one-on-one meetings with her CEO. Under the Timeframe heading, she wrote "monthly." Her resource included calling the CEO's assistant to get on his calendar.

As a result of these meetings, Tina's CEO realized that he needed to provide more specificity to her goal-setting. And Tina gained a better understanding of her CEO's expectations. She began to relax in his presence, and they developed a better working relationship. Taken together, Tina's Executive Developmental Plan and the actions it generated gave her more confidence to work with her colleagues in the accomplishment of her personal and their corporate goals. It was a win-win situation all around.

As you will see, you can greatly reduce the "overwhelm" factor if you begin to clearly identify the progress you have made in your career and the long- and short-term action steps you need to take to make your entire life work. I have found that when aspiring corporate women put their achievements and goals down on paper in this way, it enhances their sense of accomplishment and confidence and gives them the perspective to deal constructively with issues as they arise. Such an action plan can be helpful at any stage in your career, as it helps you clarify your direction and focus attention on one or two major issues at a time.

Being the perfectionists that businesswomen tend to be, we often try to improve upon everything at once. Completing your own Personal Achievement Inventory and Executive Development Plan will remind you that you have achieved and learned a great deal, and that you've come a lot further than you think. Taking the quality time to meet with your boss to ask him or her the specific questions outlined in this chapter, and taking time for yourself to reflect on your accomplishments and goals, can be some of the most important life decisions you will make. This reflection and feedback reminds us that we are human—full of hopes, dreams, aspirations, frailties, and fears. We can have and achieve whatever we want in our lives, both personally and professionally. We just have to focus and stay true to ourselves and our priorities.

Godspeed!

# *Index*